VIRTUE IN DISTRESS

Frontispiece to *Le Voyageur sentimental* by François Vernes (1786)

VIRTUE IN DISTRESS

Studies in the Novel of Sentiment from
Richardson to Sade

R. F. BRISSENDEN

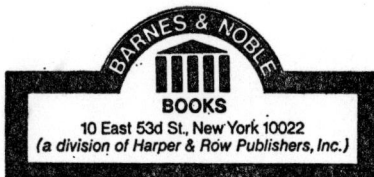

BOOKS
10 East 53d St., New York 10022
(a division of Harper & Row Publishers, Inc.)

First published in the United Kingdom 1974 by
The Macmillan Press Ltd

Published in the U.S.A. 1974 by
HARPER & ROW PUBLISHERS, INC.
BARNES & NOBLE IMPORT DIVISION

ISBN 06-490677-9

Printed in Great Britain

For
Rosemary

Tears I would . . . shed for virtue in distress . . .

Lady Bradshaigh

Celui qui sait attendrir sait tout. Il y a
plus de génie dans une larme que dans tous
les musées et toutes les bibliothèques de l'univers.

Alphonse de Lamartine, *Les Confidences*

Look out, kid,
No matter what you did . . .

Bob Dylan, *Subterranean Homesick Blues*

Contents

List of Illustrations

Preface

I first read *Clarissa* fresh from a rereading of *Tristram Shandy* and *A Sentimental Journey*, and it immediately struck me as rather odd that Richardson and Sterne should both be regarded as *sentimental* novelists. What could we mean by 'sentimentalism' or the 'novel of sentiment'? This book has grown out of an attempt to provide some answers to these questions, and in the light of these answers – necessarily tentative and partial though they may be – to take a new look at sentimentalism and at some of the more significant sentimental and anti-sentimental novels of the eighteenth century.

The book has been long in the making, and it would not have been written at all without the generous assistance of a number of people and institutions. To Bonamy Dobrée and Douglas Jefferson I owe a special debt of gratitude: they initiated me as a graduate student into the study of eighteenth-century fiction and encouraged me to carry my researches further. I am also particularly indebted to John Passmore of the Australian National University: the period I spent in his Department of Philosophy as a Senior Research Fellow in the History of Ideas gave me an invaluable opportunity to investigate the philosophical background to and origins of sentimentalism. A. D. Hope did much to make it possible for me to take up this Fellowship: for this and the many other ways in which he has helped to bring this work to fruition I am especially grateful. I must also thank Ralph Cohen, Bernhard Fabian, George Rousseau, Jane Crisp, and John Stowell for having so freely proffered their advice and criticism on various aspects of the project, and C. J. Rawson for having given the manuscript such an incisively critical reading. Anne Duffy and J. C. Eade have been more than ordinarily helpful as research assistants; and to the various typists who, under the general direction of Joyce Arey, have worked on the book I am particularly grateful. I must also express my very great appreciation of the assistance I have received from the following institutions: the British Council, the Carnegie Corporation of America, and the William Andrews Clark Memorial Library.

A portion of the book (Part II, Chapter V: *La Philosophie dans le Boudoir; or, A Young Lady's Entrance into the World*) originally appeared in *Studies in Eighteenth-Century Culture II*, edited by Harold E. Pagliaro: I am grateful to the editor and the publishers, The Press of Case Western Reserve University, for permission to include it here.

Some obligations are personal rather than scholarly, and these are the ones that can never properly be acknowledged. But for the help they have given when it was needed most my warmest thanks must go to my parents, to John and Eileen Bills, to Herbert Burton and above all to my wife.

R.F.B.

The Australian National University

Textual Note

Quotations from works in French are translated into English either in the body of the text or in the notes. Unless otherwise indicated the translations are my own. The reference given is usually to the original French text. Quotations from *Clarissa* are taken from the fourth edition, 1754. For ease of location the corresponding passages in the Everyman edition are also cited.

PART ONE

Sentimentalism and the Novel of Sentiment

I

Prologue: The Sentimental Traveller

The forgotten works of literature generally deserve their fate. Sometimes they are worth looking at again, however, particularly if for a time they were widely read or highly admired. That they should ever have enjoyed a vogue may now indeed seem the most interesting thing about them: the cultural phenomenon of Ossianism, for instance, strikes us today as rather more significant than the spurious translations which brought it into being. Not that James Macpherson's *Fragments of Ancient Poetry* are completely without merit: but the enthusiasm that greeted their appearance in 1760 seems disproportionate.

Le Voyageur sentimental, ou ma Promenade à Yverdun, by François Vernes, though not devoid of charm, is no doubt neglected even more thoroughly by the modern reader than the poems of Ossian. When it was first published, however, in 1786, although it created no tremendous stir it met with a response sufficiently warm to warrant several subsequent editions. Like Macpherson's epic fragments, it is an extremely revealing document: one which can tell us a great deal not only about the literary taste of the time, but also about contemporary moral and social attitudes.

Vernes' sentimental traveller gives a whimsically disjointed and haphazard account of a rambling journey through a number of Swiss towns and villages. His model was obviously *A Sentimental Journey*, by Laurence Sterne, which although published eighteen years earlier (1768) was still extremely popular. The resemblance was soon noted. 'I believed *Sterne* to have been dead long ago', wrote one anonymous correspondent, M. M***, to *L'Année Littéraire*; 'I see to my great astonishment that he is still alive'. The author was so delighted with the compliment that he reprinted the letter in the revised and expanded edition of the book which he brought out later in the same year.[1] There were three more editions before the end of the century and another in 1825, and an English version, *Louis and Nina, or the Excursion to Yverdun*, was published in 1789.

More interesting than M. M***'s letter for the modern reader are the title-page and, in this edition, the picture which faces it. The frontispiece shows, against the background of a sublime alpine peak, a tender scene: the reunion of an old blind beggar and his daughter. Nearby stands the sentimental traveller, in the one hand his hat, reverently doffed in the presence of such an instance of true feeling, in the other, raised to the heavens, his handkerchief, damp with tears. Beneath are written the words, 'O Rousseau, O Richardson, où êtes-vous!' On the title-page there is an epigraph (no doubt composed by the author himself):

> Une larme du sentiment,
> Quelle plus douce récompense!

> (A tear of sentiment,
> What sweeter recompense!)

The lines could be applied as aptly to the incident illustrated in the picture as they could to the book as a whole: the most valuable tribute the sentimental traveller can offer to the blind man is not money – in fact he gives him none – but the tears which spring unbidden to his eye. Money could buy bread for the old man's empty stomach; but the tears are balm for his injured heart – they ease the pain of an *amour propre* wounded by the shame of poverty. Their spontaneous appearance demonstrates that the traveller's interest in the situation is not dictated by vulgar curiosity or a cold sense of duty, but simply by sympathy for a fellow human being in distress. The tears are at once a compliment to the person whose misfortune has called them forth and evidence of the true worth of the one who weeps: 'the man is to be honour'd', Samuel Richardson had said, 'who can weep for the distresses of others'.[2]

[1] *Le Voyageur sentimental, ou ma Promenade à Yverdun*, nouvelle ed., corrigée et augmentée par l'Auteur (à Londres, 1786) 117.

[2] *A Collection of the Moral and Instructive Sentiments . . . contained in the Histories of Pamela, Clarissa and Sir Charles Grandison* (London, 1755) 204–5.

The tears, the casual nature of the incident which has inspired them, the epigraph, the alpine setting: in every way this a beautifully typical instance of the cult of sensibility – a cult which at that time, in the years immediately preceding the French Revolution, was at its height on the Continent. The whole book, indeed, is remarkable for the number of stock sentimental figures, themes and situations which it manages to bring together within a small compass.

As in *A Sentimental Journey* the story is so slight as to be almost nonexistent. It serves merely as a pretext for the presentation of a number of sentimental episodes in which the narrator is barely involved, if at all. And although his story is offered under the guise of a travel book, he warns the reader that he must expect no topographical descriptions or detailed accounts of famous churches and castles:

> Alas! a nuance of sentiment touches me and engages my interest more than all the Pantheons and Trajan's Columns . . . the man with the sheep, for example, the blind man and his daughter, the cripple: these are my follies.[3]

We have already looked briefly at the episode of the blind man and his daughter. The incident of the man with the sheep is in some ways more significant because of the political moral we are asked to read into it. When Yorick in *A Sentimental Journey* meets the man weeping for his dead ass near Nampont he makes a relatively simple comment:

> Shame on the world! said I to myself – Did we love each other, as this poor soul but loved his ass, – 'twould be something.[4]

But Vernes' sentimental traveller invests a rather similar encounter with a much wider meaning. He prefaces his account with the admission that he has always loved and admired the peasantry, 'and in general those whom heaven has created our equals but whom chance has placed beneath us'.[5] It is amongst such people that man's true nature is to be discovered – 'ils sont plus *hommes*' – and he quotes from 'le grand Rousseau' to the

---

[3] *Le Voyageur sentimental* 8.
[4] *A Sentimental Journey*, ed. Gardner D. Stout, Jr (Berkeley and Los Angeles, 1967) 141.
[5] *Le Voyageur sentimental* 16.

effect that the lower in the social order you go the more admirable mankind appears to be.

The man with the sheep is a poor butcher who has been dismissed by his cruel master because he could not bring himself to slaughter the one animal in the flock who had become his pet. This demonstration of loyalty strikes the traveller as being an example of true moral feeling, of genuine sensibility (the chapter devoted to the episode bears the title 'Où se loge la sensibilité!').[6] Conscious that his own response to the situation must be more than adequate he gives special thought to the manner in which he exercises his benevolence: he presents six francs not to the butcher, but to the sheep, 'for fear of wounding the delicacy of the master.'[7]

There are a number of other incidents in which the problem of how to be tactful in giving money to the poor is examined, although in none is the solution so grotesquely comical. The sentimental traveller also witnesses a death-bed, a funeral, and hears two or three pathetic stories of unhappy lovers. Sad situations arouse his interest more strongly than happy ones, he admits, and he takes this as a sign of a profound wisdom on the part of his creator. Most moving of all are situations which are completely irremediable, those which all the generous impulses in the world can do nothing to alter, and to which we can offer only the tribute of our pity. Such is the case of Louis and Nina, with the recital of which he brings his story to a close (and which gives the title to the English translation of the book). Louis loves Nina, the most beautiful girl in his village. Nina dies suddenly on the eve of their wedding, Louis goes gently mad, and then also dies. Profoundly moved by the whole affair the sentimental traveller composes an epitaph for the stone which stands at the grave of the two lovers; and plants two cuttings from the weeping willow that grows in the cemetery. Once a day he visits this evergreen symbol of their love. And when the pain of everyday existence becomes unbearable he can always find relief in the beauties of nature. A view of the Alps at sunset will bring peace to any unhappy heart; and when he climbs their flower filled valleys in summer a silent ecstasy brings him in touch with the Deity: 'I prostrate myself in silence . . . I have seen God!'[8]

---

[6] Ibid. 18.   [7] Ibid. 22.   [8] Ibid. 210.

The OED defines the word 'sentimental' thus: 'characterized by sentiment. Originally in favourable sense: chacterized by or exhibiting refined and elevated feeling. In later use: Addicted to indulgence in superficial emotion: apt to be swayed by sentiment'. In the two volume *Larousse Universel*, published in 1923, 'sentimental' is defined as follows: 'Où se manifeste un sentiment, vrai ou affecté: *discours sentimental*. Qui a ou affecte une sensibilité un peu romanesque: *jeune fille sentimentale*. (S'emploie souvent avec quelque idée de dénigrement.)' And 'sentimentalisme' is defined first as 'affectation du sentiment'; subsequently as 'Genre sentimental. Morale du sentiment'. *Le Voyageur sentimental* is clearly sentimental in the less favourable sense of the term, the sense in which we most often use the word today. The traveller's emotional attitudes, his 'sentimentalisme', appear to us an an 'affectation du sentiment'; and the feelings in which he indulges himself, the 'nuances de sentiment' which he pursues and savours with the ardour of a connoisseur, are not only superficial but grossly disproportionate to the situations which inspire them. In fact the more disproportionate they are the more they seem to be valued. Those incidents in which the traveller is the least closely involved arouse the most intense feelings: he expends far more emotion, for instance, on the fate of Louis and Nina, with whom his relationship is tangential to say the least, than on his own love affair.

This apparently deliberate dislocation of feeling is extremely interesting in itself. Before considering it any further, however, we should note something equally interesting: namely that François Vernes and his readers seem to have been quite unaware of what was going on. Thus, although he describes himself as 'sentimental' he is obviously not employing the word with any idea of deprecation or disparagement – quite the reverse. So far as the author of *Le Voyageur sentimental* and its admirers are concerned the feelings of the traveller are intended to be taken as genuinely 'refined and elevated' and not 'superficial', false or affected. He knows that he may be unworldly and that in the eyes of the sophisticated he may appear comically foolish for allowing himself to be swayed by his sentiments, but of their moral worth, their innate value, he has not the slightest doubt. As he says in an apostrophe to Jean-Jacques Rousseau, that good and sublime spirit remains the glory of humanity even in those moments when he reveals his frailty: 'Rousseau! gloire de l'homme, dans l'aveu même de tes foiblesses'.[9]

Le Voyageur sentimental, despite a certain elegance and good humour, is a slight and rather sad little book. When one considers the time at which it was first published – 1786 – it also begins to look faintly sinister. The episode of the man with the sheep, for instance, hardly seems adequate as a comment on rural poverty three years before the French Revolution. But then the whole theme of the work is inadequacy: the sentimental traveller is presented as an almost completely helpless and powerless character. He passes through a world in which real people live, experiencing joy and pain, love and suffering, but his strongest feelings are the 'nuances de sentiment' which he receives from observing others and from participating vicariously in their lives. He weeps for them, occasionally alleviates their immediate economic problems, but is utterly incapable of really helping anybody. The more hopeless the situation, the more exquisite is the sentimental *frisson* he receives from contemplating it, and since such an emotion does not have to be – indeed *cannot* be – translated into action, it can be enjoyed simply for its own sake. The sentimental traveller clearly prefers the feelings aroused by thinking about love to being actually in love himself. As a lover he is absurdly ineffective; but even this ineffectiveness he invests with a certain moral significance. When a gesture of pity to a beggar causes him to lose the opportunity of meeting the beautiful Rose, he is moved to comment that love is obviously not so important in human personality as humanity, i.e. general benevolence:

> Love, I said to myself, is then not the first sentiment which the seal of the divinity impresses in our souls. Admirable mechanism! All the other strings of the heart vibrate when that of humanity has just been sounded.[10]

And it is Vernes' humanity which struck his anonymous critic as his worthiest and also his most timely quality. So overcome with enthusiasm that he breaks into verse, M. M*** praises Vernes for the way in which his advocacy of universal benevolence reflects so faithfully the spirit of the times:

[9] Ibid. 72–3.   [10] Ibid. 170–1.

Que votre amour si général
Peint bien la fougue de notre âge.[11]

In so far as the spirit of the age was sentimental the comment certainly seems justified.

Le Voyageur sentimental, considered simply as a work of fiction, has little intrinsic value. To anyone concerned with the history of ideas and of literature, however, it may be considered significant in at least three ways. Firstly, the success it enjoyed, modest but by no means negligible, indicates the power with which, at this period in European history, sentimental ideas, values and attitudes were charged. In the novel at least there was, it is clear, a tradition of sentimentalism established with sufficient distinction for an author to be able to profit by openly associating himself with it. Secondly, Vernes demonstrates, at least by implication, something of the complexity of this tradition. He apostrophises Richardson and Rousseau and he imitates Sterne. In some ways it would be difficult to imagine three novelists more dissimilar – Richardson puritanic, obsessive, tragic; Rousseau idealistic and rather solemnly romantic; Sterne sceptically and urbanely comic. Yet each is a sentimentalist, and each, in his own way, is a great and fundamentally realistic writer (Rousseau less great in his novel, perhaps, than in his other work, but then even in his own day he was not regarded primarily as a novelist). The gulf which separates Vernes from the three writers whom he most admires is, of course, enormous. And this suggests the third way in which *Le Voyageur sentimental* may be regarded as significant. The character of the work itself, its emptiness and artificiality, implies that there was something profoundly wrong with sentimentalism – at this stage of its development at any rate. Today the notion of sentimentality (which is slightly but significantly different from sentimentalism) suggests shallowness, insincerity, self-indulgent emotionalism: 'among the politer terms of abuse', I. A. Richards has observed (speaking of the use of the word in literary criticism), 'there are few so effective as "sentimental"'.[12] The quality of *Le Voyageur sentimental*, both

[11] Ibid. 218.

[12] *Practical Criticism* (London, 1929) 255. Jacques Barzun effectively summed up the modern sense of the term in his definition of sentimentalism as 'The cultivation of feeling without ensuing action'. In *Classic, Romantic and Modern* (New York, 1961) 75.

as a work of literature and as a comment on life, suggests why the word should now carry such derogatory connotations. What it fails almost completely to suggest, however, is why sentimental ideals and attitudes should have seemed at all admirable to anyone at any time. Yet they undoubtedly did: the sentimental tradition, properly so called, embodied some of the most vital, dynamic and productive elements in eighteenth-century civilisation. It also contained within itself, however, the seeds of its own decadence: *Le Voyageur sentimental* is interesting because it demonstrates so clearly both the existence of the tradition and the nature and extent of its decay.

2

'Sentimentalism':
An Attempt at Definition

I

It is simple enough to assert or assume that sentimentalism or the sentimental tradition existed and that it manifested itself most obviously during an 'Age of Sensibility'. But scholars and historians of ideas are reluctant to confront directly the question of what is or was *meant* by sentimentalism and sensibility. Martin Price, for instance, in his Introduction to a recent special issue of *Eighteenth-Century Studies* which is given over to the subject warns us against construing such terms too narrowly, and prudently observes that 'to speak of *an* age of sensibility is to indicate . . . the tentativeness of a proposal rather than an historical label';[1] while Northrop Frye in his influential article, 'Towards Defining an Age of Sensibility', tells us a great deal about the age while saying almost nothing about sensibility itself.[2] This reluctance is part of the scepticism with which we now view the whole business of Neoplatonic pigeon-holing which once made life so easy for the literary historian. It is now fashionable to assert that many of the cultural and historical entities with which we were once familiar – ages, movements, spirits, periods, '-isms' – never really existed. And their disappearance has partly resulted in some instances from the thoroughness with which people have tried to define them. 'A case in point', as Arthur Sherbo has observed, 'is the term "romanticism". . . . The word has really ceased to have any meaning, and that

[1] Op. cit. IV (1970) 2.
[2] In *Eighteenth-Century English Literature*, ed. James L. Clifford (Oxford, 1959) 311–18.

because of the multiplicity of meanings that have been given or denied it.'[3]

It is difficult not to sympathise with Mr Sherbo's argument. But no matter what may have happened to 'romanticism', the same fate will not, I think, overtake 'sentimentalism': despite the industry of the scholar, it is not likely to be defined out of existence. It is, I believe, a genuinely meaningful term although a quite unusually complex and slippery one. And if it is properly understood, and if its application is intelligently directed it can be validly and usefully employed to describe a constellation of related ideas and ideals – beliefs about and attitudes towards man and society. Moreover the distinctiveness and interconnectedness of this group of ideas was acknowledged – tacitly, perhaps, more often than consciously – during the eighteenth century itself. This is our strongest justification for trying to redefine it for ourselves and in our own terms today.

In giving my own account of sentimentalism I intend to deal mainly with three aspects of it: the vocabulary of sentimentalism, the general ideas with which the terms in this vocabulary are concerned, and sentimental (and to some degree anti-sentimental) literature – in particular what I have chosen to call the novel of sentiment. The first two areas of this inquiry naturally overlap and merge into each other: it is impossible, for instance, to go on talking for very long about the meaning of a basic term like 'sympathy' without beginning to explore both the particular and the general ideas which the word denotes and the way it functioned during the period. Since my main concern is with the novel I shall not pretend to conduct such explorations in any

---

[3] *English Sentimental Drama* (East Lansing, Michigan, 1957) 1. See also George Boas's engagingly astringent consideration of the problem in his essay, 'In Search of the Age of Reason', *Aspects of the Eighteenth Century*, ed. Earl R. Wasserman (Baltimore, 1965) 1–19 The eighteenth century, says Mr Boas, 'is a period which has been called rationalistic, sentimentalistic, optimistic and pessimistic, melancholy, necrophilic, contented with itself, and fond of nature. It has, of course, also been called the Enlightenment, the *siècle des Lumières*, and the *Aufklärung*. But if the Spirit of the Times did not suffer from divided personality, these traits should turn out to be fairly general, and none of them do. And if its *Geist* is divided against itself, one had best find out how many *Geister* existed simultaneously'.

great depth. It may be possible, however, to suggest briefly something of the range and character of the most important elements in the sentimental tradition, and also of the way in which they changed and developed during the eighteenth century.

II

The appearance and growth of an identifiably 'sentimental' vocabulary during the period is one of the most substantial pieces of evidence both for the existence of a sentimental tradition and for its dynamic character.[4] The key terms in this vocabulary are 'sentiment', 'sentimental' and 'sensibility'. Also important are 'sense', especially in the phrase 'moral sense'; 'sentimentality', 'sentimentalism', 'sentimentalist'; 'sensible' and 'sensitive'; and the phrase 'man of sentiment'. In French the cognate words are 'sens', 'sentiment', 'sensibilité', 'sentimental' and 'sensiblerie'. Other words not related etymologically to the 'sense' family could also be described as belonging to the language of sentimentalism: the most important of these are 'feeling' and 'sympathy', especially in such phrases as 'feeling heart' and 'man of feeling'. Some of these words, e.g. 'sentiment', existed long before the eighteenth century; others, e.g. 'sentimental', were coined during the period. But in many cases some of the meanings they carried, the connotations with which they

[4] For more extensive and detailed surveys of this particular aspect of sentimentalism, see Erik Ermämetsä's extremely valuable but occasionally inaccurate pioneering investigation, *A Study of the Word 'Sentimental', and of other linguistic Characteristics of Eighteenth-Century Sentimentalism in England* (Helsinki, 1951); *English Sentimental Drama*, by Arthur Sherbo (East Lansing, Michigan, 1957), esp. ch. I: 'Sentimental Drama "defined"'; Arthur M. Wilson, Jr's article, 'Sensibility in France in the Eighteenth Century: a Study in Word History', *French Quarterly* XIII (1931) 35–46; the discussions of 'delicate' and 'sensibility' in *The Structure of Complex Words*, by William Empson (London, 1951); 'Some Remarks on Eighteenth-Century "Delicacy", with a Note on Hugh Kelly's *False Delicacy* (1768)', by C. J. Rawson, *Journal of English and Germanic Philology* LXI (1962) 1–13; my own article, ' "Sentiment": Some Uses of the Word in the Writings of David Hume', *Studies in the Eighteenth Century*, ed. R. F. Brissenden (Canberra, 1968) 89–107; and Arthur Friedman's essay in *The Augustan Milieu*, ed. Eric Rothstein and G. S. Rousseau (Oxford, 1970) 247–61: 'Aspects of Sentimentalism in Eighteenth-Century Literature'.

were charged, were unique to the period, or at least operated then far more strongly than at any time before or since. The way in which 'sentimental', for instance, has altered in meaning – a process of change which began, in fact, not long after it first appeared in English, some time in the 1740s – is of extraordinary interest. The problems of understanding how and why such alterations occurred leads one directly into a consideration of the nature of sentimentalism itself.

This problem, however, like many of the problems associated with the vocabulary of sentimentalism, is by no means easy to grapple with. This becomes obvious as soon as one opens the dictionary. As William Empson has remarked, 'This family of words is obviously very difficult; the mere number of them is distracting'.[5] The *OED* includes in the group over one hundred individual words; and some of these have several different meanings. Thirty distinct uses of the noun 'sense' are noted, for instance, and five of the verb, while ten definitions are given for 'sentiment' itself. The section devoted to the group as a whole occupies fifteen pages of the dictionary; and this does not include combinations such as 'common sense', 'moral sense', and others which are treated separately elsewhere.[6]

The roots from which this large family have sprung are two Latin words: the verb 'sentire' and the noun 'sensus'. Apparently simple, these two words are unusually complex. Convincing evidence of their complexity is afforded by the size and diversity of the group of words which has been derived from them: words which in almost every case seem to have been brought into existence in order to limit more precisely certain areas of that extensive field of reference which is covered by 'sentire' and 'sensus'.

These root words themselves also developed a large range of meanings. 'Sentire', in its most general signification, means simply 'to be aware'. According to Lewis and Short in their *Latin Dictionary*, it is used primarily in reference to physical awareness: it means 'to discern by the senses; to feel, hear, see, etc.; to perceive, be sensible of'. But it can also refer to 'mental'

---

[5] *The Structure of Complex Words* (London, 1951), esp. 250.

[6] This and some of the paragraphs which follow are taken in part from my article cited in note 4; see *Studies in the Eighteenth Century* 96–8.

awareness: it means (with a 'mental' connotation) 'to feel, perceive, observe, notice'; and thus, by transference '(in consequence of mental perception) to think, deem, judge, opine, imagine, suppose'. '*Sensus*', the primary meaning of which is given as 'the faculty or power of perceiving, perception, feeling, sensation, sense, etc.' can also be used with either a corporeal or mental connotation. Thus it can refer to a simple physical sensation or perception, or it can refer to a mental feeling – a 'sentiment, emotion, [or] affection'. As '*sensus communis*' it acquires the meaning, 'the common feelings of humanity, the moral sense, taste, discretion, tact', and something very like our own 'common sense'. Eventually it comes to denote 'understanding, mind, reason'.

The primary ambiguity in '*sentire*' and '*sensus*' is that they can be used to refer either to simple physical awareness, to simple mental awareness (if either of these 'pure' states can ever be said to exist), or to an awareness in which elements of both are present. They can refer either to feeling (in the emotional rather than the sensory meaning of the word), or to thinking or to states of consciousness in which both partake. They can refer to the process or power of thinking and feeling, and also to its result – to activities and also to states.

It may be worth noting that the word 'wit' is similarly ambiguous. Nowadays it has the general association of intellectual liveliness – 'always with reference to the utterance of brilliant or sparkling things in an amusing way' (OED). And indeed it seems (in its substantive form) always to have had thought rather than feeling connotations. The first (and now obsolete) meaning given by the OED is 'the seat of consciousness or thought, the mind'. But 'wit' also at one time commonly signified corporeal sense – 'any one of certain particular faculties of perception, classified as *outer* (*outward*) or *bodily* and *inner* (*inward*) or *ghostly*, and commonly reckoned as five' (OED). There was also a phrase, 'common wit', which corresponded exactly to 'common sense' in the meaning it once had of 'an "internal" sense . . . regarded as the common bond or centre of the five senses, in which the various impressions received were reduced to the unity of a common consciousness'. This usage of 'wit' survives vestigially in phrases such as 'keeping your wits about you', and 'being scared out of your wits'.

That both 'sense' and 'wit' should exhibit this fundamental ambiguity suggests first of all that whatever it is they refer to – state, process or entity – is not easy to define. And the questions implicit in the notion of consciousness are admittedly some of the most obdurate that man has ever attempted to resolve. Nor do these questions become any more amenable when they assume a moral dimension, when the terms which are used to describe consciousness in its most simple aspect are also used to describe a process which, while sometimes simple, can often be highly sophisticated and complex, the process of moral judgment. The existence of this ambiguity suggests too that at least some of the distinctions we commonly attempt to make between apparently different aspects of consciousness are at best artificial and at worst misleading. Is there in fact a real difference between thinking and feeling?

Stated in this manner the question seems simple enough, and there were those in the eighteenth century who were prepared to give it a simple answer: Robert Whytt, for instance, the Scottish physiologist, made what seems today the fairly sensible assertion that the traditional division of the human soul or personality into different faculties was misleading and unjustified: 'there seems to be in man one sentient [i.e. feeling] and intelligent PRINCIPLE, which is equally the source of life, sense and motion, as of reason'.[7] Whytt's views did not meet with complete approval from his fellow physiologists, but they were not generally regarded as dangerous or outrageous. But when the materialist philosopher Helvétius, arguing from a similar premise – namely that feeling ('la Sensibilité Physique') is the sole cause of our actions, our thoughts and our passions[8] – went on to maintain that feeling and judging are the same ('*sentir est juger*')[9] his views were regarded as profoundly disturbing. Diderot in particular, otherwise a friendly and sympathetic critic, found

[7] *An Essay on the Vital and other Involuntary Motions of Animals* 2nd ed. (Edinburgh, 1758) 321. For an excellent account of Whytt and his theories, see *Robert Whytt, the Soul, and Medicine,* by R. K. French (London, 1969).

[8] 'La Sensibilité Physique est la cause unique de nos Actions, de nos Pensées, de nos Passions, & de notre Sociabilité.' Chapter Heading (§II, ch. VII) in *De l'Homme, de ses Facultés intellectuelles et de son Education,* Ouvrage Posthume de M. Helvétius (London, 1783) I 102.

[9] *De l'Esprit* (Paris, 1758).

the moral and psychological implications of Helvétius's position quite unacceptable.[10] And it was almost impossible, of course, to discuss the relation between thinking and feeling without bringing morality and metaphysics into it somewhere. And in French, as Arthur M. Wilson has noted, the situation is further complicated by the fact that 'âme' means both 'mind' and 'soul'.[11] Indeed the traditional modes of presenting the supposed division within the psyche – the reason (or right reason) and the feelings, the will and the passions, the head and the heart, the spirit and the flesh – bristled with moral and theological implications. The question as to which of the two either is or ought to be the dominant or primary element in man provided the ground for continuous controversy and speculation throughout the century – and concepts such as 'sentiment' and 'sensibility' (as I shall show in more detail later) occupied a central and often ambiguous position in the argument. This is one of the reasons – possibly the main one – why so many words in the 'sense' family seem so semantically unstable, why they appear to be so peculiarly susceptible to shifts in evaluative connotation. 'Sentimental' offers the clearest example of this: when the adjective first came into vogue (sometime in the 1740s) it seemed – to quote from Lady Bradshaigh's letter to Richardson – that 'everything clever and agreeable [was] comprehended in that word'.[12] By the end

---

[10] Diderot's response to Helvétius's first book, De l'Esprit (1758), in which the key phrase appears was not hostile. But when he saw the general conclusions which could be drawn from this elaborated in De l'Homme (1772), he produced his Réfutation d'Helvétius. (Diderot began to write the Réfutation in 1773. Five years after his death (1778) it was published serially in the Correspondance littéraire (1783–86). A complete edition did not appear until 1875.)

[11] Diderot: the Testing Years, 1713–1759 (New York, 1957) 148.

[12] 'What, in your opinion, is the meaning of the word sentimental, so much in vogue amongst the polite [?] Every thing clever and agreeable is comprhended in that word; but I am convinced a wrong interpretation is given, because it is impossible every thing clever and agreeable can be so common as this word. I am frequently astonished to hear such a one is a sentimental man; we were a sentimental party; I have been taking a sentimental walk. And that I might be reckoned a little in the fashion, and, as I thought, show them the proper use of the word, about six weeks ago, I declared I had just received a sentimental letter'. In Correspondence of Samuel Richardson, ed. Anna Laetitia Barbauld IV (London, 1804) 282.

of the century, however, it had acquired that suggestion of the shallow, the excessive, and the insincere which it bears today. 'Sensibility' suffered a similar decline; and it is extremely interesting to note that as 'sensibility' went out of fashion 'sensitivity', which apparently had a neutral, scientific (particularly botanical) aura, was brought in to replace it. The adjective 'sensitive' dates back to the fifteenth century; but the first use of 'sensitivity', the noun, recorded by the OED occurs in 1803 (Jane Austen's *Sense and Sensibility* was published in 1811). At the same time 'sensible' began to lose its meaning of 'sensitive', while the meaning it has today – 'reasonable', 'intelligent', in accord with the dictates of common sense – which up till then had been more colloquial than correct,[13] gained in force and respectability.

In France the situation resolved itself in a slightly different manner. 'Sensibilité', the French equivalent of 'sensibility', retained the authority and integrity of its moral connotations, but was able to do so only because a new word, 'sensiblerie', was coined, some time in the 1780s, to describe false and affected sensibility. 'Some time before the Revolution,' wrote Mercier, in 1799, 'people of fashion had adopted a certain *sentimental* philosophy ("une certain philosophie *sentimentale*") which was the art of dispensing with being virtuous. This philosophy had its jargon, its sensibility, its accent, even its gestures.'[14] And it was to this simulated and sterile set of attitudes ('cette sensibilité feinte et sterile') that the name 'sensiblerie' was given.

The way in which Mercier uses the French 'sentimental' is exactly parallel to the way – or to one of the ways – in which 'sentimental' was being used at this time in English; and it

[13] This is the last of the eight meanings given by Johnson in his *Dictionary*. The full set of definitions is interesting, especially (in this context) senses 4 and 5: '1. Having the power of perceiving by the senses. 2. Perceptible by the senses. 3. Perceived by the mind. 4. Perceiving by either mind or senses; having perception by the mind or senses. 5. Having moral perception; having the quality of being affected by moral good or ill. 6. Having quick intellectual feeling; being easily or strongly affected. 7. Convinced; persuaded. A low use. 8. In low conversation it has sometimes the sense of reasonable; judicious; wise'.

[14] *Le Nouveau Paris* (1799) II. Quoted in *Dictionnaire alphabétique et analogique de la Langue Française*, par Paul Robert (Paris, 1966) s.v. 'sensible'.

demonstrates strikingly the extent to which the connotations of the word had changed in the fifty years since Lady Bradshaigh had written about it so enthusiastically. That 'sensibilité' and 'sensibility' are by this time no longer precise equivalents, however, illustrates another of the major issues which we have to take into account. This is the problem – and it is an extremely complex one – of the ways in which the developing and interacting vocabularies of sentimentalism in French and English are involved with each other. And to complete the picture some note should also be taken of parallel and related developments which were occurring in the German language. The word 'sentimental' poses the problem in its most acute form. Although the term first appeared in the English language in the 1740s, later in the century Sterne was widely credited with having introduced it. This is understandable, since the way in which he used the word in the 1760s played an essential part in establishing its popularity. And he does appear to have been directly responsible for the creation of a word, 'empfindsam', in German, and for the introduction of 'sentimental' into French. Lessing suggested to Johann Joachim Christoph Bode in 1768, when Bode was at work on his translation of A *Sentimental Journey*, that 'sentimental', because it was such a novel and important word, should be translated by a completely new term, 'empfindsam'. Bernhard Fabian has pointed out that 'Lessing was under the impression that "sentimental" had been coined by Sterne and that Sterne's concept was so new as to require a new word. *Empfindsam*, he thought, would gradually be filled with meaning. In other words it was a word of the future'.[15] His prediction could not have been more accurate. 'Empfindsam' and 'Empfindsamkeit' rapidly established themselves in the German language. Within a few years, for instance, 'Empfindsamkeit' ('sensibility') was being used to describe the distinguishing quality of the new music in which the transition from Baroque 'correctness' to romantic 'feeling' was beginning to make itself apparent. And foremost among the new composers, and one to whose music the term was often applied, was a man who was almost Sterne's exact contemporary, Carl Philipp Emanuel Bach (Bach was born in

[15] 'Tristram Shandy and Parson Yorick among some German Greats', in *The Winged Skull*, ed. A. H. Cash and J. M. Stedmond (Kent State U.P., 1971) 202.

1714, Sterne in 1713). 'Sentimental' is the last word, of course, that one would wish to apply today to C. P. E. Bach's work.

At the same time as Lessing was making his suggestion to Bode the first French translator of Sterne's novel observed that 'the English word *sentimental* could not be rendered into French by any expression which agreed exactly with it, and it has been left to stand as it is'.[16] Yet when Sterne used 'sentimental' he thought he was using the word in a French way; and E. K. Erämetsä has argued convincingly that to some extent Sterne was justified in thinking this. As a result of his reading of French literature and his direct experience of life in France, 'Sterne adopted the English word "sentimental" as the corresponding adjective for his "sensibility", with a distinct French implication. By so doing he made *a sort of sense-loan*. He gave "sentimental" a new signification that was current in French *sentiment*.'[17] It was this word which was then taken back as it were into the French language.

The problems posed by this family of words are rendered even more complicated and fascinating by the way in which they combine breadth and variety of meaning with an unusually high degree of connotative valence. Especially during this period they were charged with great and often vague emotive power – moral, sexual, political, often semi-religious. They represented or could be made to represent a constellation of highly significant general ideas and feelings; while at the same time they could be used with precision, delicacy and scientific neutrality. They operated across the broadest spectrum of thought and discourse: the same word in one context could be coldly empirical while in another it could radiate the most enthusiastic idealism. At the highest level they played a part, sometimes an essential one, in the languages of physiology, psychology, philosophy and the emerging social sciences. If I may borrow a term from Thomas S. Kuhn's *Structure of Scientific Revolutions*,[18] concepts such as 'sympathy'

[16] See *Dictionnaire alphabétique* s.v. 'sentimental'.

[17] *A Study of the Word 'Sentimental'* 54. I am assuming here, as Erämetsä does, that Sterne first used the word in the late 1750s. The problem of whether he had used it earlier in a letter dated 1739/40 is discussed below, p. 98.

[18] *The Structure of Scientific Revolutions*; II, no. 2 in *The International Encyclopaedia of Unified Science* 2nd ed. enlarged (Chicago, 1970).

and 'sensibility' can be seen as functioning 'paradigmatically' both for philosopher–psychologists and sociologists like David Hume, Adam Smith, Helvétius and Denis Diderot and for experimental physiologists like Albrecht von Haller and Robert Whytt: that is, they provided them with hypotheses about the nature of man that they could take both as established and as capable of future development. At the lowest level, however, 'sentimental' concepts formed part of what Steven Marcus, in his study of sexual literature in the Victorian age, has character-ised as the 'fantasies' of a period, that 'mass of unargued, un-examined and largely unconscious assumptions'[19] which forms the basis of that view of the world which everybody, without perhaps being fully aware of the fact, at a particular time and in a particular society seems to share. One of the deepest and most pervasive fantasies of the age was the assumption that man is innately benevolent, or, at least, that he is not innately malevo-lent. But this was also often accompanied by the fear that man's capacity for benevolent action was very limited. In a concept such as that of a *delicate sensibility* or an *exquisite sensibility* we find the hope and the fear ambiguously and dynamically combined; and it is not surprising that these phrases should appear and reappear in all kinds of writing throughout the century, and with a widely varying, but always related, set of connotations.

For anyone whose primary concern is the novel, 'sensibility' and 'sentimental' are the words which demand the closest in-vestigation. Such an investigation can probably be conducted most fruitfully, especially in the case of 'sentimental', as part of an examination of the sentimental novel or novel of sentiment; and I shall therefore postpone any detailed account of the mean-ings which may be given to these key terms until a later point in the discussion.[20] In any case it may be helpful at this stage to say something about the general context of sentimental ideas within which these words functioned, and which they helped to define and formulate. This context extends well beyond the bounds of what is generally understood as sentimental literature; but it is only when these terms are placed within this large

[19] *The other Victorians: A Study of Sexuality and Pornography in Mid-Nineteenth Century England* (London, 1966) 1.
[20] See below, pp. 98 ff.

framework that their full significance so far as literature is concerned can be properly appreciated.

III

Sentimental ideas are complex and to some extent contradictory, and their development in England and on the Continent, especially in France, though generally similar and often intimately related, did not always follow exactly the same path. But like so many other ideas in the eighteenth century, they all derive from one basic notion. This is that the source of all knowledge and all values is the individual human experience. 'Whence has [the mind] all the materials of Reason and Knowledge?' asked John Locke in 1690 in *An Essay concerning Human Understanding*. The reply he gave to this question was simple – or apparently simple – and profoundly important. 'To this,' he said, 'I answer, in one word, from *Experience*: in that, all our knowledge is founded; and from that it ultimately derives itself. Our observation employ'd either about *external, sensible objects; or about the internal operations of our minds . . . is that which supplies our Understandings with all the materials of thinking*'.[21] The key word is 'sensible': what we know derives ultimately from what our *senses* tell us – from our *sensibility* (although Locke himself does not use the word). Locke established firmly and clearly that all successive speculation about the nature of man would have to be grounded on basic empirical principles – although the way in which these principles were to be interpreted was to vary extensively over the next hundred years. A. S. Pringle-Pattison reminds us in his edition of the *Essay* that Locke is 'far from being a consistent Empiricist (that is, a pure Sensationalist), of the type of Hume, Condillac, or James Mill'; and he observes that 'the ambiguity of the term "experience" is one of the main difficulties in the way of arriving at a correct interpretation of [Locke's treatise]'.[22] And there is a considerable gulf separating the relative simplicity with which Locke uses the term and the manifold complexities with which Kant deploys *Erfahrung*, its German equivalent, in 1781 in the *Critique of*

[21] Op. cit. 37 (II, i).
[22] *An Essay concerning Human Understanding*, by John Locke, ab. and ed. A. S. Pringle-Pattison (Oxford, 1924) 42 note 1.

Pure Reason, the opening sentences of which echo, perhaps deliberately, the English philosopher's famous statement. 'That all our knowledge begins with experience there can be no doubt', states Kant, only to add almost immediately the important qualification that 'though all our knowledge begins with experience it by no means follows that all arises out of experience'.[23]

By the time Kant wrote his *Critique* such a beginning for a philosophical discourse had become conventional. As Nicholas Capaldi has observed, 'most Enlightenment works begin not with a metaphysic, a theory about the ultimate nature of the world, but with an epistemological theory, a theory about what man knows and how he comes to know'.[24] The implications of such an approach were not, of course, simply epistemological. They were also of the greatest significance in the sphere of ethics, religion and politics. In the eighteenth century man found himself as never before faced squarely with the fact that the only valid way for him to understand himself is by looking thoroughly and honestly at the available evidence, and that, whether or not God exists, this evidence must ultimately rest on the way in which feeling, thinking, *sentient* individual human beings experience the world of 'external, sensible objects' and the 'internal Operations of [their] Minds'. It is from this experience (an experience conditioned both by the nature of man and by the nature of the world in which he exists) that he will derive

---

[23] *Critique of Pure Reason*, trans. J. M. D. Meiklejohn (London. 1934) 25.

[24] *The Enlightenment: The Proper Study of Mankind*, ed. Nicholas Capaldi (New York, 1967) Introduction 17. Capaldi illustrates his point by quoting the opening statements from a number of important works: 'Hume begins his *A Treatise of Human Nature* with the statement: "All perceptions of the human mind resolve themselves into two distinct kinds, which I shall call Impressions and Ideas." D'Alembert, in Part I of the "Preliminary Discourse", says, "our first step will be to examine . . . the parts of our knowledge . . . in short we must return to the origin and generation of our ideas . . ." Helvétius opens *A Treatise on Man* (1772) with the following statement: "I still learn; my instruction is not yet finished; when will it be? When I shall be no longer sensible; at my death . . ." Finally, Condorcet introduces his *History of Human Progress* (1794) with the statement: "Man is born with the faculty of receiving sensations".' (Note that the original French of Helvétius reads, 'Lorsque je n'en serai plus susceptible', not 'sensible'.)

not only his notions of the physical universe, but also his moral notions – or, as they were almost universally called during this period, his moral *sentiments*.

The assumption that the source of all knowledge and value is the individual human experience is not, of course, peculiar to sentimentalism, but it is essential to it. What distinguishes it in its sentimental aspect is the way in which it was used to stress certain features of that experience which had previously not received so much attention. The role of the feelings, especially in the formation of moral judgments, was particularly emphasised. As David Hume put it in a striking and widely misunderstood phrase, the reason was now seen to be 'the slave of the passions'.[25] This did not mean – especially in Hume's own moral theory – that reasoned and reasonable opinions and judgments were necessarily subordinate or inferior to the feelings or the emotions, but merely that feeling was necessarily the *primary* element in the process which led to the formation of a moral sentiment. And the feelings, the passions and the rational considerations which went into the making of moral judgments were, of course, one's own. Disproportionate weight eventually came to be placed on the feelings – on sensibility at the expense of sense. But this is not so significant as the fact that the process of moral judgment was held to be essentially private and subjective. Ideally the man or woman of sentiment as presented in the fiction of the age was seen as someone in whom the claims of reason and feeling were properly balanced. What distinguished these sentimental heroes and heroines was not only their highly developed awareness of their own processes of discrimination, but also their belief in the sanctity and authority of their private judgments.

It is this rather than their exquisite sensibilities, for instance, which characterises the leading figures in Richardson's novels. Sir Charles Grandison and Clarissa Harlowe place principles before feelings – but they insist on their right to interpret those principles for themselves. Grandison 'lives to himself, and to his own heart, rather than to the opinion of the world,'[26] and Clarissa insists, both to her parents and to Lovelace, on her

[25] A *Treatise of Human Nature*, ed. L. A. Selby-Bigge (Oxford, 1888, etc.) 415.
[26] *Sir Charles Grandison*, ed. Jocelyn Harris (London, 1972) I 182.

ultimate right to decide for herself the question of where her duty lies:

> My motives . . . arise principally from what offers to my own heart; respecting . . . its own rectitude, its own judgment of the Fit and the Unfit; as I would, without study, answer for myself to myself in the first place; to him [Lovelace], and to the world, in the second only. Principles that are in my mind; that I found there; implanted, no doubt, by the first gracious Planter: which therefore impell me . . . to act up to them . . . to the best of my judgment . . . let others act as they will by me.[27]

It is this which unites these characters with others who in many respects are very different from them – Parson Yorick, Laurence Sterne's sentimental traveller, who trusts the promptings of his delicate sensibility; Harley, the man of feeling, in the novel (of the same name) by Henry Mackenzie, who eventually fades away and dies; the sorrowful and suicidal Werther; or Rousseau's Savoyard vicar, whose motto is 'My judgment right or wrong, simply because it's mine'.

> I realised, moreover, that far from delivering me from my useless doubts, the philosophes had only multiplied those which tormented me, and had not resolved one of them. I took therefore another guide and I said to myself, let us consult the inner light, it will mislead me less than they do, or at least the error will be my own, and I shall get myself into less trouble through following my own illusions than by giving myself over to their deceptions.[28]

Whether our own unaided judgments are true or illusory, they are, it was emphasised, our own, and they are, ultimately, all we have to work with.

To recognise this was to make things simpler in some ways but more difficult in others, for it immediately raised the question of what sort of authority one could attribute to the individual's private intuitions. For a devout Christian like Clarissa the

[27] Clarissa, III 311 (Everyman II 306).
[28] La "Profession de Foi du Vicaire Savoyard" de Jean-Jacques Rousseau, éd. critique par Pierre Maurice Masson (Fribourg et Paris, 1914) 61–3.

answer was simple: since God had planted the correct principles in her mind they carried his absolute and universal authority. Provided she was given the freedom to examine her conscience honestly everything must be well. Rousseau would probably have preferred to speak of Nature rather than God – but he too believed that the inner light could reveal the truth. He also believed, however, that it could be deceptive, that the prompt-ings of one's own heart might not carry the universal validity with which they seemed to be invested. And for a sceptical materialist like Hume, for instance, there was no need to claim that one's subjective judgments had any general application whatever – although Hume himself did not assume such a com-pletely relativist position, nor apparently did he wish to. But the question was now irrevocably opened: whether the moral senti-ments of the individual have any intrinsic authority, and the extent to which the moral sentiments of man in general agreed or disagreed with the traditional precepts of Christian morality and the concept of man's nature which such precepts imply, were matters for critical and empirical investigation. The process of this investigation was to be the source of some of the liveliest and most agonised intellectual and spiritual conflict in the century – a conflict of which we are the heirs and in which we are still involved. 'Is an ethics possible, and if so on what basis?' This, as Lester G. Crocker so amply demonstrates in *An Age of Crisis,*[29] is the 'great problem' which from now on was to con-front anyone who wished to think seriously about the nature of man as a moral and social being.

Although there was wide agreement that the proper study of mankind was man, and that the proper basis for such a study was empirical observation, the conclusions to which such an inquiry might lead could vary enormously. Lockean sensational-ist epistemology would seem to provide a firm basis for a com-pletely relativist or subjectivist ethical theory; and it is a short and, some would argue, logical step from something like the humane scepticism of David Hume's ethical position to the bleak and anarchic moral nihilism espoused and advocated by the Marquis de Sade. Yet Sade, who is a ruthlessly anti-senti-mental writer, would have found nothing to argue with in the

[29] *An Age of Crisis: Man and World in Eighteenth-Century French Thought* (Baltimore, 1959) 20.

basic assumption laid down in 1725 by Francis Hutcheson in the Preface to *An Inquiry into the Original of our Ideas of Beauty and Virtue* that 'the Importance of any Truth is nothing else than its Moment, or Efficacy to make Men happy, or to give them the greatest and most lasting Pleasure; and *Wisdom* denotes only a Capacity of pursuing this End by the best Means'.[30] 'In this world', Juliette tells her sister, the hapless Justine, 'one must not be afflicted save by what affects one personally . . . [and] true wisdom consists infinitely more in doubling the sum of one's pleasures than in increasing the sum of one's pains'.[31] In a strictly technical sense Hutcheson can be described as a sentimental philosopher; and he would differ radically from Sade in his conception of what could give man 'the greatest and most lasting Pleasure'. But hedonism and sensationalism are as essential to his position as they are to Sade's.

Hutcheson, like Shaftesbury who preceded him and Hume and Adam Smith who followed him, would have found Sade's concept of man as a fundamentally aggressive, violent, cruel, isolated, anti-social being completely incomprehensible. 'A Creature void of natural Affection, and wholly destitute of a communicative or social Principle . . .' writes Shaftesbury, 'feels but small Enjoyment in Life, and finds little Satisfaction in the mere sensual Pleasures which remain with him, after the Loss of social Enjoyment; and all that can be called *Humanity* or *Good-Nature*'.[32] Such a person would be '*absolutely* immoral and inhuman'. And Hume finds it equally difficult to imagine such a being: 'A creature, absolutely malicious and spiteful, *were there any such in nature*, must be worse than indifferent to the images of vice and virtue'.[33]

This belief in man's innate benevolence, or at least in man's capacity to act benevolently rather than malevolently if given

---

[30] Op. cit. ix.

[31] *Justine, or Good Conduct Well Chastised* in *The Marquis de Sade: the complete Justine, Philosophy in the Bedroom and other Writings*, comp. and trans. Richard Seaver & Austyn Wainhouse (New York, 1966) 460.

[32] *An Inquiry Concerning Virtue or Merit*, in *Characteristicks* (London, 1711) II 81.

[33] *An Enquiry Concerning the Principles of Morals*, § V, pt. ii, in *The Essential Works of David Hume*, ed. Ralph Cohen (New York, London and Toronto, 1965) 222. My italics.

the opportunity, was so widely and pervasively held during the eighteenth century that it deserves to be called a fantasy in Marcus's terms. As Ronald Crane has shown in his seminal article, 'Suggestions toward a Genealogy of "The Man of Feeling"', it formed a central part of 'the propaganda of benevolence and tender feeling', preached in England from the time of the Restoration on into the mid-eighteenth century 'with increasing intensity . . . by the anti-Puritan, anti-Stoic, and anti-Hobbesian divines of the Latitudinarian school'.[34] And what the congregations accepted each Sunday in their churches the philosophers for the most part did not question too deeply in their studies. The idea, of course, did not go completely unchallenged. Its most notorious opponent in Britain was probably Bernard de Mandeville, the satirist-philosopher, who attacked it with great force, wit and thoroughness in his *Fable of the Bees* (1714). But his argument that man is ineradicably selfish, that his advocacy of moral values is necessarily hypocritical and that, paradoxically, private vices are public benefits, was on the whole taken more seriously in France than in England. The materialists La Mettrie and Helvétius present an image of man that owes something not only to Bayle (whose influence Mandeville acknowledges) but also to Mandeville himself; and these are the thinkers whom Sade is later to acclaim as his teachers. In England it is true that Mandeville's attack drew a certain amount of fire – on the title-page of Hutcheson's *Inquiry*, for instance, it is announced that 'The Principles of the late Earl of SHAFTESBURY are Explain'd and Defended, against the Author of the *Fable of the Bees*', and Adam Smith takes issue with him in his *Theory of Moral Sentiments*. But the debate does not on the whole lead these and other opponents of Mandeville into exploring in any serious way the status of the notion of man's innate benevolence. Like Hume they obviously feel that this is something that can be more or less taken for granted; and so it tends to be assumed and asserted rather than demonstrated and argued for with any vigour.[35]

[34] ELH I (1934) 230.
[35] Mandeville's thesis is generally dismissed as wilful perversity. Remarks such as the following are typical: 'There is no one that seems more to depend upon the Folly and Madness of his Readers . . .' (William Law, *Remarks upon . . . The Fable of the Bees*, London,

The belief that man was naturally capable of acting benevolently if given the chance was often held in company with
extremely pessimistic ideas about the nature of the world and
society. The paradox that man though naturally good somehow
creates the conditions which prevent him from acting virtuously
– that born free, as Rousseau said, he is everywhere in chains –
haunted the imagination of the age. But an awareness of the
problem was usually not enough to destroy the optimistic belief
that if only the right circumstances prevailed man could live up
to his expectations. At the same time, however, the contemplation of the evil and inimical conditions – 'the world' – in which
the benevolent impulse was forced to operate was accepted as a
legitimate source for melancholy. The sentimental tribute of a
tear exacted by the spectacle of virtue in distress was an acknow-
ledgement at once of man's inherent goodness and of the impossibility of his ever being able to demonstrate his goodness
effectively.

The response, of course, did not necessarily have to be sentimental in our sense of the term. In *Rasselas*, for instance, that
most unsentimental of books, man is presented as being proud,
self-deluded, foolish and wrong-headed – but also as being fundamentally more inclined to act in a humane rather than a
malicious way. Rasselas in particular is shown to be spontaneously
benevolent. When the young Prince of Abissinia becomes dis-
satisfied with life in the happy valley he is told that if he had
seen the miseries of the world he would know how to value his
present state. His main ambition then becomes to escape from the
valley into the world outside, to move from illusion into reality:

> His chief amusement was to picture to himself that world
> which he had never seen; to place himself in various conditions;
> to be entangled in imaginary difficulties, and to be engaged in
> wild adventures: but his benevolence always terminated his
> projects in the relief of distress, the detection of fraud, the
> defeat of oppression, and the diffusion of happiness.[36]

1724 71); 'the shocking Image [Mandeville] has drawn of Man-
kind . . . [is] monstrous and unnatural'. ([George Blewitt], *An
Enquiry whether A general Practice of Virtue tends to Wealth or
Poverty, Benefit or Disadvantage of a People?* London, 1725 Preface).
   [36] *The History of Rasselas, Prince of Abissinia* (1759), ed. J. P. Hardy
(London, 1968) 9–10.

In the language of the day 'benevolence' is a 'sentiment', and it is the strongest sentiment to be aroused when the young Prince becomes aware of the nature of reality, that is, when he realises that life for the majortiy of mankind is (in Johnson's view at least) painful and unhappy. Brought up under ideal conditions – Rasselas indeed can be regarded as being in a state of primal innocence – his sympathy is aroused as soon as he becomes *sensible* of the miseries of others; and the benevolent impulses which spring from this response make him in his own imagination not merely charitable but also percipient and heroic – he detects fraud and defeats oppression. Johnson, one imagines, would not have wished to maintain that all the spontaneous movements of the heart are benevolent. But this brief incident illustrates the pervasiveness of the belief that men have a basic desire to act benevolently; that the sentiments of humanity and sympathy are among the most powerful feelings we possess. And this, at least in the sense of the word then in vogue, is a thoroughly *sentimental* idea.

The notion that human beings are innately sympathetic is a key element in sentimentalism; and so far as the concept of sympathy is concerned this particular period in the eighteenth century is of special interest. 1759, the year in which *Rasselas* appeared, also saw the publication of the first two volumes of *Tristram Shandy* and of *The Theory of Moral Sentiments*; and in 1764 Robert Whytt brought out his *Observations on the Nature, Causes and Cure of those Diseases which are commonly called Nervous, Hypochondriac or Hysteric: to which are prefixed Some Remarks on the Sympathy of the Nerves*. Sympathy, in either a psychological, physiological or social sense (and these significations are all related to each other), is of basic importance in all these works. Sterne's novel demonstrates more positively and convincingly than does any other eighteenth-century work of fiction the power of sympathy in human relations; Adam Smith takes as a fundamental assumption that the capacity of human beings to sympathise with each other, to identify themselves in some way with the feelings of their fellows, is the basis for the formation of all moral attitudes; and his fellow Scot, Robert Whytt, Professor of Medicine at Edinburgh, clarified and extended the traditional physiological idea of sympathy (which goes back to Galen) in such a way as to help make possible the development in the nineteenth and twentieth centuries of the concepts of the autonomic and sympathetic nervous systems; while at the same time he showed considerable insight into hypochondriac and psychosomatic conditions, and into the way in which certain physical states or processes – yawning, laughing, weeping, vomiting, hysteria, fear – can be sympathetically excited in one person by another. This latter phenomenon was already well known in medicine; but by locating it so firmly in his general theory of sympathy Whytt provides empirical physiological evidence which supports Adam Smith's argument that it is through sympathy that human beings are basically able to communicate with each other. In *The Theory of Moral Sentiments* sympathy emerges as the essentially cohesive element which holds together the fabric of society.

Sympathy, moreover, was conceived to be not merely that which made society possible, but that which made the *good* society possible. And the good society came to be seen more and more as one which enabled the maximum number of its members to be happy. The phrase, 'the greatest happiness of the greatest number', seems to be an eighteenth-century invention: 'Hutcheson was the original author of that famous phrase', states John Rae in his *Life of Adam Smith*;[37] and in the Preface to Hutcheson's *System of Moral Philosophy* published in 1755, after his death, the Reverend William Leechman, Professor of Divinity at Glasgow, commends him for placing 'the highest virtue and excellence . . . where all sound Philosophy and Divine Revelation has placed it', namely in that sort of behaviour '*which will promote the happiness of mankind in the most extensive manner to which our power can reach*'.[38] The sermon which the Reverend Laurence Sterne chose to print as the first of *The Sermons of Mr. Yorick* bears the title, 'Inquiry after Happiness', and opens with the statement that 'the great pursuit of man is after happiness. It is the first and strongest desire of his nature'. One can only agree with Louis I. Bredvold when he asserts that 'it was no mere accident that Locke's three basic rights of life, liberty and property were changed to the rights of life, liberty and the pursuit of happiness in [the] Declaration of

---

[37] Op. cit. (London, 1895) 12.
[38] *A System of Moral Philosophy* (London, 1755) I xvi–xvii.

Independence'.[39] Not only was it asserted more forcefully than ever before that all men have a natural right to be happy, but this assertion was to some extent seen as replacing – or was at least merged with – the traditional Christian notion that all men had an obligation to be good. As Lester G. Crocker observes at the conclusion of his massive survey of ethical speculation in the eighteenth century, 'One fact stands out. There was almost unanimous agreement that human nature must not and could not be violated in its basic demand for happiness.'[40]

Furthermore it was assumed that it lay within man's power (not necessarily assisted by the power of God) to create the conditions under which this demand could be satisfied. If man had a natural right to be happy he also had a natural capacity to act virtuously, i.e. benevolently. A person who cannot, or does not, wish to act benevolently, was thought to be less than human: 'all his sentiments', says Hume of such a creature, 'must be inverted, and directly opposite to those which prevail in the human species'.[41] 'Humanity' functioned as a concept at once empirical and idealistic, and eventually in the context of the French Revolution, ideological. To be human in the true sense of the word was to be *humane*. Significantly, it was not until the eighteenth century that the word 'humane' as distinct from 'human' (an orthographic distinction which can be made in English but not in French) took on exclusively the meaning it has today. According to the OED, it was then that 'it became restricted to a particular group of senses', viz. 'Marked by sympathy with and consideration for the needs and distresses of others; feeling or showing compassion and tenderness towards human beings and lower animals; kind, benevolent'. This meaning had been present in earlier times – although 'humane' often functioned then simply as a synonym for, or another way of spelling, 'human' – now it became the only meaning. In 1776 the Society for Recovering Persons Apparently Drowned, which had been formed two years earlier, decided to call itself the Royal Humane Society.[42] The choice of title is a small but revealing

[39] *The Natural History of Sensibility* (Detroit, 1962) 7.

[40] *Nature and Culture: Ethical Thought in the French Enlightenment* (Baltimore, 1963) 498.

[41] *An Enquiry Concerning the Principles of Morals*, § V, pt. ii, in *Essential Works* 222.   [42] OED s.v. 'humane'.

piece of evidence of the belief and hope that human society could itself become humane, and moreover that this could be achieved, indeed would have to be achieved, by man alone. This is the century in which Christian teaching increasingly places works before faith, in which writers of religious conduct books, like The Whole Duty of Man and Defoe's Family Instructor, devote a growing and proportionately larger amount of space to man's duty to his neighbour and less to his duty to God. It is in this period that the humanitarian impulse is recognised and consciously fostered in western civilisation, although the word 'humanitarian' itself does not enter the language until the early nineteenth century. And this impulse, and the recognition of it, is in the original sense of the word, 'sentimental'. This 'reliance on the supreme freedom of our good impulses as an assurance of the salvation of man', as Bredvold has said, 'was perhaps the most important contribution of the movement of sensibility to our modern ways of thinking'.[43] The French Revolution, at least in one of its aspects, was an attempt to create the conditions under which men would be free to express their good impulses; and despite the tragic warning provided by the Terror this belief that if only man can be given the right opportunities he will act well remains an essential and potent element in both radical and liberal idealism. It was this, according to two English observers, that most strikingly distinguished the French revolution of May 1968: 'It carried the germ of hope', wrote Patrick Seale and Maureen McConville, 'that the intellect, the spirit, and the imagination if given free range and scope, could really change the world'.[44]

In the eighteenth century ideals and ideas such as these – notions of man's innate benevolence, of his 'humanity', of his capacity to sympathise, of his ability and his right to exercise his own judgment, to formulate alone and unaided his own moral sentiments – functioned not only as powerful fantasies but also as complex and sometimes precisely defined concepts which were developed and investigated in the work of philosophers, scientists and imaginative writers. And it was through the effort to define, develop and apply these ideas that a terminology and a set of concepts evolved which enabled people to

[43] Natural History of Sensibility 26.
[44] French Revolution, 1968 (Harmondsworth, 1968) 229.

explore in new and significant ways the whole question of what it means to be a human being living in the society of his fellows. The work of the novelist often complemented the work of the philosophical or scientific inquirer in a remarkably close and fruitful manner. Often, indeed, the one person operated in both fields: Diderot, Voltaire and Rousseau are novelists, playwrights, poets – and *philosophes*; and Sade regarded himself as being in the same tradition. The naturalistic novel, primarily an English invention, grew at least partly out of the attempt to provide supporting documentary evidence for what we should now describe as sociological theories. This is certainly true of much of Defoe's fiction – especially in *The Family Instructor* and *Religious Courtship* – and of Richardson's *Familiar Letters* and *Pamela*. Fielding and Smollett cannot be regarded in this sense as 'socio-logical' novelists; but it is surely significant that Smollett was a medical man, and one concerned with questions of public health (particularly in the navy), and that Fielding actively involved himself with social problems. It may be true, as Malvin Zirker has effectively demonstrated,[45] that the views advanced by Fielding in his two pamphlets, *Enquiry into the Causes of the Late Increase of Robbers* and *A Proposal for Making an Effectual Provision for the Poor* are extremely conservative and hard-headed – so much so as to seem to contradict at times the attitudes embodied in the novels. But nonetheless the pamphlets clearly manifest a theoretical concern with the problems of society; and at the practical level Fielding and his brother unquestionably made a positive contribution to the reform and development of police work and the administration of justice at Westminster. And Laurence Sterne, before he became a novelist, was a conscientious priest with a close experience of what it could mean to cope with the personal and communal problems of his parishioners. If *Tristram Shandy* and *A Sentimental Journey* can be read as 'theoretical' novels, as I believe they can, it is worth remember-ing that Sterne's sentimental theorising is grounded in a sub-stantial amount of social practice.

Clarissa demonstrates a similar amalgam of practice and theory. The social, economic, legal and familial sub-structure of the situation with which the book deals is firmly and meticulously

[45] *Fielding's Social Pamphlets* (Berkeley and Los Angeles, 1966) 43–64.

established: and on this foundation Richardson is able to develop a narrative which is both a novel of ideas and something like a programmed experiment. The situation which he has built up enables him to test to destruction certain notions – such as man's innate humanity – which are basic to sentimental morality. Almost as a spin-off from this experimental process he produces an account of the inner conflicts of morally sensitive individuals which for dramatic, psychological vividness and minuteness of detail is new in English fiction. Choderlos de Laclos in *Les Liaisons Dangereuses* does something very similar: his novel has the tightness, precision and finality of an elegant mathematical theorem; and even his characters, Valmont and the Marquise de Merteuil, consciously see themselves as experimenting with their own and others' emotions. It is in this sense a very philosophical novel.

It is perhaps not surprising that the term 'philosophy' should have enjoyed at this time a much wider range of reference than it does today. To be philosophical was to be in the most basic and the most general sense sceptical, critical, inquiring – at once scientific, humane and omnivorously curious. The philosopher took the whole of human behaviour as his province – he was concerned, to quote the title of the Earl of Shaftesbury's collection of essays, with the *Characteristicks of Men, Manners, Opinions*; and the areas of inquiry which are now defined as psychology, anthropology and sociology were then still part of the general subject of ethics or moral philosophy. Astronomers, physicists, chemists and physiologists – people we should now call 'scientists' – then thought of themselves as 'natural philosophers'. Robert Whytt, for example, the Scottish physiologist who was concerned with the investigation of sensibility and sympathy as attributes of the nervous system, described his *Essay on the Vital and other Involuntary Motions of Animals* (1751) as a 'Philosophical inquiry', and acknowledges a debt to Newton: 'No doctrine in Philosophy which was not built on [experiment and observation], has ever been able to stand its ground . . . and the theories of NEWTON, and some few others . . . have therefore triumphed over all objections.'[46] Newton's

---

[46] *An Essay on the Vital and other Involuntary Motions of Animals* vi. Whytt read philosophy for a time as a student at Edinburgh, and the brother of his second wife, Louisa Balfour, became Professor of

influence extended far beyond the boundaries of astronomy, optics and mathematics – 'God said, "Let Newton be!" and *all* was
light'. As the sub-title to David Hume's *Treatise of Human
Nature* (1739) indicates, the Newtonian approach was considered
to be valid for all areas of human inquiry. Hume saw his *Treatise*
as '*an Attempt to introduce the experimental Method of Reasoning into Moral Subjects*'; and 'moral' had the widest connotations:
the three books into which the work is divided deal with the
Understanding, the Passions, and Morals.

Hume's *Treatise* seems not to have been widely read – at least
in the years immediately following its publication – but its
influence on other philosophers was nonetheless very great indeed. This influence can be seen particularly in a work such as
Adam Smith's *Theory of Moral Sentiments* which was published
twenty years later in 1759. This lengthy critique and statement
of sentimental morality is both a serious contribution to
philosophy and to some extent a work of popularisation. In
many ways it is an unusually important document. It represents
on the one hand the culmination of the work of the sentimentalist, Moral Sense, group of British philosophers – Shaftesbury,
Hutcheson and Hume in particular – and on the other it must
be regarded as something which opened the way for what were
to become central lines of development in modern sociological
and psychological theory. It is thus both representative and
seminal; and in the latter half of the eighteenth century it
enjoyed an extensive circulation amongst educated readers in
both Britain and France (although its influence in the latter
country is difficult to estimate). Robert Burns's famous lines

> Oh wad some power the giftie gie us
> To see oursels as others see us!

afford one of the most striking pieces of evidence of Smith's
popularity, for they are almost certainly an echo and transmuta-
tion of a passage in *The Theory of Moral Sentiments*.[47]

Moral Philosophy at that University. The Edinburgh Medical Society,
which published Whytt's first major piece of research ('An Essay
towards the discovery of a safe medicine for dissolving the stone')
later changed its name to the Philosophical Society. See R. K. French,
Robert Whytt ch. I *passim*.
[47] The notion is central to Smith's account of the development of

As D. Daiches Raphael has pointed out Adam Smith also influenced Darwin, and he seems, too, to have anticipated certain of Freud's ideas.[48] At the same time he helped to establish, as Glenn R. Morrow has emphasised, that 'realistic philosophy of society'[49] which is a necessary basis for any valid and fruitful sociological investigation. The social sciences as we understand them are born in the eighteenth century: and it is in works such as The Theory of Moral Sentiments — especially when it is taken in conjunction with the The Wealth of Nations — that we can most clearly see this birth taking place.

I have already referred to Thomas S. Kuhn's theory of the 'paradigm', and it may be helpful to look more closely at the way in which this term may be applied to works like The Theory of Moral Sentiments — for it is abundantly obvious that a revolution in the scientific approach to the study of man took place in the eighteenth century; and that sentimentalism was at the heart of this revolution. A paradigm, in Kuhn's sense, is a special kind of achievement, one 'that some particular scientific community acknowledges for a time as supplying the foundation for its further practice'; and he cites as examples a number of classic treatises in the physical sciences: 'Aristotle's Physica, Ptolemy's Almagest, Newton's Principia and Optics, Franklin's Electricity, Lavoisier's Chemistry, and Lyell's Geology'. These and several other works may be called paradigms, he suggests, 'because they shared two essential characteristics. Their achievement was sufficiently unprecedented to attract an enduring group of adherents away from competing modes of scientific activity.

---

conscience, and he refers to it many times in the book. A typical passage runs as follows: we can only judge our own actions 'by endeavouring to view them with the eyes of other people, as other people are likely to view them... We attempt to examine our conduct as we imagine any other fair and impartial spectator would examine it'. Adam Smith's Moral and Political Philosophy, ed. H. W. Schneider (New York, 1948) 137.

[48] 'Sympathy and Imagination', The Listener, March 1959 407–8. See also my article, 'Authority, Guilt and Anxiety in The Theory of Moral Sentiments', Texas Studies in Literature and Language XI (1969) 945–62. It is worth noting that The Theory of Moral Sentiments was studied extensively in American universities during the nineteenth century.

[49] 'The Significance of the Doctrine of Sympathy in Hume and Adam Smith', Philosophical Review XXXII (1923) 75.

Simultaneously, it was sufficiently open-ended to leave all sorts of problems for the redefined group of practitioners.'[50] Locke's *Essay concerning Human Understanding*, to take one example, clearly belongs in the same class as the works listed by Kuhn, and moreover it was acknowledged to be this sort of work during the eighteenth century. And the philosophers and the *philosophes* (not, of course, inspired solely by Locke) saw themselves very much as a group of practitioners in the science of man who were undergoing a process of redefinition. As Peter Gay has recently reminded us the *philosophes* thought of themselves – even when they differed amongst each other – as a 'party' or a 'family', a group of people who were engaged in a common intellectual enterprise, and one that was related to all other scientific and civilising activity.[51] It was Hume's ambition to introduce Newtonian procedures into moral philosophy just as it was Whytt's to introduce them into his area of philosophy, namely physiology. And the *philosophes* took the work of Newton and Locke as paradigms. Their most distinctive achievement in some ways – an achievement with which we are still coming to terms – was the *Encyclopédie*. This great though extremely uneven repository of human knowledge and source book for new and revolutionary ideas, which appeared under constant threat of censorship and destruction during the fifteen years 1751–65, was the result of a team effort directed – at least in theory and to some extent in practice – along basically scientific lines. And for Diderot, the leader of the team, the notions of sentiment and sensibility, as we shall see, had a quite special significance. In Britain the way in which the Moral Sense philosophers succeeded in demonstrating that it could be possible to achieve an empirically satisfying general description of man and society was of the greatest theoretical importance. More than any other single work *The Theory of Moral Sentiments* had the effect of making the discoveries and achievements of Hume and his predecessors widely available. It is primarily for this reason, and for

[50] Op. cit. 10.
[51] 'The philosophes used [the metaphor of a family] themselves. They thought of themselves as a *petite troupe*, with common loyalties and a common world view. This sense survived all their high-spirited quarrels: the philosophes did not have a party line, but they were a party.' *The Enlightenment: an Interpretation* (New York, 1966) 6.

the way in which he deploys, develops and investigates the fundamentally sentimental concept of sympathy, that we are justified in describing Smith's work as paradigmatic.

This redefinition of man as a social and moral being took place in the context of a redefinition of man as a physical being. And people like Diderot and Smith were quite conscious of this. 'Sensibility', 'sentiment', and 'sympathy' were terms with precise meanings in the newly developing sciences of physiology and neurology; and it is in the 1750s and 1760s that these terms, of central importance not only in works such as *The Theory of Moral Sentiments* but also in novels such as *Tristram Shandy* and *A Sentimental Journey*, and Diderot's *La Religieuse* and his philosophic dialogue, *Le Rêve de d'Alembert*, gained a secure and valuable place in medical terminology. And the scientists who were responsible for the establishment of sensibility and sympathy as workable physiological and psychological concepts – notably Albrecht von Haller and Robert Whytt – were also keenly aware of the moral connotations of these terms, and of the implications which they felt their discoveries had for the redefinition of man as a spiritual being. Although Haller and Whytt differed widely – and publicly – on certain points, both believed that their experimental demonstrations of sensibility as a physiological process provided evidence for the existence of the soul, and for man's capacity to function as a moral being.

When Albrecht von Haller published *De Partibus Corporis Humani Sensibilibus et Irritabilibus* in 1753 (translated into English in 1755 as *A Dissertation on the Sensible and Irritable Parts of Animals*) he was Professor of Anatomy and Botany at the University of Göttingen, which was under the patronage of the Hanoverian George II of Great Britain. But the Swiss scientist was already well known as a poet, essayist and reviewer. His review of *Clarissa*, published originally in a French periodical in Amsterdam and reprinted in the *Gentleman's Magazine* (XIX, June and August, 1749), is one of the first extended and genuinely critical examinations of Richardson's novel; and he almost certainly played an important part in arranging the first translation into German of the book, and was also involved in the translation of *Sir Charles Grandison*.[52] In his poetry, notably a longish

[52] See *Samuel Richardson: a Biography*, by T. C. Duncan Eaves and Ben D. Kimpel (Oxford, 1971) 290–1, 320, 376.

meditation *Ueber den Ursprung des Uebels* (*On the Origin of Evil*) written in 1734, he had argued that feeling ('gefuhl') is the divine spark in man, planted in him to provide a link with the deity, and to alert the body and the soul to the presence of evil. In an English translation of 1794 Haller's simple 'feeling' has become the more complex 'sensibility', but the drift of the argument – in particular the intimate involvement of physical sensitivity with spirituality and the dangers which this entails – remains clear:

> To aid our weakness, the Creator has imparted that prompt and vigilant sensibility which, easily irritated, alarms the whole body upon the slightest injury . . . In that delicate con-texture of infinitely small vessels which distribute strength and nourishment to every part, the smallest violence would break the tender links: confidence in health would conduct us to the tomb, if a secret sensation excited in the marrow of our fibres, the source of pain, of pleasure, of life itself, warned us not to avoid an enemy that would ruin us in perfidious silence. This sensibility contracts our nerves to resist the approach of what is hurtful . . .[53]

But, ironically, sensibility itself is the source of man's moral decay:

> The body, by its intimate union with the soul, draws towards it the pleasure of the senses . . . The soul too weak to govern the passions yields to their empire. The means of our preserva-tion become poison to us: our natural inclinations exceed their due bounds, so that at length, all our heavenly qualities are debased. . . . This is the origin of the corruption of man . . .[54]

Civilisation is the great danger: the only really innocent, happy and healthy people Haller knows (as he writes in an earlier poem) are the peasants who live in the high Alps. As the English trans-lator of the Eloge delivered before the Royal Academy of Sciences at Paris after Haller's death was to put it, 'His soul was gentle, and his heart replete with sensibility. All his writings are expressive of his love of Virtue'.[55]

[53] *The Poems of Baron Haller*, trans. Mrs Howorth (London, 1794) 98.   [54] Ibid. 102.
[55] *Memoirs of Albert de Haller*, M.D., by Thomas Henry (London, 1783) 150.

If in his poetry Haller sounds somewhat like Mrs Radcliffe, in his scientific researches he was a thorough and deliberately dispassionate professional:

> Since . . . the beginning of the year 1751, I have examined . . . a hundred and ninety animals, a species of cruelty for which I felt such a reluctance, as could only be overcome by the desire of contributing to the benefit of mankind . . . I examined attentively, whether upon touching, cutting, burning, or lacerating the part, the animal seemed disquieted, made a noise, struggle, or pulled back the wounded limb . . . The repeated events of those experiments I marked down faithfully, whatever I found them to be. For what is it to me, in fact, on which side nature decides the question?[56]

One cannot help being reminded of Richardson, similarly praising God and labouring for the benefit of mankind, as he pressed forward relentlessly to the tragic conclusion of *Clarissa*. 'The *heart* is likewise sensible', wrote Haller, although he confessed that he found it difficult to distinguish the degree of its sensibility because 'an animal whose *thorax* is opened is in such violent torture, that it is hard to distinguish the effect of an additional slight irritation'.[57] In statements such as these the voices of the scientist and the novelist or poet seem almost indistinguishable.

Haller did not invent the terms 'sensibility' and 'irritability' and still less the concepts. The notion that the capacity to feel is what distinguishes the animal from the vegetable and the inanimate world goes back to Aristotle and was well established in physiological theory. The opening sentence of Galen's *On the Natural Faculties*, for instance, begins with the statement that 'Since feeling [Τὸ αἰσθανέσθαι] and voluntary motion are peculiar to animals, whilst growth and nutrition are common to plants as well, we may look on the former as effects of the *soul* and the latter as effects of the *nature*'.[58] But it is one thing to draw such a distinction and another to explore what it means.

[56] A *Dissertation on the Sensible and Irritable Parts of Animals* (London, 1755), as reprinted in *The Bulletin of the Institute of the History of Medicine* IV (8 Oct. 1936) 7, 9–10. Introd. Owsei Temkin.
[57] Ibid. 22.
[58] Galen *On the Natural Faculties*, trans. A. J. Brock (London, 1952) 2. Galen's treatise was written in the second century A.D.

What made Haller's work such an important step forward in physiology was the thoroughness and scrupulousness of his methodology. According to a modern historian of medicine 'Haller gave to irritability and sensibility a purely experimental definition'.[59] And even though the theories Haller derived from his experiments were to be severely qualified by contemporary and later physiologists, he did much to provide the foundation for all subsequent formulations of the concept of sensibility.

Robert Whytt, whom I have already mentioned, and who was one of Haller's most outspoken opponents, also played an extremely important role in the development of the physiological concepts of sensibility and sympathy. His most important work, the *Essay on the Vital and other Involuntary Motions of Animals*, was published in 1751, a year before Haller first read his paper at Göttingen. In this Whytt advances the theory that every part of the body is sensible, or has feeling, and that this 'sentient principle' is the basis of all animate motion, voluntary or involuntary, and that it can therefore be equated with the mind or soul (Haller, on the contrary, in distinguishing between *sensible* and *irritable* parts of the body, maintained incorrectly that those parts that are irritable are *insensible*). Whytt thus argued that the old distinctions between *animus* and *anima* – mind and soul – or between thinking and feeling, were misleading and unnecessary:

> In man the sentient and the rational principle must be acknowledged to be one; since we are all conscious that what feels, reasons and exerts itself in moving the body is one and the same, and not distinct beings. It is the mind, therefore, that feels, thinks, remembers and reasons; which through one principle, is nevertheless possessed of these different powers, and acts in these different capacities.[60]

[59] Owsei Temkin, Introduction to A *Dissertation* 2.
[60] *An Essay on the Vital and other Involuntary Motions of Animals* 2nd ed. (Edinburgh, 1758) 314. Although Whytt made peculiarly his own the phrase 'sentient principle' he did not invent it. G. S. Rousseau has drawn my attention to its appearance in *The English Malady*, by George Cheyne, M.D. (London, 1733) I 71: 'Feeling is nothing but the Impulse, Motion or Action of Bodies, gently or violently impressing the Extremities or Sides of the Nerves, of the Skin, or other parts of the Body, which . . . convey Motion to the Sentient Principle in the Brain.'

And this one principle, in its most basic aspect, is *sensibility*. Moreover it quite clearly has a moral dimension. Although most of Whytt's writings are taken up with strictly medical matters he makes it plain that man's physiological sensibility and his moral sensibility are different but intimately related facets of the same process:

> And as the DEITY seems to have implanted in our minds a kind of SENSE respecting *Morals*, whence we approve of some actions, and disapprove of others, almost instantly, and without any previous reasoning . . . so, methinks, the analogy will appear very easy and natural, if we suppose our minds so formed and connected with our bodies, as that, in consequence of a *stimulus* affecting any organ . . . they shall immediately excite such motions . . . as may be most proper to remove the irritating cause.[61]

It is not surprising that Whytt, like Haller, should have been so conscious of the wider implications of his physiological discoveries. Physiologists in general at this time were generally concerned with the problem of reconciling the traditional concept or concepts of the soul with their newly acquired knowledge of how man functioned as a physical organism. On one side a radical materialist like La Mettrie in his *Histoire naturelle de l'âme* (1745) and the more notorious *L'Homme machine* (1747) maintained that the soul was a completely empty and outmoded notion, while on the other animists like Stahl, Le Cat and Delius attempted – as did Whytt and Haller – to accommodate the old Aristotelian and Christian notions of the soul to the discoveries they were making.[62] Medical research and theorising, as we are only just beginning to realise,[63] had an immediate and increasingly important effect throughout the century on speculation about the nature of man as a moral, spiritual and even political being. The complexly vital and dynamic way in which this

---

[61] Ibid. 318–9.

[62] See *Robert Whytt*, by R. K. French, esp. ch. XII: 'The Demise of the Soul'.

[63] See G. S. Rousseau's illuminating article, 'Science and the Discovery of Imagination in Enlightened England', *Eighteenth-Century Studies* III (1969) 108–35.

could manifest itself is demonstrated particularly clearly in the writings and political activities of the French revolutionary figure J. P. Marat. Marat was an aggressive and not particularly original theorist who tried unsuccessfully to get himself and his ideas accepted by the scientific establishment. As Robert Darnton has observed, Marat's career parallels in a close and interesting way that of Franz-Anton Mesmer. Both men were doctors of medicine, both had their theories rebuffed by the Parisian Academy of Science at about the same time, and both came to regard themselves – and to be regarded by others – as victims of the ruling élite. Mr Darnton remarks of Marat that 'the resentments produced by his frustrated literary and scientific ambitions in the 1780s provided the crucial element in [his revolutionary] career, and probably in many careers like his'.[64] Marat, though he became a powerful and demagogic politician, was not the confused, charismatic, half-seer, half charlatan that Mesmer was; but his physiological treatise, *L'Homme, ou des Principes et des Loix de l'Influence de l'Ame sur le Corps, et du Corps sur l'Ame* (1775) is surprisingly lyrical and rhapsodic for a work of science. Sensibility occupies a key place in the image he presents of man. It is the first principle to develop in a human being; and it shares with the understanding 'a pre-eminent and commanding dominion over the body and the other faculties of the soul'.[65] The degree of physical sensibility in a human organism depends directly on the delicacy and elasticity of the walls of the nervous fibres (which he pictures as minuscule tubes carrying nervous fluid);[66] and physical sensibility is related immediately to the sensibility of the soul. Thus although Marat rejects the materialism of La Mettrie and others in favour of a simple dualism his argument is rendered otiose by the mechanistic crudity of his own physiological model. Nonetheless he claims that his treatise has a theoretical comprehensiveness and empirical solidity lacking in all previous attempts to give an account of man. These have all been weakened by the fact that the philosophers have

[64] *Mesmerism and the End of the Enlightenment in France* (Cambridge, Mass., 1968) 94.

[65] *L'Homme* (Amsterdam, 1775) II 300.

[66] Ibid. I 144 ('*le plus haut point de sensibilité physique tient au plus haut point de délicatesse & d'élasticité des parois des fibres nerveuses*').

not known enough about man as a physical being and the medical scientists have not been sufficiently philosophical.[67]

Marat's statement of the problem would have appealed to many of his contemporaries, even if they found themselves unable to share his enthusiastic belief in the excellence of the solution he was putting forward. Denis Diderot in particular – in this as in so many other things a central and representative figure – would have warmly endorsed the view that any worthwhile philosophical discussion of the nature of man must be grounded in a sound understanding of the human animal as a physical organism. Throughout his life Diderot was keenly interested in medicine. One of his first publications was a translation of a medical dictionary and one of his last was his *Eléments de Physiologie*; and he had a number of medical friends and acquaintances, among them Dr Bordeu, who plays such an important part in *Le Rêve de d'Alembert* and who was one of the twenty-two doctors of medicine who were among the contributors to the *Encyclopédie*. It was possibly Bordeu who prepared the long medical article on sensibility[68] – and it would be appropriate if he were the author, since it is in *Le Rêve* that Diderot presents in its most fully developed form his own complex theory of sensibility. As Arthur M. Wilson points out, *Le Rêve* 'is based upon a great variety of medical and physiological knowledge', and he quotes Diderot's statement, made late in life, that 'it is very difficult to think cogently in metaphysics or ethics without being an anatomist, a naturalist, a physiologist, and a physician'.[69] But although the concept of sensibility presented in *Le Rêve* has a physiological dimension it is given a significance which extends much further. As d'Alembert in the *Entretien* observes, Diderot's concept of sensibility implies that it is 'a general and essential attribute of matter',[70] the omnipresent energising power which either directly or potentially activates or animates the universe. When d'Alembert objects that it necessarily follows from this

---

[67] 'Discours Préliminaire' to *L'Homme*.

[68] See Paul Vernière, Introduction to *Le Rêve de d'Alembert* (Paris, 1951) X note 2.

[69] *Diderot: the Testing Years, 1711–1759* (New York, 1957) 93. Wilson quotes from the *Oeuvres Complètes*, ed. Jules Assézat and Maurice Tourneux (Paris, 1875–7) II 322.

[70] *Oeuvres Complètes*, ed. Assézat and Tourneux II 105.

that a stone must feel, Diderot agrees – but in agreeing he is merely stating his thesis in its most extreme and apparently paradoxical form. Put more straightforwardly his argument maintains that sensibility is a differently or more highly organised *form* of some power or force that is present in all matter; and that intelligence consists in sensibility plus memory in an even more highly organised and developed mode of being. And sensibility as moral awareness or moral sensitivity is merely one aspect of this general attribute. Diderot's concept of sensibility developed and changed throughout his life, but the various meanings with which at different times and in different places he invests the term overlap rather than contradict each other. As Yvon Belaval, who has isolated five meanings for 'sensibilité' in Diderot's writings, observes, these must be seen more as nodes or focal points of signification, than as separate and clearly definable areas of meaning.[71] 'Physical, biological, psychological, esthetic and ethical considerations were all one for Diderot and all had a single cause at bottom – a physical cause', Norman L. Torrey has stated;[72] and in *Le Rêve de d'Alembert* Diderot assigns to this cause one of the most complex, powerful and ambiguous names with which the language and thought of the day could supply him – the name of 'sensibility'.

Le *Rêve de d'Alembert* was written in 1769, although like many of Diderot's most important and characteristic works it was not published during his lifetime, not appearing until 1830. Another document in which the concept of sensibility is of central significance, *A Sentimental Journey*, had appeared in the preceding year; and in 1765 Volume V of the *Encyclopédie*, the volume containing Dr Bordeu's article on 'sensibilité', had been published. This article is followed by a second which deals with sensibility as a moral attribute of man. The way in which sensibility is discussed in these two articles – especially the second – suggests very clearly the peculiar force with which at this period the term was charged.

[71] *L'Esthétique sans Paradoxe de Diderot* (Paris, 1950) 90–2 ('dans une philosophie du continu comme celle de Diderot . . . [ces] modes . . . représentent plutôt des noeuds de significations que des significations séparées et nettement délimitables').
[72] *Les Philosophes: The Philosophers of the Enlightenment and modern Democracy*, ed. Norman L. Torrey (New York, 1960) 199.

The medical article is lengthy – it runs for some fourteen pages – and it gives a comprehensive account of sensibility as a physiological process or function. It begins by defining 'sensibilité' or 'sentiment' (both words appear in the entry title) as

the faculty of sensing, the cause of feeling, or feeling itself in the organs of the body, the basis of life and what assures its continuance, animality *par excellence*, the finest, the most singular phenomenon of nature, &c . . . It consists essentially in a purely animal awareness of physical objects which distiguishes between what is useful and what is harmful.

The entry under 'Sensibilité (Morale)' is much briefer but the claims it makes are no less sweeping: sensibility, it states, is that

Tender and delicate disposition of the soul which renders it easy to be moved and touched. Sensibility of soul, which is rightly described as the source of morality, gives one a kind of wisdom concerning matters of virtue and is far more penetrating than the intellect acting alone. People of sensibility because of their very liveliness can fall into errors which men of the world would not commit; but these are greatly outweighed by the amount of good they do. Men of sensibility live more fully than others: the good and the bad things of life are increased so far as they are concerned. Reflection can produce a man of probity: but sensibility makes a man virtuous. Sensibility is the mother of humanity, of generosity; it is at the service of merit, lends its support to the intellect, and is the moving spirit which animates belief.[73]

When we set beside these definitions Yorick's rapturous invocation of the Divine Spirit of Sensibility the talismanic power with which the term was invested during this decade of the eighteenth century becomes even more apparent:

– Dear sensibility! source inexhausted of all that's precious in our joys, or costly in our sorrows! thou chainest thy martyr down upon his bed of straw – and 'tis thou who lifts him up to HEAVEN – eternal fountain of our feelings! – 'tis here I trace thee – and this is thy divinity which stirs within me – not, that in some sad and sickening moments, '*my soul shrinks*

[73] *Encyclopédie* V (Neufchastel, 1765) s.v. 'sensiblité'.

back upon herself, and startles at destruction' – mere pomp of
words! – but that I feel some generous joys and generous cares
beyond myself – all comes from thee, great – great SEN-
SORIUM of the world! which vibrates, if a hair of our heads
but falls upon the ground, in the remotest desert of thy
creation.[74]

This passage can strike a modern reader as artificial and
affected. But Sterne is, I think, completely serious here, and his
enthusiasm is not even faintly undercut, as it is so often in his
work, by a note of ironic self-mockery. To see in our own sensibilities a mark of the divinity which stirs within us would have
seemed in no way extraordinary to Sterne's readers; nor would
Yorick's gently ecstatic celebration of the fact have appeared to
be inappropriate or excessive. Nor was there anything novel in
the idea of God as an omnipresent awareness (or sensibility)
infinitely extended through space and time. The notion of the
universe as a divine 'sensorium' had been put forward by
Newton, discussed vigorously in the Clarke–Leibniz correspondence, and commented on at length by Addison in the *Spectator*,
no. 565.[75] And the way in which the divine sensorium filled and
interpenetrated the material world was seen to parallel the way
in which the soul, the 'sentient principle', or the sensibility
informed the bodies of individual human beings. That otherwise
sober Scot, Robert Whytt, advances the idea in the concluding
pages of his *Essay on the Vital and other Involuntary Motions
of Animals* with a warmth and a typographical extravagance
that are positively Sternean:

If . . . the motions and actions of our small and inconsiderable
bodies, are all to be referred to the active power of an
IMMATERIAL principle: how much more necessary must it be,
to acknowledge as the Author . . . of the universal system, an
INCORPOREAL NATURE every where and always present, of

[74] A *Sentimental Journey* 277–8.
[75] A number of scholars have recently drawn attention to this. See
App. E., pp. 353–4, and note to p. 278, 15–16, in Stout's edition of
A *Sentimental Journey*. Cf. also Yvon Belaval's observation that 'la
mens momentanea leibnizienne rejoint "la sensibilité inerte de la
pierre" de l'*Entretien entre d'Alembert et Diderot*' in L'*Esthétique
sans Paradoxe de Diderot* 55.

infinite power, wisdom and goodness; who conducts the motions of the whole, by the most consummate and unerring reason, without being prompted to it by any other impulse than the original and eternal benevolence of his nature![76]

The note struck in this passage is that of enlightenment optimism and faith in man and God at its most self-confident. The universe is reasonable and ordered because God is prompted by his feelings – the original and eternal benevolence of his nature – to exercise his power in a rational manner. Man, it is implied or assumed, if given the chance to follow freely the promptings of *his* innately benevolent sensibility will act with comparable rationality. But this note of optimism and self-confidence became increasingly more difficult to sustain as the century drew towards its close. It was sounded most clearly and powerfully in August 1787 in the Declaration of the Rights of Man and the Citizen; but the assured and untroubled idealism of this document was to be savagely shaken only four years later by the blood-letting of the Terror. The French Revolution has to be seen, of course, as the attempt to express in practical social and political terms many of the ideas about man and society which I am suggesting can be called sentimental – and indeed (as I shall show later) it was looked on in this way at the time. The Revolution was at once an expression of hope and belief in man and paradoxically, because it *was* a revolution and eventually a violent and bloody one, an expression of rage and despair at human folly and inadequacy. It is in the context of the Revolution that the semantic changes in words like 'sentiment', 'sentimental', and 'sensibility' most obviously took place; and the course the Revolution took in part explains them.

These changes, however, had begun to occur well before 1789; and a sense of uneasiness with certain aspects of sentimentalism had clearly manifested itself in the novel and the drama and to some extent in philosophical writing in the preceding twenty years. There is an area of logical and metaphysical instability in the concepts of 'sentiment' and 'sensibility' themselves. The source of this instability may be found in the relationship between the reason and the feelings and the question of determining which of these faculties or attributes of man either is or

[76] Op. cit. 436–7.

ought to be the more important constituted one of the central
and enduring grounds of debate throughout the period. People
became increasingly aware of this problem, and in their attempts
to cope with or to evade the difficulties it posed lies at least a
partial explanation for the peculiar dynamics of the whole nexus
of ideas which constitute sentimentalism.

As the story is commonly told, reason gradually gave way to
feeling – or to sentiment, which was sometimes taken to be
synonymous with feeling. The pivotal figure in the debate, as
Basil Willey has pointed out, was David Hume: 'Before Hume:
empiricism and sensationalism; after him, the "Copernican
revolution" of Kant; before him, Nature and Reason go hand in
hand; after him, Nature and Feeling.'[77] In a very general sense
this is true enough, although it would be misleading to assume
that Hume's theories form a knife-edge watershed. And as
Ronald Crane demonstrates in his 'Suggestions toward a
Genealogy of the "Man of Feeling"',[78] it is dangerous to regard
the early years of the eighteenth century as a period of 'cold
intellectuality'. 'Our Reason has but little to do in the forming
of our minds, and bringing up to Vertuous Religious Life,' wrote
Charles Hickman, later the Bishop of Derby, in 1700; ''tis our
Passions and Affections that must do the work, for till they
begin to move, our Reason is but like a Chariot when the Wheels
are off, that is never like to perform the Journey.'[79]

Nonetheless a general shift of emphasis did take place. In part
this is reflected in the way in which the passions were increasingly assumed to exercise dominance over the reason, or to be
more trustworthy guides in the making of judgments, in part in
the way in which the notion of reason itself changed. For the
great systematic philosophers – Descartes, Spinoza, Leibniz –
reason still carried absolute and divine authority: it was the
faculty in man which enabled him to understand those aspects
of the world, universal and eternal truths, which are the manifestation of God. But philosophers in the eighteenth century saw
reason, as Ernst Cassirer has said, in 'a different and more modest
sense'. For them

[77] *The Eighteenth-Century Background: Studies on the Idea of
Nature in the Thought of the Period* (London, 1940) 111.
[78] ELH I (1934) 205–30.
[79] *Fourteen Sermons* (1700) 271–2. Quoted by Crane, op. cit. 215.

[Reason] is no longer the sum total of 'innate ideas' . . .
[but] the original intellectual force which guides the discovery
and determination of truth . . . The whole eighteenth century
understands reason in this sense; not as a sound body of knowledge, but as a kind of energy. . .[80]

Thus it is not so much that reason *gives way* to feelings as that
the reasoning process, now seen as something fundamentally
active, takes on or assumes or is understood to include certain
characteristics which were formerly ascribed only to passion,
desire or feeling. The eighteenth century deserves to be called
the Age of Reaso*ning* rather than the Age of Reason: it was
above all empirical, critical and anti-rationalistic.

If then – to quote once more from Basil Willey – '*Cogito ergo
sum* is displaced by the *je sens, donc je suis* associated with
Rousseau',[81] it is displaced because it is felt that it tells only half
the story: thinking, or reasoning, as Hume insisted, was impossible without feeling. Pure Reason (in a special sense), Kant was
later to attempt to demonstrate, could still be shown to exist;
but he begins his *Critique of Pure Reason* with the firmly-stated
premise that the capacity to receive sense impressions is a
necessary pre-condition for the operation of thought: 'By means
of sensibility . . . objects are given to us, and it alone furnishes
us with intuitions; by the understanding they are *thought* . . .
But all thought must . . . relate ultimately to intuitions; consequently . . . to sensibility, because in no other way can an object
be given to us'.[82] At a less metaphysical level the power and
value of feeling, in all senses of the term, came to be more and
more widely accepted. With Rousseau, who made peculiarly his
own the notion that feeling constitutes the essential element in
life, it became not so much a philosophical hypothesis as an
article of faith. By the time he appropriated the idea it was, of
course, common property (possibly the first to use the phrase,
je sens, donc je suis, having been the Marquis d'Argens in his
dispute with the Cartesians: 'Je crois qu'on peut aussi bien
prouver l'existence, en disant, *Je sens, donc je suis*, qu'en disant,

[80] *The Philosophy of the Enlightenment* (Princeton, 1951) 13 (first
published as *Die Philosophie der Aufklärung* in 1932).
[81] *The Eighteenth-Century Background* 108.
[82] *Critique of Pure Reason*, trans. J. M. D. Meiklejohn (London,
1934) 41.

Je pense, donc je suis').[83] But the implications of such an assumption extend beyond the bounds of epistemology – or even physiology. Marat, for instance, who in the conclusion to his treatise on Man rhetorically invokes the aid and inspiration of Rousseau, celebrates the superiority of the passions to reason with a most unscientific fervour:

> O REASON! reason! vaunted ally of the sage, what can your feeble voice do against the impetuous raging of the passions? How can it prevail against a soul made desolate or liberated by the fury of the senses?[84]

And Rousseau in the opening paragraphs of his *Confessions* – published in 1782, a year after Kant's *Kritik der reinen Vernunft* – begins with the words 'I feel' – 'je sens':

> I feel my heart, and I know men. I am not made like any one I have seen; I dare to believe that I am not made like any one who exists. If I am not more worthy at least I am different.[85]

If you have feelings, and these feelings tell you that you are different from other people, the obvious implication is that you have the right to enjoy your sense of otherness, you have the right to be free. And in 1782 such an assertion would have had the clearest of political implications. It may be true, as has been recently suggested, that none of the revolutionaries had really read Rousseau[86] (how many student radicals, for that matter, have *really* read Marx or Mao?). But you would have needed to read only the first few pages of the *Confessions* – one of the most eloquent and memorable personal statements that have ever been made – to believe that Rousseau was the inspiration of the men

[83] *Philosophie du Bon-Sens* Nouvelle éd. (La Haye, 1746). Quoted by Gilbert Chinard in his Introduction to Morelly's *Code de la Nature* (1755) (Paris, 1950) 18 note 1 ('I believe that one can demonstrate that one exists as well by saying *I feel therefore I am* as by saying *I think therefore I am*').

[84] *L'Homme* I 311.

[85] *Les Confessions de J. J. Rousseau, suivies des Rêveries du Promeneur solitaire* (Genève, 1782) ('Je sens mon coeur, & je connois les hommes. Je ne suis fait comme aucun de ceux que j'ai vus; j'ose croire n'être fait comme aucun de ceux qui existent. Si je ne vaux mieux, au moins je suis autre').

[86] See chap. I in Joan McDonald, *Rousseau and the French Revolution, 1762–1791* (London, 1965).

who drafted the Declaration of the Rights of Man (especially Articles 4 and 5).

By 1789 the appeal to the feelings had acquired an almost sacred character – 'Feeling hearts (les coeurs sensibles) – there is the great phrase of the period. On the eve of the Revolution one spoke only of sensibility.'[87] The causes which helped to bring about this vogue are naturally extremely complex, but among them is the ambiguous relationship which existed between the reason and the feelings; for although 'sentiment' and 'sensibility' could be taken, and indeed were taken, to refer to the feelings they still carried with them strong connotations of rationality, and were thus invested with some of the authority with which the Reason was traditionally endowed. The way in which these two apparently mutually exclusive human faculties dynamically merged and blended manifests itself clearly in the development of moral theory among the British philosophers from Shaftesbury and Hutcheson to Hume and Adam Smith. Hume adopted the basic position that 'all probable reasoning is nothing but a species of sensation';[88] but this acquired an especial force in his moral theorising. The basic problem in ethics, according to Hume, is to decide whether our fundamental moral principles 'be derived from REASON or SENTIMENT; whether we attain the knowledge of them by a chain of argument and induction, or by an immediate feeling and finer internal sense'.[89] He maintained, of course, that although 'reason and sentiment concur in almost all moral determinations and conclusions',[90] the initial source of all moral judgments was sentiment. Adam Smith elaborated, illustrated and brilliantly popularised Hume's basic position, and also finally endowed sentiment with an authority almost as absolute as that possessed by the reason in the philosophers Hume had apparently disposed of. It is this which makes *The Theory of Moral Sentiments* in some ways a rather two-edged piece of work: on the one hand helping to

[87] Mme Isabelle Kraft-Bucaille, *Causeries sur la Langue française* (Paris, 1890) 246. Quoted by Arthur M. Wilson, 'Sensibility in France in the Eighteenth Century', *French Quarterly* XIII (1931) 36 note 2.

[88] *A Treatise of Human Nature* 103.

[89] *Essential Works* 181 (*An Enquiry concerning the Principles of Morals* § I).

[90] Ibid. 183.

establish the principles and methodology of a genuinely empirical study of man and society, on the other reinforcing some of the deepest fantasies of the age. And the deepest fantasy of all is the notion that the spontaneous moral responses of the individual, despite their basic subjectivity, possess some special and general authority, that one's *better* feelings are necessarily reasonable. This is what 'sentiment' ultimately comes to mean – a *reasonable feeling* – not merely in the language of ordinary educated people but also in the writings of philosophers. It is highly suggestive that, despite their thoroughgoing empiricism, none of the English Moral Sense philosophers ever seriously considers the notion that the right feelings for some people may in fact not be aroused by the social virtues; that the good of the individual may not always coincide with the good of society.

In this even Hume is at one with Shaftesbury and Hutcheson, the earlier advocates of the moral sense. Their fine internal feelings responded with pleasure to benevolence and with pain to ingratitude; by the exercise of reason they arrived at the conclusion that societies functioned best when men were benevolent; and empirical observation informed them that men – or at least the best sort of men, those who were most rational and most sensitive – were naturally benevolent and sympathetic. The moral sense was assumed to function in the same way in all men, just as the other senses did. A man might be morally colour blind, as it were, he might be morally deafened or blinded; his moral palate might be corrupted by exotic foods, but he was potentially as incapable of mistaking good for evil as he was of mistaking red for green – or of thinking that two and two make five. A man whose moral sense functioned properly could be expected to act rationally. In fact the more sensitive he was to the good and ill of himself and his society the more effectively he would demonstrate his humanity and therefore his rationality – 'for of the reality of such a good and ill', says Shaftesbury, in a most revealing phrase, 'no *rational* creature can be *insensible*'.[91]

Now Hume nowhere says quite this; but in some ways, he might as well. No normal human being, according to Hume, can have the wrong sentiments about the things Shaftesbury would

[91] 'An Inquiry Concerning Virtue or Merit', in J. M. Robertson (ed.), *Characteristics of Men, Manners, Opinions, Times. . .* (London, 1900) I 258. My italics.

assume to possess the qualities of good or evil. Thus in Hume's ethical theory, especially as it is presented in the *Enquiry*, 'sentiment' carries a strong connotation of rationality: a typically human moral sentiment is always a reasonable feeling.[92]

It need hardly be stressed that the notion of a necessarily reasonable feeling is both extraordinarily attractive and profoundly ambiguous. That such a notion should lie at the heart of the whole complex of sentimental ideas is, I think, remarkably suggestive. It does much to explain both the self-contradictions of sentimentalism and its peculiar dynamics – by which I mean the compelling power of the sentimental ideal and the rapid (though only partial) fall from popularity that it suffered, a process which is reflected in the changes in meaning undergone by 'sentimental' and related words. Sentimentalism represented both an idealistic and a freshly empirical and pragmatic approach to life, and one which clearly enabled people – not least in the emerging art form of the novel – to explore human problems in a new and illuminating manner. It also helped to provide the basis for a liberal and a revolutionary political ideology – humanist, anti-authoritarian and compassionate – which is still working like yeast through the social structures of the world; but, at the same time, in the flattering picture it offered of man both as essentially benevolent and good natured and as potentially weak, it provided a means of evading the very problems to which it apparently offered a solution – and of evading them in a peculiarly subtle and self-gratifying manner. Sentimentalism could too easily degenerate into sentimentality: to understand something of how and why this should have occurred is to grasp an essential characteristic not only of eighteenth-century civilisation but of our own.

[92] This, and the preceding paragraph are taken with some adaptation from my article '"Sentiment": some Uses of the Word in the Writings of David Hume', *Studies in the Eighteenth Century*, ed. R. F. Brissenden (Canberra, 1968) 105.

3

Sentimentalism and Ideology:
A Note on the French Revolution

When the National Assembly rose at two o'clock on the morning of 5 August 1789 the members were in a state of exaltation and excitement: 'Une contagion sentimentale entraînait les âmes' (A contagion of sentimental feeling carried them away) reported an eyewitness of the meeting, the Genevese Dumont.[1] The adjective could not have been more happily chosen, for in the preceding few hours the Assembly had passed a series of sweeping resolutions which were to make possible not only the political and social restructuring of France but also the implementation of many of those humanitarian ideals which I have argued may properly be called 'sentimental'. On the night of 4 August the seigneurial privileges of the aristocracy and serfdom were abolished, the principle of equality before the law was enunciated, and the first steps were taken towards the disestablishment of the church. 'The Assembly', Georges Lefebvre observes, 'had swept clear the ground on which a constitution and a declaration of rights could be constructed.'[2] Three weeks later, on 26 August, the Declaration of the Rights of Man and the Citizen was formally adopted.

It is by now a commonplace amongst historians to warn us against the dangerous and misleading idea of there having been *a* French Revolution. 'The Revolution', in Alfred Cobban's phrase, 'was not one but many.'[3] Having acknowledged this,

[1] Quoted by Georges Lefebvre in *Quatre-vingt-neuf* (1939) (Paris, 1970) 185; trans. R. R. Palmer as *The Coming of the French Revolution* (New York, 1959) 142.
[2] *The Coming of the French Revolution* 145.
[3] 'The Myth of the French Revolution', *Aspects of the French Revolution* (London, 1971) 107. See also 'The Historiography of the French Revolution' by J. McManners, *The New Cambridge Modern History* VIII (Cambridge, 1965) 651 and *passim* ('There were many revolutions within one Revolution').

however, we can still recognise that one of these revolutions, perhaps the most important, consisted of a conscious attempt to realise in political actuality an ideal theory of man, 'to put into laws', as Robespierre said, 'the moral truths culled from the philosophers'.[4] And some of the most fundamental of these moral truths can, in a strictly technical sense, be described as *sentimental*: that is, they were grounded in the belief that man's capacity to act morally is related to the degree of psychological and physical sensitivity with which he can spontaneously respond to the world about him, related, in a word, to his *sensibility*. With this belief went the hope that if people were allowed to exercise their sensibilities freely they would act in a 'humane' way. As Henri Peyre succinctly puts it, 'the eighteenth century writers [who] prepared the way for the Revolution without wishing for it . . . taught a secular code of ethics . . . [in which] they gave first importance . . . to the love of humanity, altruism and service due society or our fellow man'.[5] And simple but far-reaching humanitarian reforms – some of which, of course, took many years to implement fully – were among the most positive accomplishments of the Revolution. The elimination of torture as part of the judicial process, the abolition of slavery and traffic in slaves (although not finally achieved in French territories until 1848), the establishment of religious toleration, and the attempt to guarantee genuine freedom of thought and expression: these all stemmed directly from what took place in 1789. And these reforms were all inspired by an optimistic view of the benevolent potentialities of man. The people, as Robespierre was to insist again and again, were essentially good, and this goodness could be expressed fully only in a democratic society which guaranteed personal liberty. This view

[4] 'What does this mysterious science of government and legislation amount to? To putting into laws the moral truths culled from the words of the philosophers.' In a speech to the Convention. Quoted in the article, 'The French Revolution', *Encyclopaedia Britannica* (1929). For an excellent brief account of what Robespierre believed these truths to be, see 'The Fundamental Ideas of Robespierre' by Alfred Cobban, *Aspects of the French Revolution* 137–58.

[5] 'The Influence of Eighteenth-Century Ideas on the French Revolution', *The Influence of the Enlightenment on the French Revolution*, ed. William F. Church (Boston, 1966) 94; reprinted from *Journal of the History of Ideas* X (1949) 63–87.

is the political embodiment of those notions of the primacy and sanctity of the individual's experience and judgment which had so deeply exercised the European mind during the preceding century. The philosophers did not *cause* the Revolution, the origins of which are extraordinarily complex, but they undoubtedly influenced very strongly the course it took, and the ideology which it generated. And the ideology of the French Revolution was one of its most significant and influential achievements. As Alexis de Tocqueville pointed out more than a century ago in *L'Ancien régime et la revolution*, the Revolution was in some ways more like a religious than a political upheaval: 'Not only did it have repercussions far beyond French territory, but like all great religious movements it resorted to propaganda and broadcast a gospel.'[6] And the gospel was based on a general theory of human nature and consequently was seen as holding true for all men: 'It did not aim merely at defining the rights of the French citizen, but sought also to determine the rights and duties of man in general . . . No previous political upheaval, however violent, had aroused such passionate enthusiasm, for the ideal the French revolution set before it was not merely a change in the French social system but nothing short of a regeneration of the whole human race.'[7]

The text of the gospel was the Declaration of the Rights of Man and the Citizen and it was, and still is, an extremely influential document – more influential than the English Bill of Rights or even the American Declaration of Independence, to both of which (especially the latter) it owes a great deal. Since 1789 there have been some fifty-two documents produced which can be described as in some sense declarations of human rights – idealistic statements of principle and intention drawn up by the governments of newly formed states and by international bodies such as the League of Nations and the United Nations. These all look back in some way to the original Declaration of the Rights of Man and the Citizen.[8]

---

[6] *The Old Régime and the French Revolution*, trans. Stuart Gilbert (New York, 1955) 11.

[7] Ibid. 12.

[8] See *Basic Documents in Human Rights*, ed. Ian Brownlie (Oxford, 1971). Fifty-four documents are included, many of which are specialised statements by International bodies on specific problems – labour

The Declaration is therefore worth examining with some care; especially in the context of this present discussion, for in the sense in which I have attempted to define 'sentimental' it can be seen as in some respects an essentially sentimental document. This becomes clear if it is compared with the Declaration of Independence. The committee which drafted the French Declaration took the American statement as their model and consulted Thomas Jefferson himself who was then ambassador at the French court. But the Declaration of the Rights of Man and the Citizen goes much further than the Declaration of Independence in maintaining the primacy of the individual over the state, and in stressing the central significance of individual liberty and in attempting to define what is meant by this.

The most important section of the Declaration of Independence for our purposes is the second sentence:

> We hold these truths to be self-evident, that all men are created equal, that they are endowed by their Creator with certain unalienable Rights, that among these are Life, Liberty and the pursuit of Happiness, that to secure these rights, Governments are instituted among Men, deriving their just powers from the governed, that whenever any Form of Government becomes destructive of these ends, it is the Right of the People to alter or abolish it, and to institute new Government . . .

These principles are restated in basically similar terms in the Preamble to the Declaration of the Rights of Man and the Citizen and in the first three articles. But particular and positive emphasis is laid on liberty. Article I begins with the brief statement: 'Men are born and remain free and equal in rights.' 'The rest of the Declaration', as Lefebvre remarks, 'is so to speak only an exposition and commentary on [this].'[9] Seven of the seventeen articles deal with various aspects of personal liberty. The most significant of these are Articles IV and V:

---

relations, slavery, etc. Brownlie says of the Declaration of the Rights of Man that it 'is the first of its kind [and] . . . was to influence many constitutions of the parliamentary type of the nineteenth century and later in Europe and Latin America' (p. 8).

[9] *The Coming of the French Revolution* 147.

IV. Liberty consists in the ability to do whatever does not harm another; hence the exercise of the natural rights of each man has no limits except those which assure to other members of society the enjoyment of the same rights. These limits can only be determined by law.

V. Law may rightfully prohibit only those actions which are injurious to society. No hindrance should be put in the way of anything not prohibited by law, nor may any man be forced to do what the law does not require.[10]

These articles are at once more optimistic and more permissive than anything in the Declaration of Independence, the various Bills of Rights of England and the American States, or the United States Constitution. Moreover the evils which can arise from the denial of the natural and imprescriptible rights which these articles assert are attacked in far stronger and more general terms in the Declaration of the Rights of Man and the Citizen than in any of the earlier documents. 'The ignorance, neglect or contempt of the rights of man', states the Declaration, 'are the *sole* causes of public misfortunes and governmental corruption' ('l'ignorance, l'oubli ou le mépris des droits de l'homme sont les seules causes des malheurs publics et de la corruption des gouvernements'). Guarantee individual liberty and you ensure the healthy functioning of the body politic.

Unfortunately man is not so good natured and the preservation of liberty is not so simple as the members of the National Assembly believed in 1789 – and this was to be tragically demonstrated by the course which events were to take during the next decade. The Terror was perhaps not so brutal and bloodthirsty as it has been represented to be – particularly by later writers such as Carlyle and Dickens—but it was still a genuinely terrible and socially traumatic experience, the symbolic and cruelly ironic significance of which was clearly recognised by people at the time. The guillotine itself, which was to become the sign of revolutionary violence, had originally been introduced for democratic and quite unhypocritically humane reasons: Dr Guillotin, in 1790, urged its adoption to the National

[10] These two articles are an expansion and more formal expression of Montesquieu's statement: 'Liberty is the right to do everything the laws allow' (*L'Esprit des Lois* XI 3).

Assembly on the grounds that 'in cases of capital punishment the privilege of execution should not be confined to the nobles, and that it was desirable to render the process of execution as swift and painless as possible'.[11] Three years later Robespierre, invoking another moral and political principle, the sanctity of the general will – the principle enunciated in Article VI of the Declaration – was to condone and direct the employment of the guillotine for the purpose of creating the conditions under which people could be genuinely free. No doubt it is true, as Lester G. Crocker maintains, that 'the cruelty and bloodthirstiness of the Terror were due to revolutionary dynamics, not to any ideas of the *philosophes*'.[12] Nonetheless the uses to which Dr Guillotin's mercifully efficient machine were put demonstrated convincingly that man, in his attempt to be humane, could be only too appallingly human.

The rapid and seemingly inevitable assumption of dictatorial authority by Robespierre and the Committee of Public Safety; the crude and tyrannical exercise of the power of public democracy by the crowds in the Jacobin Club and the streets of Paris; and the eventual establishment of a centralised government and bureaucracy under the Napoleonic and subsequent regimes – these developments were also to cast an ironic light on the hopeful idealism of the Declaration. 'The Revolution', R. R. Palmer observes, 'liberated the individual, and it consolidated the modern state. It confirmed the rule of law, and it launched a tradition of violence.'[13] It is one of the paradoxes of history that the clearest enunciation of the desire for individual liberty so far made by man should have coincided both with the rise of the highly organised, minutely administered, and increasingly authoritarian nation state and with the onset of that scientific and technological revolution which has made possible the thorough, constant and impersonal regulation of the life of the individual citizen. If alienation is the neurosis of contemporary western society its origins are to be found in the simultaneous promise

[11] 'Guillotine' in *Encyclopaedia Britannica* (1969). Guillotin did not invent the machine: he perfected a device which in various forms had been used in Scotland, England and parts of the Continent since the middle ages.

[12] *An Age of Crisis* 470.

[13] Preface to *The Coming of the French Revolution* v.

and denial of personal liberty and fulfilment which that society has presented to man since the eighteenth century.

To say all this is perhaps to state the obvious. My excuse for doing so is that the ironies of the situation presented themselves in just such brutally obvious ways to people at the time of the Revolution. One did not oneself have to be in prison awaiting execution or on the scaffold to appreciate the force of remarks like that of Vergniaud, the young Girondist: 'Others sought to consummate the Revolution by terror; I would accomplish it by love'; or Mme Roland: 'O Liberty, what crimes are committed in thy name.' In England, in 1798, the same charge was laid at the door of sensibility:

Sweet Sensibility, who dwells enshrined
In the fine foldings of the feeling mind . . .

Sweet child of sickly Fancy! her of yore
From her loved France Rousseau to exile bore;
And, while midst lakes and mountains wild he ran,
Full of himself, and shunn'd the haunts of man,
Taught her o'er each lone vale and Alpine steep
To lisp the story of his wrongs, and weep . . .
– Taught by nice scales to mete her feelings strong,
False by degrees, and exquisitely wrong; –
– For the crushed beetle *first*, – the widow'd dove,
And all the warbled sorrows of the grove; –
Next for poor suffering *guilt*; – and *last* of all,
For Parents, Friends, a King and Country's fall.

Mark her fair votaries, prodigal of grief,
With cureless pangs, and woes that mock relief,
Droop in soft sorrow o'er a faded flower;
O'er a dead jack-ass pour the pearly shower; – *
But hear, unmoved, of *Loire's* ensanguined flood,
Choked up with slain; – of *Lyons* drench'd in blood;
Of crimes that blot the age, the world with shame,
Foul crimes, but sicklied o'er with freedom's name. . .
Of talents, honour, virtue, wit forlorn,
In friendless exile, – of the wise and good

* See Sterne's 'Sentimental Journey'.

Staining the daily scaffold with their blood. . .
Of hearts torn reeking from the mangled breast, –
They hear – and hope, that ALL IS FOR THE BEST.

These lines, written by a young politician and statesman,
George Canning, occur in a long poem, later called *The New
Morality*, which appeared in the final issue of the *Anti-Jacobin*,
a short-lived but brilliant Tory satirical review. In the Prospectus
announcing the advent of the journal, the first number of which
appeared on 20 November 1797, the editors stated that they
were enemies 'of JACOBINISM in all its shapes . . . political and
moral, public and private, whether as it openly threatens the
subversion of States, or gradually saps the foundations of domestic happiness'. They added that 'in Morals . . . [they had] not
yet learned the modern refinement of referring . . . not to any
settled and preconceived principles of right and wrong . . . but to
the internal admonitions of every man's judgment or conscience.'
The authors of most of the material in the *Anti-Jacobin* were
three young members of parliament – Canning, who was Under-
Secretary of State for Foreign Affairs in Pitt's government, John
Hookham Frere, his friend since schooldays at Eton, and George
Ellis. The nominal editor was William Gifford. The review ran
for some eight months, and as well as serious and satirical political comment and reporting contained a deal of light-hearted and
clever literary parody, including a play, *The Rovers*, a skit on
sentimental German romantic drama.

Practically the whole of the concluding issue of the *Anti-
Jacobin* – no. 36, Monday, 9 July 1798 – is given over to the
poem (here simply titled *Poetry*) and to a large, fold-out cartoon
by Gillray which bears the title (later given to the poem) of
The New Morality. The poem which runs for 463 lines is one of
the most substantial and weighty pieces to be published in the
Anti-Jacobin. It is the work of Canning, Frere, Gifford and Ellis,
and Pitt himself possibly contributed ten lines. The most sustained passage in the poem, lines 71–137, is by Canning, the
most gifted poet of the group. It systematically attacks the 'new
philosophy' – 'French philanthropy' – in other words the
philosophical basis of 'the new morality'; and it culminates in
the invocation to, or rather description of, the Goddess of
Sensibility, which I have quoted.

Gillray's cartoon offers an elaborate accompaniment to this passage. It depicts a motley radical crowd worshipping the French idols, Justice, Philanthropy and Sensibility. On the altar Sensibility, wearing the revolutionary cap and tricolour rosette, is shown 'holding Rousseau's works in one hand, and weeping over a dead bird, while her foot rests on the decapitated head of the martyred Louis'.[14] If we read the cartoon from left to right the figure of Sensibility occupies a peculiarly dominant position; she is the focal point of the adulation of the crowd of worshippers. And in the context of the *Anti-Jacobin* as a whole her position is just as significant: this powerful image, ambiguously rich in moral, philosophical, literary, social and political significance, stands as a graphic tail-piece to the thirty-six issues of the review – a symbol of everything to which the satirists were opposed, a symbol of sentimentalism. That we should appreciate with equal keenness both the justice and the unfairness of their attack is an indication not merely of the complexities of the French Revolution – complexities which still puzzle and disturb us – but also of the ambivalent connotations with which, by the end of the eighteenth century, the concept of sensibility had become charged.

[14] *The Works of James Gillray, the Caricaturist*, ed. Thomas Wright (London, 1873) 246. Gillray entitled the cartoon *The New Morality, or the Promis'd Instalment of the High-Priest of the Theophilanthropes*, with the homage of Leviathan and his Suite.

The New Morality (detail) by James Gillray (1798)

4

Virtue in Distress:
The Emergence of a Theme

The reaction against sentimentalism, of which *The New Morality* – the caricature as much perhaps as the poem – provides such as striking instance, was part of a general dissatisfaction with those optimistic elements in man's vision of himself and the world which had prevailed during the eighteenth century. This dissatisfaction had always been present to some degree – *Gulliver's Travels, The Fable of the Bees, The Dunciad, Candide* and *Rasselas*, to mention but a few of the more obvious examples, can scarcely be called (at least in the simple sense) optimistic works: and novelists like Prévost, Richardson and Laclos present a profoundly sad picture of humanity. There was also a well established tradition of antisentimental satire, often operating, paradoxically enough, in work which was ostensibly sentimental. This ambiguous but dynamic relationship between satire and sentimentalism is particularly obvious in fiction, especially in the novels of Smollett and Sterne. On the stage sentimental fiction and sentimental drama had both been laughed at – most memorably in George Colman's farce, *Polly Honeycombe* (1760), and in Sheridan's *The Rivals* (1776) and *The School for Scandal* (1777). The exposure of Joseph Surface, the man of sentiment, as a malicious, hypocritical and thoroughly selfish villain is a damning indictment; and it is conducted with a sureness of touch which suggests that by 1777 there was considerable disenchantment with the more obvious complacencies of sentimentalism. The same confidence is displayed in Jane Austen's juvenile burlesques of Gothic and sentimental fiction, although these were not produced for publication and remained in manuscript until this century. The most notable of them, *Love and*

Friendship, was written in 1790; and in this same year a different but not totally dissimilar parody of the sentimental novel, *Justine, ou les Malheurs de la Vertu*, by the Marquis de Sade, was published in Paris. Like most of Sade's fiction *Justine* is a calculated, rigorous and thoroughgoing attack on sentimentalism; and even though Sade was a supporter of the Revolution his books present a vision of man and society which is brutally and shockingly antithetical to the untroubled idealism embodied in the Declaration of the Rights of Man and the Citizen. Sade's novels, drearily obsessive though they may be, are documents of the greatest significance. In them that dissatisfaction with sentimental optimism which had been present throughout the century is intensified out of all proportion, transformed into a nihilistic despair, disgust and fury which are different not only in degree but in kind from anything which had preceded them. Sade's world is bleaker and more terrible than the world of Swift's Yahoos, Pope's dunces, or Voltaire's *Candide* – and its special nastiness derives only in part from Sade's sexual preoccupations. The intellectual energy by which his fantasies are animated has its source in his desire to destroy logically and systematically the sentimental image of man as essentially benevolent and sympathetic.

Sade is a man terribly and hopelessly alienated from human society; and his alienation presents itself in such a grotesque manner that one is tempted to regard him as totally abnormal, uniquely aberrant. But it would be a mistake to do so. A sense of alienation, of intellectual and cultural dislocation, begins to manifest itself more and more widely in European literature as the eighteenth century draws to a close and the nineteenth century begins; and Sade's perverse fables are merely the most extreme instance of this. A less obvious and much more complex example can be seen in the poetry of Wordsworth, a man whose life and art (in these respects at least like Sade's) were also intimately involved with both the idealism and the despair generated by the French Revolution. His most ambitious poem, *The Excursion*, was in part directly inspired by what had happened in France: 'I wish you would write a poem, in blank verse', Coleridge had said, 'addressed to those who, in consequence of the complete failure of the French Revolution, have thrown up all hopes of the amelioration of mankind, and are sinking into an almost epicurean selfishness, disguising the same under ... [a] contempt for visionary *philosophes*.'[1]

As an indication of the extent to which moral, social and literary attitudes had shifted and altered during the century it is interesting to set *The Excursion* beside an earlier poem to which in outline and intention it bears a distinct resemblance, Pope's *Essay on Man*. Pope's *Essay* is a philosophical discourse 'on Human Life and Manners' which begins from the assumption that 'the proper study of Mankind is Man', and asserts that 'WHATEVER IS, IS RIGHT' and, in particular, that 'true SELF-LOVE and SOCIAL are the same'.[2] Wordsworth's *Excursion* is also a 'philosophical poem, containing views of Man, Nature and Society';[3] like Pope's *Essay* it is written to a friend, and it is also, in its own way, dedicated to demonstrating that whatever is, is right. But it is unfinished, its intended title was 'The Recluse', and its theme is that the proper study of mankind is, in the first instance at least, not man but nature. The ideal image of the poet projected by Wordsworth is that of a solitary, introspective figure, who hears the 'still, sad music of humanity', and knowing that he is incapable of alleviating its suffering draws comfort from the contemplation of the natural world. Wordsworth, of course, is not a sentimental writer – especially in the modern sense of that term – but his *Excursion* (surely, like Yorick's, 'a quiet journey of the heart in pursuit of NATURE'!) is in its own way a sentimental journey: its *dramatis personae*, the Poet, the Solitary and the Wanderer, though infinitely more intelligent and realistic than Le Voyageur sentimental, are, like him, impotent observers of the suffering world, alienated from their society in a manner that Pope never was from his.

Alienation, withdrawal, retreat and the rediscovery of the self in isolation strike us as peculiarly the romantic syndrome; but throughout the eighteenth century solitude and solitariness exercised a special and growing fascination for people. Men have

---

[1] Letter no. 290 [*c.* 10 Sept. 1799], in *Collected Letters of Samuel Taylor Coleridge*, ed. Earl Leslie Griggs (Oxford, 1956) I 257.

[2] See Pope's Prefatory note, 'The Design', to *An Essay on Man*; and Epistle IV 394 and 396.

[3] From Wordsworth's Preface to *The Excursion* (1814); reprinted in the editor's Advertisement to the 1850 edition of *The Prelude, or Growth of a Poet's Mind*.

always sought the loneliness of deserts and mountains in order to escape from the distracting or corrupting company of their fellows; but from now on the dream of escape into self-imposed exile began to assume the character of an obsession. It is no accident that only about a hundred years after John Donne had asserted that 'no man is an island' Daniel Defoe should have written his island epic, *Robinson Crusoe*: the most powerful, most clearly articulated and also most optimistic mythical statement of modern man's longing for solitude. The literature of the age is thick with hermits and solitaries, from Fielding's noble or embittered stoics – Mr Wilson, Squire Allworthy, the old man of the hill – to Goldsmith's Traveller and Cowper's Castaway.

This preoccupation with solitariness in an age which has left a reputation for its sociability, an age which first gave clear enunciation to the secular doctrine of the brotherhood of man, is worth examination. The reasons for its emergence at this time are numerous and involved; but some of the more important stand out fairly clearly. The largest and vaguest but in some ways the most significant is probably an ill-defined but profound fear of society, of man in the mass, of urbanisation and industrialisation; an almost subconscious awareness that the human community, once it gets beyond a certain size, becomes too large and complicated to be fully understood or properly controlled. Pope's equation of duncedom with the city mob is one of the earliest clear expressions of this fear: it is in part the sheer multitudinousness of the dunces which ensures their victory. As the century wore on this antipathy was more and more accompanied by a renewed sense of the vital importance of man's relationship with nature; and in the romantic 'retreat' from society to the natural world one can see a prophetic foreshadowing of and response to what has emerged in our own day as the most urgent problem the human race is facing – the problem of bringing man back into fruitful harmony with the enclosed global ecosystem, with nature, a system which the technological, industrial and population explosions touched off in the eighteenth century are already beginning to throw dangerously out of balance. *Robinson Crusoe*, near the beginning of the century, images in its most hopeful form man's dream both of escaping from the mess and of asserting himself fully and freely in an environment of which he can become absolute master. But against this should be set an equally visionary and much more pessimistic work which appeared towards the end of the century, in the same year as Wordsworth's and Coleridge's *Lyrical Ballads* (1798) – *An Essay on the Principle of Population*, by Thomas Robert Malthus. Malthus argued that the ideal of infinite progress and improvement for mankind must prove vain since increase in population will always outstrip growth of production. The most fascinating thing about Malthus's theory is that although it now seems to hold true in the nonindustrial, underdeveloped world (of which he knew nothing) – and thus may eventually hold true for the world as a whole – it is not empirically borne out by what happens in the sort of industrial society to which Malthus himself belonged. The facts from which Malthus was arguing just do not support his case; but nonetheless his reaction to eighteenth-century civilisation as he experienced it, and to eighteenth-century sentimental optimism, particularly as manifested in the writings of Rousseau and Hume (with whom his father was friendly), produced an insight, now shown to be quite terrifyingly valid, into the potentiality for social processes to accelerate out of control. Malthus is a key figure in the development of what may be called the enlightenment's greatest legacy, namely the social sciences – but significantly what his theory conveys most strongly is a fear and distrust of society.

The urge to withdraw from the world can also be seen as an expression of that belief in the sanctity of the individual judgment which was of such central and dynamic importance in European civilisation at this time. By cutting oneself off from society one could preserve one's moral judgment unimpaired; and it is highly significant that it is from this point that solitary communion with nature begins to be seen as *morally* renewing. There is, said James Thomson in 1726, 'no subject more elevating, more amusing; more ready to awake the poetical enthusiasm, the philosophical reflection, and the moral sentiment, than the works of nature'.[4] The theme was not to achieve its fullest and most eloquent poetic statement until Wordsworth; but before this it functioned as an essential and energising element not only in poems such as *The Seasons*, but also in many of the seminal prose works of the age. What is still sometimes taken as the

[4] Preface to *Winter* 2nd ed. (London, 1726).

peculiarly romantic revelation of the moral force of natural beauty manifests itself clearly for instance in the lyrical descriptions of Alpine scenery in *La Nouvelle Héloïse*, and of course in *Les Rêveries du Promeneur Solitaire* and in Rousseau's *Confessions*. It plays a significant part in *Werther*; and it forms the main subject of a long, semi-philosophic, semi-rhapsodic work called *Solitude, considered with Respect to its Influence upon the Mind and Heart*. This treatise is worth mentioning not merely because it was read with such enthusiasm throughout Europe during the last decades of the century but also because its author, Johann Georg Zimmerman, physician to the crowned heads of Prussia and Great Britain, had been Von Haller's assistant in his vivisectional experiments into sensibility. (Zimmerman's international fame left him far from solitary: his work 'acquired the universal approbation of the German Empire', and a flattering recognition from the Empress of Russia in the form of a diamond ring, a gold medal, and a personal note from Catherine herself to thank 'M. Zimmerman, Counsellor of State and Physician to his Britannic Majesty . . . for the excellent precepts he has given to mankind in his Treatise upon Solitude'.[5] Von Haller himself had written a poem on 'The Alps'.)

The moral advantages of living a solitary or at least a secluded and sheltered life amidst beautiful or, preferably, sublime natural scenery are nowhere more clearly stated than in those faithful mirrors of popular taste the novels of Mrs Ann Radcliffe. In them, indeed, the natural world acquires the status of an extra character; although when Mrs Radcliffe wrote her best known and most influential novel, *The Mysteries of Udolpho*, first published in 1794, she had not yet seen the originals of the vividly imagined landscapes which play such an important role in her stories. Although the plots and machinery of her Gothic tales are fantastic enough, the characters (apart from the villains and their retinue) are strictly conventional. St Aubert, for instance, the father of Emily, the sensitive heroine in *The Mysteries of Udolpho*, is another Mr Wilson:

[5] *Solitude, considered with Respect to its Influence upon the Mind and the Heart*, written originally in German by M. Zimmerman, trans. from the French of J. B. Mercier (London, 1791) vii. See also Peter Burra's *Baroque and Gothic Sentimentalism. An Essay* (London, 1931) 32.

he had . . . mingled in the gay and in the busy scenes of the world; but the flattering portrait of mankind which his heart had delineated in early youth, his experience had too sorrow-fully corrected . . . he retired from the multitude, more in pity than in anger, to scenes of simple nature, to the pure delights of literature, and to the exercise of domestic virtues.[6]

But the scenes of simple nature were much more important to M. St Aubert than they were to Fielding's philosophic recluses. They inspired him to acts of benevolence, and the contemplation of their beauty was made all the sweeter by 'the consciousness of acting right'. This

diffused a serenity over his manners, which nothing else could impart to a man of moral perceptions like his, and which refined his sense of every surrounding blessing . . .'[7]

After distributing to his pensioners their weekly stipends . . . and softening the discontents of all by the look of sympathy and the smile of benevolence – St. Aubert returned home through the woods . . . The evening gloom of woods was always delightful to me, said St. Aubert, whose mind now experienced the sweet calm which results from having done a beneficent action, and which disposes it to receive pleasure from every surrounding object.[8]

But it is amidst the 'stupendous' scenery of the Alps that St Aubert and his daughter are most ardently inspired. There they meet Valancourt, young, handsome, innocent and with a romantic reverence for nature. 'These scenes', he tells St Aubert and Emily, as they gaze at the Alps by moonlight,

soften the heart like the notes of sweet music, and inspire that delicious melancholy which no person, who has felt it once, would resign for the gayest pleasures. They awaken our best and purest feelings; disposing us to benevolence, pity, and friendship.[9]

With Valancourt another stock image in the sentimental dream is introduced; the noble savage. Although Valancourt is a young man of birth and education, he prefers to spend his time

[6] *The Novels of Mrs. Ann Radcliffe*, in Vol. X of *Ballantyne's Novelists' Library* (London, 1824) 233.
[7] Ibid. 225.   [8] Ibid. 229.   [9] Ibid. 243–4.

hunting in the Alps, sharing the simple lives of the peasants. 'St. Aubert was much pleased with the manly frankness, simplicity, and keen susceptibility to the grandeur of nature, which his new acquaintance discovered;'[10] but he realises the weakness of this innocent, natural and untutored virtue:

> He saw a frank and generous nature . . . but impetuous, wild, and somewhat romantic. Valancourt had known little of the world . . . St. Aubert . . . often repeated to himself, This young man has never been at Paris. A sigh sometimes followed this silent ejaculation.[11] St. Aubert's premonitory fears are justified. Like young Annesly in *The Man of the World*, Valancourt succumbs to the temptations of the big city; he goes to the dogs in a truly Byronic fashion, and in the end is saved only by the love of a good woman – Emily.

In one form or another the dream figure of the noble savage haunted the eighteenth century.[12] Mrs Behn, towards the end of the previous century, had seen in the Indians of Surinam 'an absolute *Idea* of the first State of innocence before Man knew how to sin',[13] and in Oroonoko, a primitive and savage prince whose sense of honour and loyalty is higher than that of the degenerate whites who play upon his trust and finally destroy him. To Wordsworth, a hundred years later, an indomitable peasantry came to represent the same virtues. Byron's Giaours and Corsairs have a similar significance; they are violent but honourable. Earlier, in *The Man of the World*, Mackenzie had used the redman as an ideal to throw into relief the vice and decadence of contemporary European society – and the account given by Annesley of the years he spent with the Indians is the most realistic and convincing part of the novel. Mackenzie shirks very little: his Indians are genuinely bloodthirsty and cruel – but they are also genuinely honourable and just.

---

[10] Ibid. 238.   [11] Ibid. 241–2.

[12] The phrase is originally Dryden's, in *The Conquest of Granada* (1672):

> I am as free as nature first made man,
> Ere the base laws of servitude began,
> When wild in woods the noble savage ran.

[13] *Oroonoko: or The History of the Royal Slave*, in *All the Histories and Novels written by the late Ingenious Mrs. Behn* (London, 1705) 55 (Oroonoko was first published in 1688).

As H. N. Fairchild, in his classic study, *The Noble Savage*, has demonstrated, dramatists, novelists and poets used this complex, highly charged symbol in a variety of ways.[14] The noble savage was always imagined as being more virtuous than the representatives of European (or urban as opposed to rural) civilisation. He was more honourable, more loyal, and more honest. Sometimes, as in the stories of Oroonoko or of the equally admired Inkle and Yarico, his virtue is seen as the cause of his betrayal by the more sophisticated and more vicious Europeans; sometimes, as in the fourth part of *Gulliver's Travels*, and in the South American sections of *Candide* and in *L'Ingénu*, the noble savage, or someone very like him, is used simply as a satiric commentator on the follies of civilisation. As the century advanced he became more and more of an ideal figure: a composite of the natural, the rational, and the sentimental man. Fairchild's description of the Red Indians in Mackenzie's novel suggests the symbolic values with which they were invested. Although their savagery is not sentimentally softened

> They are endowed with that stateliness, that quiet fortitude, that intense passion controlled by innate goodness, which belong to the Indian of legend . . . The Indian is – always with reservations – Rousseau's man of nature, he is Sterne's man of sensibility, he is Mackenzie's own Man of Feeling opposed through all the Ages to the Man of the World.[15]

The role which the noble savage played in eighteenth-century thought is thus in all senses of the word a sentimental one. He represents all those virtues, both of reason and of feeling, which were assumed to be the natural birthright of every man. At the same time the forms and the contexts in which he was imagined managed to imply the fear that such virtues might be incompatible with the economic and social structure of the society which valued them so highly. No matter how much honesty, a sense of justice, universal benevolence and a recognition of the brotherhood of man were admired it was recognised if not always

[14] See also Bernard Smith, *European Vision and the South Pacific* (Oxford, 1960) for a fascinating account of the part played by the noble savage in the visual arts.

[15] *The Noble Savage: a Study in Romantic Naturalism* (New York, 1928) 92.

openly admitted that if everyone were to practise them the whole fabric of society might disintegrate. The nobility of the noble savage was potentially as dangerous to the preservation of social order, as social order was envisaged in the eighteenth century, as his primitive violence and passion. It is the complete isolation of the noble savage from the realities, the pain and complexity, of group existence that make him such a sentimental figure in our meaning of the term. Mackenzie's redmen are in one way more realistic than Annesley and Sir Thomas Sindall; but Mackenzie is able to write about his savages 'honestly' because he has artificially isolated them. He can describe their violence, savagery and nobility without any of the embarrassment which he would have caused both himself and his readers if he had tried to present truthfully the equally savage elements actually present in contemporary European society. Mackenzie's noble savage is a sentimental figure because although potentially dangerous he is in fact harmless. Both his nobility and his savagery are in quarantine and can be observed and admired in safety.

In this combination of potential danger and actual harmlessness the noble savage can be seen to be not only sentimental but sublime. Burke, in his classic definition of the sublime, states that

> whatever is fitted in any sort to excite the ideas of pain and danger, that is to say, whatever is in any sort terrible . . . is the source of the *sublime*.[16]

But in order to excite sublime feelings the terrible must be harmless:

> The passions which belong to self-preservation turn on pain and danger; they are simply painful when their causes immediately affect us; they are delightful when we have an idea of pain and danger, without actually being in such circumstances . . . Whatever excites this delight I call *sublime*.[17]

Kant distinguishes the sublime in the same way, although he makes the further point that an additional element in the experience of sublimity is the feeling which is evoked of power and moral superiority.

[16] *A Philosophical Enquiry into the Origins of our Ideas of the Sublime and Beautiful* 2nd ed. (London, 1759) 58.
[17] Ibid. 84–5.

The dynamic sublime is found in nature represented as might, but as might that has no dominion over us . . . overhanging rocks, thunderclouds, and lightning, volcanoes, hurricanes, the stormy ocean, high waterfalls . . . are fearful. But if we are safe from their menace, they become delightful because of their fearfulness . . . we are lifted momentarily above nature. Physically we may be dwarfed, but our reason remains undaunted and the mind becomes aware of the sublimity of its own being.[18]

The identification and exploration of the sublime was one of the most illuminating and rewarding discoveries – or rediscoveries – of eighteenth-century aesthetics. But the particular forms in which the sublime revealed itself are highly suggestive. It is possible that the stupendous works of nature which inspired a terror that could be enjoyed in safety served as neutralising and harmless displacement symbols for other terrors which were too real and threatening to be contemplated directly. One feature of the age to which I have already paid some attention is the emergence at this time in an embryonic but confident form of the social sciences: when Pope proclaimed that the proper study of mankind is man he gave the century one of its most fitting slogans. But this confidence was accompanied by a considerable and growing unease – a fear and a distrust of social processes which were nourished by an awareness of just how little man knows about society; and a suspicion of and antipathy towards the excessive growth of cities (it was in 1821 that Cobbett called London 'the great wen of all') and the consequences of industrial and technological development.

Nature, of course, was not regarded simply or even mainly as terrifying: it was seen primarily as the source of spiritual health and sanity. And the romantic insistence that the proper study of mankind might not be just man but man in relation to mountains, waterfalls and thunderstorms, to the weather and the seasons, must be understood as part of a complex response to the development of modern civilisation. In its positive aspect this

[18] From a paraphrase by S. H. Monk of *The Critique of Aesthetic Judgment*, trans. J. C. Meredith (Oxford, 1911), quoted in *The Sublime: A Study of Critical Theories in XVIIIth Century England* (New York, 1935) 8.

expressed itself in an extraordinarily valuable and prophetic re-affirmation of man's inherent and inescapable involvement with the natural world. 'The works of Nature', when properly contemplated can indeed – to return to Thomson's phrase – 'awake . . . the philosophical reflection, and the moral sentiment'. When approached in an irreverent and blindly exploitative spirit, however, the works of nature may merely confirm man in his own self-destructive ignorance; and in this context the techno-logical rape of the planet which mankind has committed in the last two hundred years must be seen as a fundamentally immoral act – one that has sprung from a refusal to acknowledge any 'sense of something far more deeply interfused', any sense, that is, of some all-pervasive, delicately balanced and living natural order to which man belongs and which he disregards at his peril.

But there is a negative aspect to romanticism also. One of the most profound and enduring of the complex of motives which animated the romantic movement was the urge simply to retreat: to find in solitary communion with nature and in the nostalgic contemplation of the past some compensation for the present horror of man's inhumanity to man. What was terrible in nature or tragic in the past – 'old, unhappy, *far-off* things' – could be regarded from the safe vantage point of the romantic retreat, where, as Thomas Campbell wrote in *The Pleasures of Hope*, 'distance lends enchantment to the view' and one can 'muse on Nature with a poet's eye'. And the romantic poets *did* retreat: Chatterton into death by suicide, Blake into eccentricity and obscurity, Wordsworth to the Lakes and Byron and Shelley to the Mediterranean. Like most generalisations this is only half the truth – but what is significant is that it was a half-truth which the poets themselves supported and encouraged. Byron was his own Childe Harold, and Childe Harold (despite Byron's satirical jibes at Sterne) was very much the sentimental traveller of his own day. Keats, like the real Chatterton and the fictive Werther, but for sound medical reasons, confessed to being 'half in love with easeful death'; and after he died it was his fellow poets, after all, who encouraged the myth of his destruction by the cruel world. And Byron's death at Missolonghi, fortuitous though it may have been, came about as the result of a thoroughly romantic gesture.

This aspect of romanticism is perhaps its least important

feature. The poets discovered a new and creatively sustaining world when they were forced back upon themselves, and if they retreated from their own immediate society, they made a fighting withdrawal. But they did withdraw – or at least adopted the posture of withdrawal. The myth of the unloved, misunderstood, agonised and alienated artist is a romantic myth; and it is intimately related to, is in part perhaps a variant of, the myth of the virtuous but impotent man of sentiment. Both grow out of the conviction that it is either impossible or immensely difficult to bridge the gap between innocence and experience, to bring about the marriage of heaven and hell. And since the end of the eighteenth century the writer in the European tradition has become increasingly preoccupied with the theme of the dislocated, deracinated, powerless artist: the theme, in other words, of virtue – literacy, artistic, cultural virtue – in distress.

II

The emergence of the theme of virtue in distress in the widest sense grew out of an awareness of the distance which separated moral idealism and the world of practical action; and in its particularly literary form out of the growing conviction on the writer's part both that he ought to be the conscience of his society and that in this role he was doomed to ineffectiveness: 'poets', as Shelley said, 'are the *unacknowledged* legislators of the world'. For Wordsworth, as for many other people, this mood of disillusionment had been crystallised by the failure – or the apparent failure – of the French Revolution. But it is clear that long before the Terror people had been feeling uneasy about painting too optimistic – or as we might say today – too *sentimental* a picture of man and society. There was an uncomfortable and increasingly embarrassing gap between the benevolent moral theories of the enlightenment and the social reality in which they were supposed to operate; and it would have been strange if people had not been in some way aware of this. The gap made itself most distressingly apparent in the treatment of those who had been economically or sexually unfortunate or aberrant. The apparent inevitability of poverty seemed to contradict the assumption that man, like his Creator, is both benevolent and reasonable; while the relief of the poor posed a perpetual challenge to the individual who wished to express his philanthropic impulses in useful action. At the same time the situation was further complicated by the relationship which was felt to exist between sensibility and sexuality. Heightened moral awareness depended ultimately on heightened physical awareness; and a heightened physical awareness could be assumed – to put it at the crudest level – to express itself in a heightened sexual or erotic responsiveness. 'The breasts', observed Albrecht von Haller, 'are covered with a great deal of skin, and furnished with many nerves. The *paenis*, which has likewise a great deal of skin, and receives a greater number of nerves than any other part of the body of an equal size, has also proportionable degree of sensibility.'[19] One can safely assume that Jane Austen was not thinking in such specifically physiological terms when she wrote *Sense and Sensibility*; but she had a clear realisation that for a young woman to over-indulge her feelings or to be unwisely generous (a word with both erotic and pecuniary connotations) could lead to disastrous consequences of an undeniably sexual nature. When M. G. Lewis was attacked for the frankness of his language in *The Monk* a friendly critic observed: 'for *that*, which he has most unwarrentably stiled *lust* . . . every circulating library would have afforded him a thousand gentle expressions, such as *amiable weakness, exquisite sensibility*, &c. &c.'[20] Justine, Sade's victim-heroine, is, as he tells us over and over again, endowed with the most delicate of sensibilities; and it is significant that this characteristic should lead not only to her sexual but also to her social and economic humiliation. Sade's heroes are driven by a greed for power and money which is almost as strong as – indeed is seen as part of – their lust for sexual domination.

Love and money are subjects of enduring interest to the novelist. But for a variety of reasons, among them the changing status of women and the new dimensions in the problem of poverty caused by the industrial revolution, they became subjects of quite special concern to the novelist in the eighteenth century, and in particular to the sentimental novelist. And the concern shown by the novelist reflected a general concern.

[19] *A Dissertation on the Sensible and Irritable Parts of Animals* 31.
[20] Henry Francis Robert Soame, *An Epistle in Rhyme to M. G. Lewis*; quoted by Louis F. Peck in *A Life of Matthew G. Lewis* (Cambridge, Mass., 1961).

The question of poverty in the eighteenth century is, needless to say, a complex one; but it is one nevertheless about which some generalisations must be hazarded by anyone who is concerned with sentimentalism, for sentimentalism in its most positively philanthropic aspect represents the awakening of the secular European conscience to the human problems which poverty poses. Three assertions can, perhaps, be made with some confidence. The first is that poverty tended to decrease as time went on: people in England – and probably also in France – on the whole lived longer, were more healthy, and were materially better off at the end of the eighteenth century than they had been at the beginning. The second is that the distresses and social inequities and cruelties associated with poverty *seemed* worse to people at the turn of the century than they had to earlier generations. 'The contrasts which have been drawn between the distresses of the early nineteenth century, and a golden age, thirty, fifty, or a hundred years earlier', Dorothy George has observed, 'are coloured partly by ignorance of past conditions, partly by a new attitude to evils which had long existed. These had become more intolerable not only to the sufferers but to onlookers by reason of the new humanitarianism'.[21] The revolutionary process through which not merely France but to some degree the whole of Europe was to pass was basically a 'revolution of rising expectations': the discontent, distress and frustration to which it gave vent were aroused partly because people had become aware at once that things were changing and improving and that they were not changing and improving as quickly as they might. The third assertion is that the ways in which attitudes to poverty and social injustice and their amelioration changed during the eighteenth century threw, or seemed to throw, a new and unprecedented responsibility on to the individual. R. H. Tawney has argued in *Religion and the Rise of Capitalism* that the treatment of poverty in this period was worse – less efficient and less humane – than it had been in the sixteenth and seventeenth centuries. In a semi-feudal hierarchical society in which Church and state were closely allied, the relief of the poor had been accommodated relatively easily into both the theory and practice of institutionalised Christianity. By the eighteenth century,

[21] *England in Transition* (Harmondsworth, 1967) 135.

however, the social structures, beliefs and loyalties which had made this possible had begun to disintegrate, and the newly-emerging modern secular state had not yet taken over the charitable responsibilities it had inherited.

One may disagree with some of the emphases in Tawney's interpretation, but it cannot be denied that in this respect the eighteenth century was an age of transition, and one in which the problem of poverty, and in general of man's inhumanity to man, seemed to bear down with a new urgency on the individual conscience. And it did so partly because both in fact and theory so much responsibility devolved upon individual rich philanthropists, and partly because poverty could be taken as evidence of moral failure on the part of the poor. Thus the cure for pauperism, especially in the first half of the century, was often seen to lie in a combination of relief by the generous individual and punishment by the state: it was, for instance, the opinion of Bishop Berkeley that 'sturdy beggars should . . . be seized and made slaves to the public for a certain term of years'.[22] Careful distinction had to be made between the deserving and the undeserving poor: there was hardly anything, according to Samuel Richardson, which required 'more judgment [than] distinguishing between objects worthy and unworthy, and what is and is not, charity'. One had to take pains to draw the line between 'the worthy indigent, become so by unavoidable accidents and casualties . . . [and] those who have brought upon themselves want and distress, by their extravagance and wilful folly'.[23]

But whatever the cause and no matter how unhappy the result poverty was also generally seen as an essential concomitant to the efficient functioning of society. Richardson could admit that '*the pleasures of the mighty are obtained by the tears of the poor*',[24] and at the same time maintain that poverty is 'a very necessary State in the Scale of Beings'.[25] Arthur Young made the same point more bluntly in 1771 when he observed that 'everyone but an idiot knows that the lower

[22] Quoted by R. H. Tawney in *Religion and the Rise of Capitalism* (London, 1936) 270.
[23] *Moral and Instructive Sentiments* 9–10.
[24] *Clarissa* II 17 (Everyman I 318).
[25] *Pamela* III 24 (excised from the sixth edition (1742), on which the Everyman edition is based).

classes must be kept poor, or they will never be industrious'.[26]
He would have found few ready to disagree with him. The
reluctance of the state to do anything too positive about the
relief of poverty reflects both the belief that most of the poor
probably deserve their fate and the fear that too much pampering
of the lower classes will upset the economic life of the community. In the theories of Malthus this fear eventually found its
most direct and influential statement. Fertility, argued Malthus,
contrary to popular belief did not add to the national wealth,
therefore the poor laws, which encouraged fecundity, should be
abolished. 'For the most unfortunate it might be licit to establish
workhouses, not "comfortable asylums", but places where "fare
should be hard" and "severe distress . . . find some alleviation".
These principles', states D. G. MacRae, 'were to be enacted, were
to enervate charity and cripple social reform for a century.'[27]

Despite the deeply rooted belief that society could not function
without the systematic exploitation of a large proportion of the
population – in other words that society, 'the world', was in-
herently and necessarily cruel and inhumane – it was also widely
maintained that man was by nature benevolent, and that one of
the greatest of moral pleasures was to be attained by acting
charitably. The author of that most popular of all conduct books,
The Whole Duty of Man, felt for instance that there was no real
necessity for him to exhort people to be charitable:

> This part of Charity seems to be so much implanted in our
> Natures as Men, that we generally account them not only
> unchristian but inhumane that are void of it; therefore I hope
> there will not need much perswasion to it.[28]

Given such a situation there was, understandably, very great
pressure on the individual to behave benevolently, to have the
right feelings and to act upon them. Generosity was one of the
most highly admired of moral traits; and it was commonly argued
that the only justification for the possession of great riches was
the opportunity which wealth afforded of exercising the virtues

---

[26] Quoted by Tawney, *Religion and the Rise of Capitalism* 270.
[27] 'Malthus, Thomas Robert' in *Encyclopaedia Britannica* (1969).
[28] *The Whole Duty of Man Laid down in a Plain and Familiar Way
for the Use of All . . . Necessary for all Families* (London, 1715) 344–
345 (first published 1659).

of benevolence and charity: 'The power of doing good to worthy objects', enunciated Richardson, 'is the only enviable circumstance in the lives of people of fortune.'[29] The concept of *noblesse oblige* is an old one; but in the eighteenth century it came to be adopted by the upper classes with a new and defensive fervour. 'The happiness of great place,' wrote Mme de Lambert, Marivaux's patroness, 'is that others find their good fortune in ours . . . Liberality is one of the duties of noble birth.'[30] And it was a duty which many people – whether of noble birth or not – took very seriously. The eighteenth century is an age of great philanthropists – men like General Oglethorpe, for instance, whose 'strong benevolence of soul' led him to found the colony of Georgia with a handful of paupers and bankrupts salvaged from the Debtors Prison; his friend, Captain Coram, who badgered the ladies of London into raising money for the Foundling Hospital; John Howard, who devoted his life to an attempt to reform the prisons not merely of Great Britain but of Europe; and many others. And society did become more humane: the Poor Law was gradually made more efficient; the administration of justice – especially under the reforming guidance of people like Henry Fielding and his brother – became more equitable and merciful; Sunday schools for the education of the poor were established; hospitals in which the sick actually had some chance of survival and recovery were set up; slavery was opposed, and eventually abolished – and philanthropists were honoured.

But as the spirit of humanitarianism spread and became more active, it was accompanied by a deepening realisation – not always consciously formulated it is true – that individual acts of benevolence could not alter a general social condition which was fundamentally unjust; and also that there was perhaps something suspect in being able to derive pleasure from feeling pity and acting charitably in a situation which was irredeemable; indeed that the real pleasure – one with which sadness was inextricably blended – came from the awareness of the final hopelessness of it all. The capacity to shed tears, to exhibit a feeling heart, became as important as – eventually more important than

[29] *Moral and Instructive Sentiments* 7.
[30] Quoted by Ruth Kirby Jamieson in *Marivaux, a Study in Sensibility* (New York, 1941) 26.

– the ability to practise really effective philanthropy. 'Moral weeping is the sign of so noble a passion', wrote an anonymous correspondent to *Man, a Paper for ennobling the Species*, in 1755, 'that it may be questioned whether those are properly men, who never weep upon any occasion . . . What can be more nobly human than to have a tender sentimental feeling of our own and others' misfortunes?'[31] At one level people were not ashamed to admit that they would deliberately cultivate the doing of good deeds in order to savour this 'tender sentimental feeling', this mixture of pity, self-pity, benevolence, and sadness. Mme Riccoboni, writing to Garrick in 1769, for instance, remarks that to have a tender and a feeling heart was 'le bonton du moment' in Paris: 'La bonté, la sensibilité, la tendre humanité sont devenues la fantaisie universelle. On feroit volontiers des malheureux pour gouter la douceur de les plaindre'[32] (some would willingly create unfortunates in order to taste the sweetness of feeling compassion for them). 'Pity', as one sentimental novelist remarks, is '. . . the greatest luxury the soul of sensibility is capable of relishing.'[33] But at another level it was realised that the element of self-satisfaction inherent in such an attitude was perhaps not very admirable. 'Charity's pleasures', observes the cynical Dubourg in Sade's *Justine*, 'are nothing but sops thrown to pride.'[34] The point is neatly illustrated in the incident in *Les Liaisons Dangereuses* in which Valmont arranges that he shall be seen by one of Mme de Tourvel's servants in the act of relieving the distresses of a poor family (Lovelace, it should be remembered, had similarly tricked Clarissa into believing he did good by stealth). As Valmont is surrounded by the peasant family on their knees and weeping with gratitude he finds, to his surprise, that he is moved himself: 'I must admit my weakness; my eyes filled with tears and I felt an involuntary but delicious emotion. I was astonished at the pleasure there is in doing good; and I should

[31] Op. cit. No. 43.
[32] *The Private Correspondence of David Garrick* (1832) II 561. Quoted in Boswell's *Life of Johnson*, ed. George Birkbeck Hill, rev. L. F. Powell (Oxford, 1934–50) III 149 note 2. The whole footnote is relevant.
[33] J. Thistlethwaite, *The Man of Experience* (1778). Quoted by J. M. S. Tompkins, *The Popular Novel in England, 1770–1800* (London, 1932) 103 note 1.
[34] *The Complete Justine* 471.

be tempted to believe that those whom we call virtuous people are not so virtuous as they are pleased to tell us.'[35]

The purpose behind Valmont's ruse, of course, is sexual: he wants to make Mme de Tourvel believe that he conforms to the sentimental ideals of generosity and benevolence – he wants to play on her sensibility so that she will fall in love with him. The incident is rich in implications – particularly in the way in which it illustrates the highly involved and subtle relationships which existed at this time between sexual behaviour and social and economic position: Valmont and Mme de Tourvel are both unimaginably more wealthy than the peasants he relieves, but he, like Lovelace, is an aristocrat and she, like Clarissa, is a bourgeoise – although there are very significant differences among these four characters, especially between the two women. But the situations in which they are involved demonstrate that the gap between theory and practice in the sexual sphere was if not wider at least far more complex and difficult to chart than the gap between ideal and reality in the treatment of the poor. To begin with there were several different and conflicting theories. Gentlemen like Valmont and Lovelace were everywhere still expected to enjoy their traditional freedoms – except by embarrassingly insistent bourgeois moralists like Samuel Richardson. And the clash between aristocratic and middle class modes of sexual behaviour which Richardson presented with such startling frankness in *Pamela* and *Clarissa* was to become a major theme in sentimental fiction.

In this conflict it was generally the woman who suffered – and who was expected to suffer. When lovely woman stooped to folly she could, if she were unfortunate, be punished by society with quite extraordinary brutality and ferocity. If, however, she were lucky – especially if her luck carried her into the French court – she could be rewarded with an extravagance and liberality equally extraordinary. The sanctions and rewards which could be applied or granted by society varied enormously according to the social position of the offender; but seduction or the misfortune of pregnancy could for many women mean ruin in a most sordidly real sense. Women of the lowest class who were destitute, pregnant and on the point of delivery could be harried

[35] *Les Liaisons Dangereuses*, trans. R. Aldington (New York, 1962) 58.

from one town to the next so that they would not become the financial responsibility of the parish in which the child was born; and as Dorothy Marshall has demonstrated in *The English Poor of the Eighteenth Century* this basically economic callousness often resulted in the deaths of mother and child.[36] And there were those among the wealthy and powerful who, if they thought about the matter at all, would probably have felt that a reduction in the numbers of the poor would be a good thing for society as a whole (Malthus for impeccably humane reasons clearly believed this). Dubourg's outburst to Justine – one echoed by many of Sade's characters – is shocking not because of its calculated inhumanity but because one is made to feel that it expresses an attitude that is held far more widely than one would wish to imagine:

> It was the custom of the Greeks, it is the custom in China: there, the offspring of the poor are exposed, or are put to death. What is the good of letting those creatures live who, no longer able to count on their parents' aid . . . henceforth are useful for nothing and simply weigh upon the State . . . bastards, orphans, malformed infants should be condemned to death immediately they are pupped.[37]

The parish officers, worried about public funds and their own salaries, who wrote entries like the following no doubt would have shared Dubourg's view:

> 1722 To a big bellyd woman several days & nights at nursing at Robinsons, & conveying her to Chigwell after she had gathered strength to prevent her lying in here, she fell to pieces in 2 or 3 days there . . . 17–7.[38]

When one remembers facts such as these, together with the strictness of the laws that could be enforced against servants who disobeyed their masters, or who left their employment without proper permission, one can appreciate the true magnitude of the trials and temptations which Pamela has to face – and one can also appreciate the sentimental force of such a vision of innocent virtue in distress as Sterne gives in his sketch of Maria. The

[36] Op. cit. (London, 1926) 212.   [37] *The Complete Justine* 471.
[38] Quoted by Dorothy Marshall, *The English Poor in the Eighteenth Century* 212. She comments: 'Nor was treatment of this kind at all unusual'.

shorn lamb in the eighteenth century needed a God who could temper the winds that blew upon it.

Clarissa, of course, is at no time faced with the prospect of being subjected to the physical distress and humiliation which could be the lot of her poorer sisters. But when Lovelace rapes her he effectively destroys her (and himself); just as more subtly but no less cruelly and thoroughly Valmont destroys Madame de Tourvel by deceiving her into accepting him as her lover. Men of honour (*real* honour, that is) looked after their mistresses and their illegitimate progeny (even Lovelace takes pride in this), but they did not necessarily suffer if they failed in this private moral obligation. And it did not pay to be righteous overmuch: Henry Fielding was subjected to a degree of public disapproval and mockery when he married Mary Daniel, his deceased wife's maid, even though she was about to become the mother of his child.[39]

The sexual morality of eighteenth-century society is far too complicated a subject to be summed up effectively in a couple of paragraphs. But one is justified in pointing – however briefly – to the vast discrepancy between what went on in practice and what, according to official legal and moral codes, the community apparently thought ought to go on; and also to the differences amongst the various ways in which sexual offenders could be dealt with: Squire Allworthy for instance could have ordered Jenny Jones to be whipped at a cart's tail while at the same time accepting – albeit with disapproval – Mrs Fitzpatrick and Lady Bellaston as social equals. The Colonel's Lady and Judy O'Grady may have been sisters under the skin, but very few people would have maintained that they deserved equality of treatment.

The situation is further complicated by the considerable difference which existed between French attitudes to love and morality and those current in England. When Sterne remarks in a letter to a friend that he carries on his affairs 'quite in the French way, sentimentally',[40] he is invoking a whole literary

[39] See F. Homes Dudden, *Henry Fielding* (Oxford, 1952) I 543.

[40] 'I myself must ever have some dulcinea in my head – it harmonises the soul . . . but I carry on my affairs quite in the French way, sentimentally – "*l'amour*" (say they), "*n'est rien sans sentiment*" – Now notwithstanding they make such a pother about the word, they have no precise idea annex'd to it . . .' To ?John Wodehouse, 23 [? August] 1765. *Letters of Laurence Sterne*, ed. Lewis Perry Curtis (Oxford, 1932) 256.

and social tradition which has no real counterpart in England. Sexual freedom amongst the French aristocracy was not merely tolerated but encouraged to a degree unknown across the channel (except, perhaps, briefly and rather self-consciously during the Restoration); and 'sentiment', as defined and examined by countless French writers of the late seventeenth and early eighteenth centuries, came to stand for a highly civilised combination of erotic vivacity and delicacy together with an extremely sensitive moral awareness. What the French meant by 'sentiment' was summed up for Sterne in the statement – which he quoted more than once – that

> L'amour n'est *rien* sans sentiment,
> Et le sentiment est encore *moins* sans amour.[41]

In his own way Sterne illustrates this very thesis, especially in A *Sentimental Journey*. But there are no novelists in English who can really be compared with such erotic sentimentalists as Crébillon and Marivaux. The theme of such writers, especially Marivaux, is that sexual experience can be not merely an enjoyable pastime but a profoundly educative and civilising process. His novels, as one writer has remarked, present 'the metaphysics of love making'.[42] In Le *Paysan Parvenu*, for instance, Joseph, the naïve but honest, well-intentioned and sensitive peasant is transformed into a civilised gentleman, *un honnête homme*, through a succession of love affairs. With Mlle Habert his relationship is merely friendly, with Mme Ferval it is sensual and passionate, finally with Mme de Vambures it assumes the characteristics of true love. And he owes his success to an innate benevolence which reveals itself as much in his capacity for sexual passion and tenderness as in anything else. 'A propos de coeur', says Mme de Ferval to him, 'êtes-vous né un peu tendre? C'est la marque d'un bon caractère.'[43] And one of her *beaux* remarks that 'plus on a de sensibilité, plus on a l'âme généreuse, et par consequent, estimable'.[44]

[41] A *Sentimental Journey* 153.
[42] 'Marivaux', in *Encyclopaedia Britannica* (1957).
[43] Le *Paysan Parvenu* (Paris, 1940) 244. ('So far as your heart is concerned were you born with a slightly tender one? It is the mark of a good character.')
[44] Ibid. 248 ('The more sensibility one has the more generous, and consequently the more estimable, is one's soul.')

Even though there is nothing in English literature quite like *Le Paysan Parvenu*, the notion that the potential excellence of one's moral character can be directly related to one's capacity for love was not entirely foreign. It is, after all, one of the central themes of that most unsentimental novel, *Tom Jones*. Tom is pre-eminently a man who possesses 'une âme généreuse', and this generosity of spirit manifests itself in all his relations with other people, and especially in his relations with women. In any case, if the faculty of moral judgment is located in one's sensibility it must inevitably bear a very close relationship to one's sexual responsiveness: one's capacity for love and one's capacity for virtue both depend on the delicacy of one's sensibility.

For young men like Tom Jones and Joseph, *le paysan parvenu*, it was relatively easy to refine their consciences through a variety of amorous experience. But for Pamela Andrews and her numerous daughters, and even for Parson Yorick and the young Werther, this was not the case. We find as the century moves on that the heroes and heroines of fiction, although often endowed with increasingly exquisite sensibilities, have to suffer more and more limitations on their freedom of action in the sexual sphere. One cannot imagine Jane Austen, for instance, much as she admired Richardson, ever allowing one of her young ladies to be raped, or one of her young gentlemen to marry a common serving maid. What was happening in fiction to some extent reflected what was happening – or what many people felt ought to be happening – in life. The status of women was changing (and most novels after about 1760 seem to have been written by women) and there was a general tendency for bourgeois respectability to replace aristocratic freedom as the most admired norm, both in life and literature. Those symbolic figures Mr B., Lovelace, Don Giovanni and Valmont are all upper class libertines who are eventually defeated by implacable, *respectable* women (or their avengers) – swamped by the rising tide of middle class morality. It has always seemed an interesting set of coincidences to me that *The Memoirs of a Woman of Pleasure*, *Tom Jones* and *Clarissa* should all have appeared at about the same time (1748–9) and that the publication of *Sir Charles Grandison* should have coincided with the enactment of Hardwick's Marriage Bill (1754): Sir Charles and chaste monogamy triumph, while Fanny Hill goes underground, Tom Jones is at least put on the defensive,

and Clarissa – or the Richardsonian heroine – is finally tamed.
Even Sterne, that supremely independent spirit, was forced to
adapt himself to the change in taste. The first volumes of
Tristram Shandy may have been hailed as the work of an English
Rabelais, but, as Miss Clara Reeve remarked primly, 'it [was]
not a woman's book'.[45] What the public really wanted was
pathos, not bawdry: Sterne in the role of sentimental traveller
appears in his last book as Parson Yorick, not as Tristram, and
the account of his wanderings was presented to the world as a
'*Work of Redemption*'.[46] As such it succeeded beyond any
dreams its author may have had: Yorick, generously intentioned,
tender hearted, susceptible, ineffective – and almost always in
distress – became widely accepted as the embodiment of all the
sentimental virtues.

III

The popularity of A *Sentimental Journey* is above all a tribute
to Sterne's genius for creating character. Yorick indeed eventually
seems to have escaped from his creator and to have assumed a
life of his own – a life which was originally modelled on Sterne's
and to which the writer seems also to have adapted himself (the
question of the effect of Tristram and Yorick on Laurence Sterne
is probably as interesting as the question of the relationship of
Sterne as author and model to his characters). When Yorick first
comes on the scene in *Tristram Shandy* it is as an ancillary and
slightly obscure personage who appears to have been introduced
by Sterne for a variety of reasons – to give himself the opportunity of having a crack at some of his ecclesiastical and political
enemies and at the same time of making a humorously affectionate acknowledgment of his friendship with John Hall-Stevenson

---

[45] *The Progress of Romance* (New York, 1930) (facsimile of the
Colchester ed. of 1785). According to Horace Walpole, Bishop
Warburton recommended *Tristram Shandy*, when it first appeared,
'to the bench of bishops, and told them Mr. Sterne, the author, was
the English Rabelais'. Significantly, the bench 'had never heard of
such a writer'. Later Warburton's attitude changed, of course; see
Wilbur L. Cross, *The Life and Times of Laurence Sterne* (New Haven,
1929) 286.
[46] A *Series of Genuine Letters, Between Henry and Frances* (London, 1786) V 83; quoted Curtis, *Letters* 398 note 3.

(Eugenius); to serve as the subject for a comic-pathetic deathbed scene, and the occasion for introducing a mechanical joke (the black page and the accompanying epitaph, 'Alas, poor Yorick!'); to provide an excuse for smuggling one of his own sermons into the novel; and possibly there were other motives at work as well. But although Yorick was well and truly buried half way through Volume One of *Tristram Shandy* he refused to lie down. Sterne, capitalising on the success of his novel, published his sermons under the name 'Mr. Yorick'; he gave him the last words in *Tristram Shandy*; and he resurrected him to make his sentimental journey through France and Italy.

If one were looking for the typical sentimental hero it would be difficult to find a more representative figure than Parson Yorick. He is at once admirable and pathetic: those qualities which we are expected to admire in him are the sentimental virtues – his sensitivity, his generosity, his candour, his benevolence; what makes him pathetic and comic is the failure, or apparent failure, of these virtues to succeed in the world. In an extremely subtle and ambiguous manner Yorick therefore represents at once the hope embodied in the sentimental ideal and the fear that it may prove inadequate. And the situations in which – especially in A *Sentimental Journey* – he finds himself tested most severely usually involve either love or money or a combination of the two. The question he continually asks himself – or which, perhaps, the reader is expected to ask *himself* – is whether his acts of charity are genuinely altruistic and appropriate to the suffering he is attempting to relieve, and whether his gestures of kindness, affection and love towards the various women he encounters are free from selfishness and lust. The condition in which he finds himself is that of the virtuous, principled, sexually responsive man who is reduced by circumstances – either external (the world) or internal (his conscience) – to a position of comic or pathetic impotence. Like the starling he is trapped and can't get out; although being blessed with a sense of humour he is always able to make the best of a bad situation. And if he stretches out his hand in the dark there is, after all, always the chance that someone will take it – even if it is only the 'brisk and lively' *fille de chambre* and not her beautiful Piedmontese mistress.

Tristram Shandy and A *Sentimental Journey* are undeniably

two of the most cheerful books ever written. But they are predominantly concerned, as is every other sentimental novel of the
century, with the theme of virtue in distress. When we are first
introduced to Yorick, we are invited – serio-comically it is true –
to mourn his death: 'Alas, poor Yorick!' And Yorick's death, in
the true sentimental tradition, is attributed to a refusal to betray
his principles. Like Clarissa he insists on being true to himself,
and he pays the penalty. Poor Yorick, we are told, being at the
age of twenty-six as 'utterly unpractised in the world . . . as a
romping unsuspicious girl of thirteen',[47] provokes the wrath of
knaves and fools by his habit of plain speaking; and 'no innocence of heart or integrity of conduct' is able to protect him from
being struck down by 'CRUELTY and COWARDICE, twin ruffians,
hired and set on by MALICE in the dark . . . they had smote his
root, and then he fell, as many a worthy man had fallen before
him'.[48]

Yorick's death is presented in the manner of pure Cervantic
comedy – Clarissa's in the manner of bourgeois tragedy: yet each
is an illustration of the theme of virtue distressed, beleaguered
and defeated. Yorick and Clarissa, like most other sentimental
heroes and heroines, are in distress primarily for two reasons:
firstly, because they refuse to compromise themselves with the
forces of evil (which are represented as being, in part at least,
the forces of convention – 'the world'): and secondly, because,
being virtuous, they are somehow *necessarily* weak.

Indeed it was the frailty of virtue, rather than its simple distress, which brought the tears of sensibility brimming to the eye
of the tender hearted reader. 'I am as weak as a woman', Yorick
admits ruefully, as he plucks the nettles from Father Lorenzo's
grave, 'and I beg the world not to smile but to pity me.'[49] This is
essentially the plea made by the hero or heroine of every sentimental novel; although the ways in which the plea is presented
can vary greatly and significantly. We pity Clarissa, for instance,
but we also admire her: although defeated by the world the
manner in which she copes with her defeat transforms it into a
triumph. And the pathos of Yorick's situation is always qualified
by irony and ambiguity – do the nettles, the irreverent reader
may wonder, have anything to do with the flood of tears into

[47] *Tristram Shandy* 26 (I, xi).   [48] Ibid. 29–30.
[49] *Sentimental Journey* 103.

which he bursts in 'the little cimetiery' attached to Father Lorenzo's convent? It is because this sort of qualification is so conspicuously absent – despite the maintenance of a humorous tone – from *Le Voyageur sentimental* that Vernes is sentimental in a way that Sterne never is.

If Vernes' sentimental traveller represents one kind of degeneration Mrs Radcliffe's heroines represent another. The character from whom these touching exemplars of the virtuous maiden in distress are descended is Clarissa, and they are not always totally unworthy of their original. Mrs Radcliffe is a much more substantial novelist than François Vernes, and her quality reveals itself particularly in the confidence and polish of her style. Her novels bear witness in a striking fashion to the way in which the Richardsonian manner had by now developed into a formal rhetoric of sentiment which could be applied to almost any situation. Mrs Radcliffe's adoption of this manner is, one must admit, sometimes so careless and unthinking as to turn her style into a parody of itself – but nonetheless it always remains a style, a formal mode of writing which can be modulated to control the rendering of almost every aspect of life and to evaluate it at the same time. In the hands of Jane Austen this manner of writing was to be revitalised and transformed into a powerful and distinctive literary instrument. For an essentially minor and second-rank novelist such as Mrs Radcliffe it provided a medium through which to place her characters firmly without really exploring them, and to maintain for herself and her readers a measure of detachment from the characters' feelings and from the bizarre situations by which they were aroused.

A good example of the strength, facility and artificiality of Mrs Radcliffe's style is provided in her account of a situation that does not pretend to be anything but melodramatic: the reception of Ellena di Rosalba, the heroine of *The Italian*, by the Abbess of the convent in which she is secretly to be confined by the powerful family who wish to prevent their son from marrying her. Ellena has realised for the first time the identity of those behind her kidnapping:

Fear, shame and indignation alternately assailed her; and the sting of offended honour, on being suspected . . . of having voluntarily . . . sought the alliance of any family, especially of one who disdained her, struck forcibly to her heart, till the pride of conscious worth revived her courage and fortified her patience, and she demanded by whose will she had been torn from her home, and by whose authority she was now detained . . .

The Abbess, unaccustomed to have her power opposed . . . was for a moment too indignant to reply; and Ellena observed, but no longer with dismay, the brooding tempest ready to burst over head. It is I, only, who am injured, said she to herself, and shall the guilty oppressor triumph, and the innocent sufferer sink under the shame that belongs only to guilt! Never will I yield to a weakness so contemptible. The consciousness of deserving well will recall my presence of mind, which, permitting me to estimate the characters of my oppressors . . . will enable me also to despise their power.

I must remind you, said the Abbess, at length, that the questions you make are unbecoming in your situation . . . You may withdraw.

Ellena forbore to make farther inquiry, or remonstrance, and perceiving that reproach would not only be useless, but degrading to herself, she immediately obeyed the mandate of the Abbess, and determined, since she must suffer, to suffer, if possible, with firmness and dignity.[50]

That I have had to quote at such length is a tribute to the quality of Mrs Radcliffe's writing at this point: the passage is both self-contained and extremely difficult to cut and compress. Moreover, despite the rather theatrical references to guilty oppressors and innocent sufferers, Ellena's attitude has a touch of authentic nobility and courage; and there are a grace and economy in the final paragraph that are worthy of a more substantial context. One is not made to feel here, as one sometimes is when confronted with her more wildly rhapsodic descriptions of natural beauty, that Mrs Radcliffe is striving to produce any specially fine effect: the sureness with which an established rhetoric of sentiment allows her to analyse the heroine's state of mind is effortless.

[50] *The Italian; or, the Confessional of the Black Penitents*, in *Ballantyne's Novelists' Library* (London, 1824) X 561 (first published 1797).

Yet despite its assurance there is an element of artifice and sentimentality running through the whole passage. It manifests itself most clearly in the account Mrs Radcliffe gives of the motivation of Ellena. In her hour of trial she draws strength, as Clarissa does, by reflecting on her own virtue. She is saved by 'the pride of conscious worth', 'the consciousness of deserving well', the sense that she is 'innocent' while her enemies are 'guilty'. It is this that nerves her resistance and enables her to 'despise the power of her oppressors'. We can take this sort of language from Clarissa, because we know that both she and Lovelace, by the exhausting and painful examination of their own characters which their terrible situation has forced them to undergo, have earned the right to deliver a moral judgment not only on themselves but on other people as well. But the phrases come too glibly to the mind of Mrs Radcliffe's virtuous damsel in distress: they smack of self-congratulation rather than of genuine moral superiority. And in this, Ellena di Rosalba exemplifies the basic weakness of the whole sentimental attitude – the weakness which, especially in literature, led to the decline and decay of sentimentalism into sentimentality. The man – or woman – of sentiment was always open to the charge that he was, in general, too aware of his own goodness, and much too complacent about it ('self-complacent', one may note in passing, is a term which has suffered the same fall in value as 'sentimental' – it occurs often in unambiguously approbatory contexts in the eighteenth century). The sentimental novel in its cheapest and most popular manifestations evidences a smugly moralistic, uncritical self-adulation, a 'pride of conscious worth', that seems presumptuous, to say the least, today. And it is this self-complacence, to which, more than anything else, the clichés of the sentimental style bear witness.

The paradigm cliché is that of virtue in distress: Pamela, Clarissa, Tristram, Yorick, *le voyageur sentimental*, Mrs Radcliffe's heroines and those of countless other worthy lady novelists are all virtuous and distressed. And even in situations which are morally neutral the implication is always made that the suffering the characters undergo is intensified and to some extent brought about by the fact that they are virtuous. The notion not that virtue is rewarded but that virtue invites its own punishment is a central theme in all the novels we have been considering, novels which in one sense or another can be called 'sentimental'. That some of these should be enduring works of literary art while others should be at best mediocre and at worst shallow 'sentimental' rubbish poses a problem of definition – if of nothing else – to the literary historian. If both *Le Voyageur sentimental* and *Clarissa* can be described as 'sentimental novels' this suggests that the meaning of the term should be looked at closely. Each book certainly deals with the theme of virtue in distress. The question which needs to be answered is whether they have anything else in common: the question of just what descriptive value resides in the term 'sentimental novel' when it is applied to a certain fictive tradition in the eighteenth century.

5

The Novel of Sentiment

I

At one level it is scarcely any longer necessary to attempt a definition and description of the sentimental novel. Edith Birkhead's brief but admirably detailed essay, 'Sentiment and sensibility in the eighteenth-century novel', published nearly half a century ago,[1] gives an excellent introductory survey of the field; and J. M. S. Tompkins, in her account of popular fiction, takes a closer and more comprehensive look at its most sentimental area, the novel published between 1770–1800.[2]

But it may be useful to examine one or two particular aspects of sentimental fiction, not merely for the light we may throw on the eighteenth-century novel, but also for what we may learn about subsequent developments in the literature of the nineteenth and twentieth centuries. The novel, as we know it, was born in this period, and the dominant form in prose fiction was the sentimental novel. There were a number of major novelists in the eighteenth century, but there seems to have been only one great master – Samuel Richardson. He was a genuinely innovatory artist and craftsman,[3] and his genius was acknowledged not only in England but also in France and Germany. In his novels, especially *Clarissa*, Richardson provided at once a mythology and a method; and as Leslie Fiedler has reminded us in his brilliant if erratic study, *Love and Death in the American Novel*, their

[1] *Essays and Studies* XI (1925) 22–116.
[2] *The Popular Novel in England, 1770–1800* (London, 1932).
[3] In *Told in Letters: Epistolary Fiction before Richardson* (Ann Arbor, 1966), Robert Adams Day demonstrates that although the epistolary novel was a well established form by the time *Pamela* was written it was one in which very little of real value had been achieved. Moreover Richardson seems to have read few if any of these earlier attempts at epistolary fiction: yet despite his ignorance of what they had achieved, he 'recapitulated in his own work all the evolutionary developments of his precursors and went beyond them'.

influence was pervasive throughout the nineteenth century, and can still be discerned today.

The fictive patterns established by Richardson were capable of almost immediate vulgarisation; and the rapidity with which they degenerated into melodramatic and superficial clichés is an indication of the depth and broadness of their appeal. In the stories of Pamela and Mr B., and of Clarissa and Lovelace, the readers and the novelists of the eighteenth century found reflected with extraordinary fidelity some of the most important truths of life as they knew it. But the fidelity was too faithful for comfort: the harsh tragedy of *Clarissa* was soon softened and transformed into a 'delicate distress', and the papier-mâché terrors of the Castle of Udolpho were substituted for the unbearably authentic claustrophobia of Harlowe Place.

But if the tradition established by Richardson ran rapidly to seed in one direction in others it was to prove richly and enduringly fruitful. Through Jane Austen it led on, as F. R. Leavis has suggested,[4] to the central tradition in English fiction. Without Richardson and his successors Jane Austen's achievement would not have been possible. Her work grows out of, is a reaction against and an assimilation of, the English domestic novel of the late eighteenth century. And this genre, superficial and trivial in the main though it may have become, is descended in an uninterrupted line from the novels of Samuel Richardson.

Jane Austen was aware of Richardson quite directly: she read his novels with delight and admiration, and she learnt from them as one craftsman learns from the work of another. The moral comedy she perfected could not have been brought into existence if the opening sequences of *Sir Charles Grandison* (not wholly a dull book) had never been written. Henry James was certainly not aware of Richardson in this way, but he worked – whether he knew it or not – within a tradition which Richardson, more than any other single novelist, had helped to create. There is a sense in which *The Portrait of a Lady*, for instance, would have been impossible without *Clarissa*. And if Richardson can be called a sentimental novelist so can Henry James.

In the twentieth-century sense of the word James is not sentimental, and neither is Richardson, although there are unquestion-

---

[4] *The Great Tradition* (London, 1948) 4–5.

ably elements of sentimentality in his work. But it was not because of these that Richardson was described during the eighteenth century as a sentimental writer. The adjective was applied to him because of the qualities he shares with a novelist such as James – because of his moral seriousness and his preoccupation with the mental and emotional lives of his characters. Richardson, like James, is basically concerned with presenting a true picture of the world as he understands it. To call his work 'sentimental', then, without qualification, is both misleading and unjust. It might be both more accurate and more useful to call *Clarissa* not a sentimental novel but a novel of sentiment – a term which could be applied just as validly to *The Portrait of a Lady* or to *Ulysses*, *La Recherche du temps Perdu*, *Malone Dies*, or any other novel where the emphasis is not on physical action but on reflection, on the inner lives of the characters.

If we are to adopt the term 'novel of sentiment', however, we must remember that it does not seem to have been employed in the eighteenth century: people spoke then of sentimental novels and sentimental writers. Also, the word 'sentimental' changed in meaning between the time it first came into the language, and the end of the century. It may be useful, therefore, to take a closer look at 'sentiment' and 'sentimental' (particularly the latter) and especially at the way in which they functioned during this period when applied to literature.

'Sentimental' seems to have first appeared in the English language in the 1740s. The adverb 'sentimentally' occurs in one of Walpole's letters written in 1746; and Lady Bradshaigh, in a letter dated 1749, uses the word 'sentimental' itself.[5] This is the first firmly established appearance of the word. It also occurs in a letter supposedly written by Sterne in 1739 or 1740. There are doubts about the authenticity of this letter, however; and although it has recently been argued strongly by Duke Maskell that the document is genuine, Sterne's use in it of 'sentimental' poses some puzzling questions.[6] It is, to say the least, strange

---

[5] For Walpole's use of 'sentimentally' see E. K. Erämetsä, *A Study of the Word 'Sentimental'*. I have quoted Lady Bradshaigh's letter above, chap. II note 12.

[6] L. P. Curtis first questioned the authenticity of the letter in 1927 in a debate with Margaret R. B. Shaw in the columns of *The Times Literary Supplement*. He presents the case fully in his edition, *Letters*

that the word does not appear, so far as we know, anywhere else
in Sterne's writings until twenty years later, and it is also strange
that the sense which the word bears in the letter seems to be the
one that emerged in the 1760s and not the sense that, so far as
can be ascertained, the word generally carried in the forties and
fifties. Since the status of the letter is still a matter of debate, it
seems safe to place the first appearance of the word in 1749 when
Lady Bradshaigh made her famous plea for elucidation to Samuel
Richardson: 'What, in your opinion, is the meaning of the word
sentimental, so much in vogue among the polite?'

According to Erik Erämetsä in his *Study of the Word 'Sentimental'* the word as it was employed in the 1740s meant 'pertain-
ing to sentiment [in the sense of] opinion, thought, judgement,
mind'.[7] During the next twenty years, as he convincingly
demonstrates, there was a marked shift in connotation. By the
1760s – particularly by 1768 when Sterne published *A Sentimental Journey* – it had acquired a distinctly emotional and
sexual colouring. It was also beginning to take on the meaning
current today – 'addicted to indulgence in superficial emotion;
apt to be swayed by sentiment'.[8]

It had none of these latter meanings for Samuel Richardson.
The first appearance of the word in his writings occurs in the
'Postscript' to the third edition of *Clarissa*, where he states that
Lovelace and Belford were infidels 'only in *practice*' and that
they had not 'been painted as *sentimental* Unbelievers'[9] – in
other words, that, although their actions mocked God, they were
not philosophical atheists. It seems clear that here the adjective
has been formed from 'sentiment', considered as meaning simply
'thought' or 'opinion'.

Although 'sentiment' at this time could be used to refer to
any thought or opinion, it was also often used in a more precise
way to describe thoughts, opinions or judgments of a specifically
moral or philosophical character. When Charlotte Grandison
remarks that she is 'too *sentimental*', she is admitting (most

---

of *Laurence Sterne* (Oxford, 1935) 10–15. His argument has been
criticised in detail by Mr Maskell in 'The Authenticity of Sterne's
first recorded Letter', *Notes and Queries* (August, 1970) 303–7.

[7] See his 'Suggestion for the Entry under "Sentimental" in the
N.E.D. (before 1800)', op. cit. 146–8.

[8] OED s.v. 'sentimental'.   [9] *Clarissa* VII 362.

unusually for one of Richardson's characters) that she has been
making too many moral pronouncements. 'The French only are
proud of sentiments at this day', she goes on; 'the English cannot
bear them: story, story, story, is what they hunt after, whether
sense or nonsense, probable or improbable.'[10] It was obviously
this sense of the word that Johnson had in mind when he said
that 'you must read [Richardson] for the sentiment, and consider the story as only giving occasion to the sentiment'.[11]

Richardson would have agreed with this description of the
purpose of his novels. 'Instruction, Madam, is the pill, amusement the gilding',[12] he wrote to Lady Echlin: it is a text which
he develops at length in his various 'Prefaces' and 'Postscripts'.
In his opinion, the most valuable things in *Pamela*, *Clarissa*, and
Sir Charles Grandison were those 'moral and instructive sentiments' with which his characters fill their letters. Eventually
Richardson and an unnamed friend collected all these 'important
Maxims', and published them in one volume small enough to fit
the pockets of all such as 'were desirous of repeatedly inculcating
[them] on their own minds, and the minds of others'.[13] As
Edith Birkhead remarks, Richardson's 'heroines are "sententious"
rather than "sentimental"'.

Richardson himself would have seen little or no difference
between the two terms. Sentiment for him did not have a great
deal to do with feeling. Although he was aware of his power to
touch the hearts of his readers, he did not associate this primarily
with what he would have described as the 'sentimental' qualities
of his work. The sentiments in his novels were indeed 'moral and
instructive' and they were intended to provide comfort as much
for the reader as for the heroine during her trials. Pamela and
Clarissa drew strength and consolation from the thought that the
story of their sufferings might serve as an example to the world;
and it was only by insisting that the main purpose of his pathetic
stories was a moral one that Richardson was able to justify, both
to himself and his readers, the anguish he made them all suffer.

The term 'sentimental novel' for Richardson, and probably

[10] *Grandison* 3rd ed. (1754) V 354.
[11] *Boswell's Life of Johnson*, ed. G. Birkbeck Hill, rev. L. F. Powell
(Oxford, 1934–50) II 175.
[12] Letter of 22 Sept. 1755.
[13] 'Preface by a Friend' in *Moral and Instructive Sentiments* ix.

for many other English people in the 1740s and 50s would not
have meant primarily a novel of feeling or passion. Since most
novels, however, had love as their subject – 'a small tale, generally
of love', is how Johnson defines 'novel' in his *Dictionary* (1755)
– 'sentimental' in this context would necessarily have carried
some amatory overtones. But to describe a novel as 'sentimental'
would have been to imply that it was a thoughtful, moral work,
and one which presented human passion in a sober and realistic
rather than a fancifully romantic manner. This is the sense of
the word which William Guthrie, in fiction a minor follower of
Richardson,[14] had in mind when, in 1754, he gave his novel,
The Friends, the sub-title: *A Sentimental History: Describing
Love as a Virtue, As well as a Passion*. In the Preface he claims
that 'the Reader here needs not fear that his Attention will be
overpowered by the *Yawn of listless Love*, or his Understanding
affronted with the *Violence of frantic Passion*'. The history he
presents is 'an *Epic* in lower Life'; and his 'great Aim in this
Work' has been 'the introducing, within a small Compass of
Time, *Variety* without *Confusion*, the *Surprising* without the
Marvellous, *Events* that strike from the *Force of Probability*, and
Sentiments that affect through *the Powers of Nature*, to keep in
View one *moral Idea*, and to inculcate one *important Lesson*'.[15]
'Sentiment' is used several times in this prefatory note, some-
times to mean feeling (as in the last quotation) but more often to
mean the statement of a thought or idea – a 'sentence'. Thus
Virgil, he says, is not to be censured for 'introducing, into his
Æneid, many Similies and Sentiments (some of them literally
translated), which Homer . . . had already introduced into his
Iliad, and his *Odyssey*'.[16] *The Friends* lives up to the claims
Guthrie makes for it: though rather rambling and disorganised it
is an unpretentious and naturalistic account of the lives of some
convincingly ordinary and not altogether uninteresting men and
women. By comparison with the popular fiction produced
twenty years later it is a most *un*sentimental work.

The word 'sentimental' also appears twice in Smollett's
Ferdinand Count Fathom, which had been published a year

[14] Guthrie, a Scot, was mainly a political writer, translator and
popular historian. *The Friends* is his only novel. 'Guthrie is more
than once referred to by Johnson in terms of some respect' (*DNB*).
[15] Op. cit. A1r–v.   [16] Ibid.

earlier, in 1753. On both occasions the word is used with the sense of 'rational', 'intellectual', 'spiritual' as opposed to 'emotional' or 'passionate'. Thus Trebasi, who is *not* sentimental, is shown acting in an instinctive, irrational, unconsidered manner:

> Trebasi, whose courage was not of the sentimental kind, but purely owing to his natural insensibility of danger, instead of concerting measures costly for the engagement . . . drew a pistol without the least hesitation, and fired it at the face of Rinaldo.[17]

When Celinda's love for Fathom, up to the time his campaign of physical seduction has succeeded, is described as having been 'sentimental', the word, of course, has an emotional reference – but it also carries the simple connotations of virtuousness and spirituality, without any of the sexually ambiguous and ironic overtones with which Sterne was soon to invest it. 'Such a commerce between two such persons of a different sex', Smollett observes, 'could not possibly be carried on, without degenerating from the platonic system of sentimental love.'[18] The appearance of the word in this novel (an appearance not noted by Erämetsä) is of particular interest because *Ferdinand Count Fathom* prefigures in so many ways the gothic, melodramatic and sentimental developments which were to dominate popular fiction in the coming decades. The characters often act in highly emotional ways, and their behaviour is described in recognisably conventional language: e.g. 'the sensibility of the youth discovered itself in a flood of tears, which he shed at her appearance'.[19] And it is significant that although Smollett is not being ironic in his account of Celinda's 'sentimental' passion for Fathom, she conforms in every way to the stereotype of the sentimental heroine: she is a young girl of unusual sensibility, she is in a pathetic situation, she is innocent and she is also naïve and foolish. She is a perfect example of virtue in distress.

A document of crucial significance in the history of the word appeared in 1755. This is the essay (untitled) on 'moral weeping' which was published as no. 43 of *Man. A Paper For ennobling*

[17] *The Adventures of Ferdinand Count Fathom* (London, 1753) II 194.
[18] Ibid. I 254.   [19] Ibid. II 240.

the Species. 'Sentimental' here is used to describe genuine as opposed to spurious feeling, the sort of feeling which is aroused by a moral response to a human situation, a response moreover which is not only honestly emotional but also capable of rational justification.

> We may properly distinguish weeping into two general kinds, genuine and counterfeit; or into physical crying and moral weeping. Physical crying, while there are no real corresponding ideas in the mind, nor any genuine sentimental feeling of the heart to produce it, depends upon the mechanism of the body: but moral weeping proceeds from, and is always attended with, such real sentiments of the mind, and feeling of the heart, as do honour to human nature; which false crying always debases.[20]

A 'sentimental' response is thus honest, deeply felt, and reasonable; and it is one evoked by sorrowful rather than joyful situations.

> We are pleased when our friends are happy, but are proportionably deeper struck to see them weep under affliction. At this sight, our hearts are instantly moved; we weep by sympathy with them; we benevolently hasten to assist them; and find so noble a reward of satisfaction and self-complacency in the action, as assures us it is better to be in the house of mourning, than in the house of mirth.[21]

The Reverend Laurence Sterne was to preach a sermon on this very text;[22] and the author of the essay sets his argument firmly in a Christian context with his concluding paragraph, when he refers to Christ's tears over Jerusalem and asserts that 'the highest possible degree of moral weeping, is the weeping of our Redeemer'.

The extent to which the word preserved its rational and intellectual connotations is strikingly illustrated in an extended critical comparison between *Clarissa* and *La nouvelle Héloïse* which was printed in the *Critical Review* for September, 1761.

[20] Op. cit. n.p.   [21] Ibid.
[22] *The Sermons of Mr. Yorick* Vol. I, Sermon II: Ecclesiastes vii 2: 'It is better to go to the house of mourning than to the house of feasting –'.

The word is used here in a precise and dispassionate manner, and interestingly enough it is applied to Rousseau but not to Richardson:

> Rousseau's [performance is] infinitely more sentimental, animated, refined and elegant; Richardson's more natural, interesting, variegated and dramatic. . . . Rousseau raises your admiration, Richardson solicits your tears . . .[23]

If this criticism had been written ten years later, in 1771, the word 'sentimental' would have been applied not to Rousseau, who raises our admiration because of his intellectual and philosophical (i.e. 'sentimental') qualities, but to Richardson, the writer who solicits our tears. And by the end of the century the word would not have been applied as a term of praise to either of them. Nothing reveals more thoroughly the extent to which the connotations of 'sentimental' had changed than the remark of an American critic who stated in 1802 that the man

> must be strangely mistaken who imagines that Richardson was what is vulgarly called a *sentimentalist*. The inundation of froth and sentiment . . . [which covers] the shelves of our libraries, has taken place in direct contempt and defiance of the precept and example of Richardson.[24]

Clearly if one wishes to apply the word 'sentimental' to any of the works of literature produced during this period one will have to proceed with some caution.

In his *History of the English Novel*, E. A. Baker tries to achieve some sort of a classification by dividing the field up into novels of sentiment and novels of sensibility, but as he himself admits, this is only a 'rough distinction'[25] which cannot be pushed too far: 'both sentimentalism and sensibility . . . blend into each other and it would be safer not to draw a strict dividing line'.[26] Nevertheless it is on some such basis as this that the distinction must be made. There is more sensibility and less sentiment – in the sense of psychological realism and moral seriousness – in the novels published towards the end of the century than in those

[23] *Critical Review* XII (Sept. 1761) 205.
[24] Quoted by H. R. Brown in his *Sentimental Novel in America 1789–1860* 33–4, from the *Port Folio* II 185.
[25] *The History of the English Novel* V (London, 1930) 120.
[26] Ibid. 97.

produced in the years when Richardson was writing: from the
modern point of view, the novels written between 1770 and
1790 are on the whole more sentimental than those written
between 1740 and 1760. The ten years from 1760 to 1770 may
be regarded as a transition period. During these years 'sentimental' came to be associated less with thought and more with
feeling. At the same time the word itself, and the attitude it
stood for, began to become more and more popular. Yet even as
this was going on, criticism of sentimentalism began to take
shape. Sterne, the man who did more than any other individual
to publicise the word 'sentimental' and to make his own particular brand of sentimentalism fashionable, was also one of the
subtlest critics of the whole sentimental movement. Ultimately
he was to bring the sentimentality which he seemed to represent into disrepute, although, paradoxically enough this was the
result not of his sceptical levity but of his apparent excess. It
was not Sterne's irreverent humour but his seeming earnestness
that eventually knocked the pedestal from beneath

> The goddess of the woeful countenance,
> The sentimental Muse.[27]

As the Rev. Whitwell Elwin remarked in the *Quarterly Review*
in 1854, *A Sentimental Journey* 'has brought the word *sentimental* into discredit, and made it the standard epithet for feelings that are sickly and superficial'.[28]

Speaking of 'sentimental' as it appears generally in Sterne's
work, a modern scholar has remarked ironically that 'there is an
air of innocence and purity about [his] use of it that well becomes "the English Rabelais"'.[29] Nothing would support this
contention better than the passage in which 'sentimental'
appears in his work for the first time. In Ch. XVIII of the first
volume of *Tristram Shandy*, Sterne, or Tristram, urges the
reader 'to study the pure and sentimental parts of the best
French Romances',[30] and he gets a great deal of amusement out
of wilfully confusing the moral, emotional and erotic connotations of 'sentiment'. The passage illustrates just how equivocal

[27] Sheridan, Prologue to *The Rivals*.
[28] Quoted by E. N. Dilworth, *The Unsentimental Journey of
Laurence Sterne* (New York, 1948) xii.
[29] Ibid. 7.　　　　　　　　　　[30] *Tristram Shandy* 49 (I, xviii).

was the position occupied by 'sentimental' at this time. The tone is decorous and ingenuous – as it always is when Tristram addresses the reader as Madam, and pleads to be treated with 'strict justice':

> It is not impossible, that my dear, dear *Jenny*! tender as the appellation is, may be my child . . . Nor is there any thing unnatural or extravagant in the supposition, that my dear *Jenny* may be my friend. – Friend! – My friend. – Surely, Madam, a friendship between the two sexes may subsist, and be supported, without —— Fy! Mr. *Shandy*: – Without any thing, Madam, but that tender and delicious sentiment, which ever mixes in friendship, where there is a difference of sex. Let me intreat you to study the pure and sentimental parts of the best *French* Romances; – it will really, Madame, astonish you to see with what a variety of chaste expression this delicious sentiment, which I have the honour to speak of, is dress'd out.[31]

The sentimentality which Sterne is gently mocking here has something to do with sentimentality as Richardson and Guthrie would have understood it – and Sterne in his own way considered love to be 'a virtue as well as a passion'. But it has more to do with a much more complex and more sophisticated set of ideas: 'sentimental', as Sterne employs it in this candid appeal to the reader, has a number of connotations – moral, spiritual, philosophical, erotic, and, as John Wesley would have said, 'continental'.[32] The wit and humour of the passage arise out of the way in which all these various shades of meaning are evoked, hinted at and set off against each other.

In order to appreciate the full force with which 'sentimental' as used here by Sterne is charged it will be necessary to look back past the work of Richardson to the novels that were being written at the end of the seventeenth and the beginning of the

[31] Ibid.

[32] In his *Journal* in 1774 Wesley made this comment: 'I casually took a volume of what is called A *Sentimental Journey through France and Italy. Sentimental!* what is that? It is not English; he might as well say *Continental*. It is not sense. It conveys no determinate idea: yet one fool makes many. And this nonsensical word (who would believe it?) is becoming a fashionable one.' Ed. Nehemiah Curnock, 8 vols (London, 1909–16) V 445.

eighteenth centuries. We may also disregard for a while the fact that the word 'sentimental' did not appear in the language, so far as we know, until 1748. In some ways this date is almost irrelevant: the coining of 'sentimental' could conceivably have taken place at almost any time during the eighteenth century – that it should have occurred exactly when it did is probably to some extent accidental.

The earliest date, for instance, given by the OED for the use of 'sentiment' to mean 'mental attitude . . . an opinion or view as to what is right or agreeable', is 1639; and it states that in the seventeenth and eighteenth centuries it was often specifically used to mean 'an amatory feeling or inclination'; the first illustration it gives of this usage being a passage, dated 1652, in which the phrase 'Sentiments of Love' appears. Characters in novels talked of their 'sentiments' – meaning usually their feelings more than their thoughts – and it would not have seemed strange or obscure to have used the word to describe the opinions of the novelist.

It is possible to see the beginnings of literary sentimentalism as early as 1669, when *Les Lettres Portuguaises* was first published. Like *La Princesse de Clèves*, which appeared nine years later in 1678, *Les Lettres Portuguaises* is sentimental in the best sense of the word, and not least in the unsentimental realism with which the inner emotional struggles of the central character are presented. It is very much the sort of work which one would wish to call a novel of sentiment. It consists of five letters, supposedly written by a nun in a convent at Béjà to her lover, a French nobleman who had been serving in the King of Portugal's army. He apparently forgot her when he returned to France: the letters from the deserted woman express a passionate and bitter despair. It is just possible that the letters may be genuine (the question is still at least open to scholarly speculation) – but whether they are or not one cannot doubt the depth of the feeling which inspired them: they are eloquent, ruthlessly honest and deeply moving. The book was very widely read, went through many editions, and must have exercised a considerable influence.[33]

La Princesse de Clèves also presents an unusually penetrating

[33] It was suggested when they were first published that the letters were from a woman called Marianna Alcoforado to the Marquis de Chamilly; although in the seventeenth and eighteenth centuries it

and realistic account of the inner life of a woman who is hopelessly in love; and for the period at which it was written Madame
de la Fayette's novel, like *Les Lettres Portuguaises*, is a remarkably concise and accomplished work of fiction. Despite the power
and distinction of these two novels, however, sentimentalism
was not yet firmly established as a literary genre. Ruth Kirby
Jamieson has suggested that this did not take place until the
turn of the century: 'sensibility as a literary and social phenomenon first manifested itself [in France]', she states, 'about
1700'.[34] It was then, in the salons of people like Mme de Tencin
and Mme de Lambert, that a highly self-conscious ethos of sentiment was evolved, a philosophy of fine living, the basic tenet of
which was a belief in the moral and aesthetic goodness of feeling.
But for feeling to become valuable it needed to be refined and
directed by the reason: the ideal was to give artistic shape and
purpose to one's own emotional life, and to one's relationships
with other people. Love being the richest of all emotions was
regarded as the one capable of the greatest refinement: according
to Mme de Lambert,

> la plupart des hommes n'aiment que d'une manière vulgaire:
> ils n'ont qu'un objet. Ils proposent un terme dans l'amour . . .
> Pour un coeur tendre il y a une ambition plus élevée à avoir:
> c'est de porter nos sentiments, et ceux de la personne aimée,
> au dernier degré de délicatesse, et de les rendres tous les jours
> plus tendres, plus vifs, et plus occupants.[35]

---

seems generally to have been assumed that they were fictional. They
were immensely popular. A. Goncalvez Rodriguez in his *As cartas da
Freira, Estude Bibliografico* (Coimbra, 1944) lists 202 editions altogether, and there have been others since. There were ten editions in
France within the first year of publication, and fifty by the end of
the century. By 1731 there had been twenty-two editions in English,
and there were numerous imitations of them. One of the people most
recently to attempt a translation of them was Rainer Maria Rilke.

[34] *Marivaux: a Study in Sensibility* (New York, 1941) 3.

[35] *Réflexions sur les femmes*, in *Oeuvres* (Paris, 1763) 204–5.
Quoted by Jamieson, op. cit. 23. ('Most men love only in a vulgar
manner: they have only one aim. In love they set one goal before
you . . . For a tender heart a higher ambition is possible: this is to
carry our sentiments, and those of the one we love, to the furthest
degree of delicacy, and to make them continually more tender, more
lively and more absorbing.')

In this Parisian society of the early eighteenth century, the ideal 'man of sentiment' would have been one whose whole life was ordered as intelligently and subtly as possible in accordance with the principles of that 'lay morality' which tried to regulate the pursuit of pleasure according to the methods of Cartesian rationalism. The conscious spirit of *noblesse oblige* would have governed his relations with his inferiors, and his relations with women would have been distinguished by a tactful and sensitive tenderness, rather than by passion. Love was regarded as a delicate and a civilising amusement.

The *sentiment* of the salons was not the same as the sentiment that was to animate the bosom of that man of principle, Sir Charles Grandison. Indeed it seems doubtful whether many people in England in the first half of the eighteenth century were in any way aware of the sentimentalism then fashionable in France. In the first translation into English of Marivaux's novel *La Vie de Marianne* (1736), it is significant that the key word *sentiment* is rendered in a number of ways which suggest that the concept had no special connotations at all for the translator, or, presumably, for the novel reading public. In the following passage, for instance, *sentiment* has a precise meaning (as is emphasised by the use of the definitive article):

> Je ne sais point philosopher, et je ne m'en soucie guère; car je crois que cela n'apprend rien qu'à discourir . . . Je pense, pour moi, qu'il n'y a que le sentiment qui nous puisse donner des nouvelles un peu sûres de nous, et qu'il ne faut pas trop se fier à celles que notre esprit veut faire à sa guise, car je le crois un grand visionnaire.[36]

In the translation, this sense of the pure well of intuitive feeling that is more to be trusted than the intellect is completely lost – indeed the translation of '*sentiment*' by 'Experience' stands the original meaning on its head:

> I am not capable of arguing in the Philosophic Strain, nor do I much care, for I believe it is little more than Words in the main . . . For my part, I think that *Experience* is the only Thing, can give us any good Account of our selves, and that

[36] *La Vie de Marianne* (Paris, 1933) 15.

we ought not to depend too rashly on those our Wit is pleased to contrive, for I take that to be capricious enough.[37]

The translation, in the same novel, of 'une . . . oeuvre de métier et non de sentiment',[38] as 'a meer Trade, and not the Result of genuine charity'[39] is close enough, but again it is significant that the English word 'sentiment' should not have been used.

When Sterne began to use 'sentimental', he undoubtedly had in mind the senses given to it by French writers like Marivaux and Crébillon. Sterne's own sentimentalism is very similar to the French sentimentalism of the first half of the eighteenth century – which was one reason why, in his own time, it was taken at once too seriously and not seriously enough. When Sterne was making his triumphal personal progress through Paris, 'Crébillon', as Horace Walpole sadly observed, was 'entirely out of fashion and Marivaux a proverb'.[40] The taste was all for Richardson and Rousseau; and although there were some, like Voltaire, who hailed Sterne as the English Rabelais, there must have been many others who looked upon him as the natural successor to 'le patriarche de "Parsons Green"'.[41]

Crébillon's attitude to sentiment was rather different from Marivaux's; and while Sterne had much in common with

[37] *The Life of Marianne: or, the Adventures of the Countess of ＊＊＊* (London, 1736–1742) I 25–6. My italics.

[38] *La Vie de Marianne* 23.

[39] *The Life of Marianne* I 39.

[40] Letter to Thomas Gray, 19 Nov. 1765. *The Letters of Horace Walpole*, ed. Paget Toynbee (Oxford, 1903–25) VI 352. *La Vie de Marianne* was published in 1731–41; *Le Paysan parvenu* in 1734–6; *Les Egaremens du Coeur et de l'Esprit* in 1736; and *Le Sofa* (surreptitiously) from 1740. *La Nouvelle Héloïse* first appeared in 1761. Crébillon was still very much alive when Sterne visited Paris in 1762: Sterne wrote to David Garrick that 'Crebillion [sic] has made a convention with me, which, if he is not too lazy, will be no bad *persiflage* – as soon as I get to Thoulouse he has agreed to write me an expostulat[o]ry letter upon the indecorums of T. Shandy – which is to be answered by recrimination upon the liberties in his own works – these are to be printed together – Crebillion against Sterne – Sterne against Crebillion – the copy to be sold, and the money equally divided – This is a good Swiss-policy' (*Letters*, ed. Curtis 162). Nothing apparently came of the 'convention'.

[41] A title accorded Richardson by Paul Dottin. See *Samuel Richardson* (Paris, 1931) 424.

Marivaux's tenderness he also shared something of Crébillon's unillusioned and detached amusement. This rather cynical attitude to *sentiment* is nowhere better defined than in the novel which Yorick, on his sentimental journey, found in the hands of the pretty Parisian *fille de chambre* – *Les Egaremens du Coeur et de l'Esprit.* Sterne probably derived a certain pleasure from mentioning Crébillon's witty romance in *A Sentimental Journey.* The book has a pious title, and the sentimental traveller is careful to tell us that the 'young decent girl of about twenty' who brought it, seemed 'by her air and dress to be *fille de chambre* to some devout woman of fashion'.[42] But there is no more piety in it than in that 'most tawdry [story] . . . of a nun who fancied herself a shell-fish, and of a monk damn'd for eating a muscle',[43] that Tristram was telling to Eugenius when Death came knocking on his door. It does contain, however, a definition of that unsolemn sentimentality which Sterne admired. This definition is delivered by Versac, the splendid *beau* who is initiating Meilcour, the narrator and hero, into the ways of the world. He laughs when the young man asks him how his mistress could have discovered that he has lost his heart to her.

> Votre coeur! dit-il, jargon de Roman. Sur quoi supposez-vous qu'elle vous le demande? Elle est incapable d'une prétention si ridicule. Que demande-t-elle donc, répondis-je? Une sorte de commerce intime, réprit-il, une amitié vive qui ressemble à l'amour par les plaisirs, sans en avoir les sottes délicatesses. C'est en un mot, du goût qu'elle a pour vous, & ce n'est que du goût que vous lui devez.[44]

This is not so brutal as it sounds: the pleasures of such *une commerce intime* were subtle and various, not the least being that sort of conversation in which, as Sterne wrote to a friend

[42] A Sentimental Journey 487.
[43] Tristram Shandy 479–80 (VII i).
[44] Les Égaremens du Coeur et de l'Esprit; ou mémoires de M. de Meilcour (London, 1788) II 96–7. ('Your heart! he said: Novelistic jargon. Why ever do you suppose she would ask that of you? She is incapable of such a ridiculous pretention. What does she ask, then? I rejoined. A kind of intimate relationship, he replied, a lively friendship which resembles love in its pleasures without having its silly delicacies. She has, in a word, a fancy for you, and it is nothing but a fancy which you are obliged to have for her.')

from 'foutre-land', one could *jouer des sentiments* with one's mistress 'from sun-rising to the setting of the same'.[45] One of the first things Meilcour learnt was that in this society 'sentiment was nothing but a topic of conversation'.[46] Sterne, who liked to harmonise the soul, would always have been in danger of letting his heart become at least slightly involved; and he is much closer in spirit to Marivaux than to Crébillon. Indeed there is something rather chilling about the unruffled self-possession with which Crébillon's fops and *beaux* conduct their affairs of gallantry: 'there is no passion', as Mr Shandy reminds his brother, 'so serious, as lust'.[47]

Crébillon's sentimentalism would have disgusted Richardson. Sterne, though intellectually sympathetic to it, was ruefully aware of its emotional limitations – *The Journal to Eliza*, for all its embarrassing parade of faked literary feeling, is the genuine *cri du coeur* of a man who would like to be in love. Rousseau, with his idealistic nature, was as deeply disgusted with this attitude to love, though for different reasons, as Richardson would have been. With Rousseau, *sentiment* takes on a new tone, romantic, moral and semi-mystical, similar in many ways to the meanings it had for the French sentimentalists of the early eighteenth century, but capable of arousing more fervent emotion. Rousseau was repelled by a world in which everyone talked sentiment but 'an affair (une liaison de galanterie) lasts for little longer than one visit'.[48] The young St Preux, the hero of *La Nouvelle Héloïse*, at once fascinated and appalled by the heartless brilliance of Parisian society, wrote back to his faithful Julie that 'even the words for love and lover are banished from the intimate society of the two sexes . . . it seems as if here the whole order of natural sentiment is turned upside down'.[49] As Daniel Mornet shows, such criticisms were not novel: 'Satires on adultery were traditional at this time.'[50] But Rousseau's attack on marriage *à la mode* is not primarily satirical: it is a deeply felt revulsion from a way of living which seemed to him shallow, sterile, and unnatural. When St Preux, overcome with joy at the

[45] From a letter to John Hall-Stevenson (Paris, 19 May 1764).
[46] *Les Égaremens du Coeur et de l'Esprit* I 15.
[47] *Tristram Shandy* 592 (VIII, xxiv).
[48] *La Nouvelle Héloïse*, ed. Daniel Mornet (Paris, 1925) II 273.
[49] Ibid. II 371.   [50] *La Nouvelle Héloïse* note 1.

domestic happiness of Julie and her virtuous M. Wolmar, exclaims ecstatically, 'O sentiment, sentiment! douce vie de l'âme!
Quel est le coeur de fer que tu n'as jamais touché? Quel est
l'infortuné mortel à qui tu n'arraches jamais de larmes?'[51] he is
using the word 'sentiment' in a way that is moral, indeed almost
religious. The same note is struck by Sterne in that invocation to
sensibility which I have already quoted, and which was known
more widely, probably, than A *Sentimental Journey* in which it
appeared.

Sterne was well aware of the moral connotations of 'sentimental', and there is little question that when he chose
A *Sentimental Journey* as the title for his last book he had the
Richardsonian sense of the word in mind. No doubt he was
thinking of several other meanings as well – including some
that Richardson would have regarded as completely unacceptable. But Sterne knew the way in which many of his readers
would interpret such a title, and his intentions that they should
give it a moral interpretation were, like most of his intentions,
half in earnest and half in jest. According to Richard Griffith,
who was impressed by its freedom from the 'Grossness of the
worst' of *Tristram Shandy*, Sterne called it his *Work of
Redemption*.[52] The irony of such a description is obvious: but it
was a title which many of its readers would have been willing to
accord it in all seriousness. A *Sentimental Journey* was hailed as
a sign that Yorick had mended his ways, and had decided to
exploit his gift for the pathetic, rather than his talent for crazy
and indecent humour. 'Sterne has published two little volumes,
called Sentimental Travels', wrote Horace Walpole to his friend
George Montagu in 1768. 'They are very pleasing, though too
much dilated, and infinitely preferable to his tiresome *Tristram
Shandy. . . .* In these there is great good nature and strokes of
delicacy.'[53] The critics united in saying much the same thing,
although they usually adopted an air of moral satisfaction as
well. The comment in the *Monthly Review* is typical, and the

[51]Ibid. IV 122. ('O sentiment, sentiment! Sweet life of the soul!
What heart of iron is there that you have never touched? What
unfortunate being is there whom you have never moved to tears?')
One of Sade's villains is called Coeur-de-fer.

[52] *Letters*, ed. Curtis 398 note 3. Griffith saw the book before it was
printed.

[53] *Letters*, ed. Toynbee VII 175.

use of 'sentiment' suggests the connotations that Sterne could have expected people to give to 'sentimental' at this time. The reviewer, after quoting the episode in the bedroom with the *fille de chambre*, asks the 'Generous and virtuous Reader' if he does not

> tremble for the fate of this unguarded innocent? But, fear not: sentiment is still victorious over sensuality. The next chapter is entitled THE CONQUEST: and a noble one it is![54]

This solemn priggishness would have amused Sterne had he been alive to read it. But if he was not a prudish moralist, neither was he a cynic. When he tells Mrs James that his

> design in [*A Sentimental Journey*] was to teach us to love the world and our fellow creatures better than we do – so it runs most upon those gentler passions and affections, which aid so much to it,[55]

he is obviously wearing his best clerical face for her benefit, as he always does; just as, when he tells Sir George Macartney, a week or so later,

> I am going to ly-in . . . and unless what I shall bring forth is not *press'd* to death by these devils of printers, I shall have the honour of presenting to you a *couple of as clean brats* as ever chaste brain conceiv'd – they are frolicksome too, *mais cela n'empeche pas* –[56]

he is wearing the mask of the jolly Rabelaisian wit, the good bottle companion. But one purpose does not cancel the other. Yorick the divine and Yorick the jester are both present in *A Sentimental Journey* – and each is in part the victim of his own self-mockery.

Sterne's irony is so subtle and so self-effacing that the majority of his readers were probably largely unaware of its presence. It was his great good nature, his strokes of delicacy, the lightness and sureness with which he delineated the gentler passions and affections, that appealed so irresistibly to them. They felt for him all the gratitude which you have for anyone who can

[54] *Monthly Review* XXXVIII (1768) 313.
[55] Letter of 12 Nov. 1767. *Letters*, ed. Curtis 401.
[56] Letter of 3 Dec. 1767. Ibid. 405.

explain your own heart to you better than you can yourself. Sterne isolated and defined those finer feelings of humanity and tenderness which everyone was sure he possessed – and he gave them a name with which people could easily identify them.

The Yorick the reading public loved was the Yorick who invoked the goddesses of Sensibility and Liberty, and who tried to free the starling. They tended to avert their eyes from his adventures with *filles de chambres* and foreign ladies of high degree. They preferred to sigh in sympathy as he wept with Maria, and to drop a companionable tear as he plucked a nettle from the grave of Father Lorenzo. Yorick's tears were contagious. Like Edmund's 'noble auditors' in *The Old English Baron*, Sterne's devotees caught 'the tender infection',[57] and gave themselves up to the 'luxury of grief'.[58] It is after the publication of *A Sentimental Journey* in 1768 that the mildew begins to spread across the surface of the novel. It is from this time on that novels with titles like *The Delicate Distress*, *Excessive Sensibility* and *The Curse of Sentiment* begin to appear in their dozens. In an atmosphere of gathering gloom the distresses – and the constitutions – of the heroines become progressively more delicate, and their tears more torrential. The novel of sentiment, to use Baker's terms, gives way to the novel of sensibility.

How much and how directly *A Sentimental Journey* contributed to this development, however, it is hard to say. One of the most paradoxical things about Sterne is that although the impact he had on the changes that were taking place in the novel was so profound, it was, in a way, almost completely sterile and unproductive. Despite his widespread and continuing popularity, he seems to have contributed nothing that was essentially his own to the writers who followed him: none of them was able to copy his example successfully,[59] and, apart from the imitation of what

[57] Clara Reeve, *The Old English Baron: a Gothic Story* (1778), ed. James Trainer (London, 1967) 20.

[58] Sir Leslie Stephen's phrase. See *History of English Thought in the Eighteenth Century* (London, 1902) II 436.

[59] The one exception is Diderot. But in *Jacques le Fataliste* Diderot demonstrates that he has been influenced more by Sterne's wit than by his sentimentalism. And *Jacques le Fataliste*, like *Tristram Shandy*, is very much a work *sui generis*. Sterne's influence was greatest perhaps in Germany. But here, as elsewhere, there was little *direct* imitation of his work that was of any value.

was thought to be the true Sternean attitude of tearful sympathy, together with the acquisition of a few technical tricks, and some stock sentimental scenes and characters – dead asses and benevolent uncles – nobody seems to have been able to learn much from him. He was unique and inimitable. His satire looks back to the learned wit of Rabelais and Swift; his sentimentalism to the cool and sophisticated hedonism of Marivaux and Crébillon – even Rousseau seems to belong to a different age. Sterne stands in a peculiarly isolated relationship to the literature of his own day: although the effect he had on the development of the novel was so remarkable, it was almost solely catalytic: he merely accelerated certain processes that were already under way, processes with which he would not in all instances have been sympathetic. Had *A Sentimental Journey* never been written, the distresses of the sentimental heroine would still have been delicate, and her sensibility excessive. After all, what does Sterne's sentimentality have in common with the domestic realism of sentimental novelists like Fanny Burney and Jane Austen on the one hand, or with the 'plot and elopement, passion, rape and rapture' of the more extravagant and ultimately Gothic forms of sentimentalism on the other? The main stream of sentimentalism in the English novel springs directly from Richardson, with some tributary influence from Prévost and Rousseau (who were themselves partly inspired by Richardson's example).

Love is the theme of every sentimental novel – yet what other sentimental novelist in the eighteenth century (apart from those like Marivaux and Crébillon) was ever able to treat it with Sterne's lightness, detachment and gaiety? The love that Richardson depicts is a dark and irresistible passion which develops in the heart despite all the efforts of the unwilling lover to smother it; while Prévost is obsessed by the theme of the lover who has given up the struggle and lets himself be carried away helplessly by an emotion he can no longer control. Lust, anger and hatred are staple emotions in these novels; rape, family oppression, and the agonies of unrequited love their constantly recurring themes. And in the novels of sensibility in the last thirty years of the century one can observe innumerable variations on the basic patterns established by these and other sentimental novelists – like Marivaux in *La Vie de Marianne* or Rousseau in *La Nouvelle Héloïse*. Henry Mackenzie, who is

closer to some aspects of Sterne in *The Man of Feeling* than most
other novelists of the day, forgets about him completely in *The
Man of the World* and *Julia de Roubigné*: the plots are melodramatic, the action violent, and the borrowings embarrassingly
obvious. Rousseau and Richardson are leant on heavily and un-
imaginatively – not content with a Lovelace-like attempted
assault in *Julia de Roubigné*, for instance, he must even include
a false fire alarm as well. Mackenzie could at least write with
some grace and polish: the lesser novelists who followed in the
same well-worn tracks could sometimes not even do that.

Baker has very shrewdly pointed out that, although 'sensibility was not the object with Richardson, who wrote to inculcate
prudence and self-control', he 'had founded the English novel of
sensibility'.[60] The way in which the novel of feeling develops out
of the Richardsonian novel of moral sentiment, which is on the
whole realistic and constructed on a solid intellectual foundation,
is one of the most significant features of the whole sentimental
movement. Indeed, it is because this foundation – the whole
social and theological tradition of Protestantism – is still strong
and vital for Richardson that he is able to generate a genuine
passion of tragic dimensions. But most of the novelists who
succeeded him, and who borrowed from him the stage-machinery
of their moral fables, were inspired with no such conviction.
The trouble with the sentimental novelists of the last quarter of
the eighteenth century is that, with a few honourable but minor
exceptions, they are morally and philosophically bankrupt. Their
excess of feeling expends itself in a void; they seek continually
the indulgence of emotion for its own sake; and their work
bears little direct relation to the social realities of their own day.
Significantly the novels in which the strongest feelings were
expressed and in which some of the most effective writing is to
be found are the gothic romances – grotesque fantasies which
reflected at a distance and in a distorting mirror the stress and
turmoil of the period. As Devendra P. Varma remarks in *The
Gothic Flame* 'there is an unconscious indefinable relationship
between the Terrors of the French Revolution and the Novel of
Terror in England', and he quotes Montague Summers' observation that 'readers . . . delighted in imaginary terrors whilst the
horrors of the French Revolution were being enacted all about

[60] *The History of the English Novel* V 97.

them'.[61] But the real point is that with very few exceptions, the terrors of the gothic novel are simply not terrifying (and probably never were), just as the supposedly moving situations in the purely sentimental novels of the day are neither affecting nor credible. Like William Guthrie, the sentimental novelist in the last decades of the century ostensibly wished to demonstrate that 'Love is a virtue as well as a passion', but in their hands the concepts of both virtue and passion had become empty and meaningless stereotypes.

II

'Tears you must consider as Relief from Grief, and not as Grief itself' Richardson advised Lady Bradshaigh as she struggled to accept the conclusion of *Clarissa*.[62] It was because novelist and reader alike confused the two that the novel of sentiment eventually became sentimental (as we understand the word); and it was partly because of this that 'sentimental' acquired the meaning which it bears today. The original meaning was substantially different. Novelists were initially described as sentimental for two reasons: firstly because they dealt with moral or philosophical issues (or because they approached moral issues in a 'philosophical' way); and secondly because they were more interested in the mental and emotional than in the physical lives of their characters. These two reasons are closely inter-related: the one depends intimately upon the other. Thus it would not have been enough for a novel simply to deal with a moral problem for it to be called sentimental – almost all fiction deals in some way or another with moral issues, and if 'sentimental' simply meant 'moral' *Tom Jones* could have been described as a sentimental novel. The sentimental novelist was distinguished by his speculative and theoretical approach to his subject; and also by his interest in analysing and presenting the processes of feeling and judgment by which his characters deal with the problems with which they are confronted. In the article on Richardson and Rousseau in the *Critical Review* from which I have already quoted, the writer, after observing that Rousseau has based the whole plan of *La Nouvelle Héloïse* on *Clarissa*, begins his discus-

[61] Op. cit. (London, 1957) 217.
[62] Forster MSS. XI fol. 10.

sion by comparing the moral issues with which the novelists are concerned.

> The English moralist describes a young lady exquisitely delicate, virtuous, beautiful, and religious, but prudent, perhaps, to a degree of coldness . . . and at last falling a sacrifice to filial duty and misplaced delicacy. On the contrary, the Swiss philosopher paints a virgin in the bloom of youth, innocent, amiable, full of sensibility, deeply enamoured of virtue, yet swerving from its dictates, and yielding to the violence of her passions; but reclaimed by the horror of her crime, and her innate purity of sentiment. Her lover too was a young man honest and sensible, romantically fond of virtue . . . reasoning like a Platonist on love, and practising like an Epicurean.[63]

Rousseau, who is 'infinitely more sentimental'[64] than Richardson, is described as the philosopher, and Richardson as the moralist. Later on the writer states that 'Rousseau's manner of expressing the sublimest sentiment is natural, but it may sometimes be thought too philosophical',[65] and he concludes by stating that 'if we think Richardson more simple and affecting in his manner, we must allow that Rousseau is more masterly and instructive'.[66] It is obvious that the author of this article has a clear theory of what constitutes a sentimental novel. It was a theory that many people must have become familiar with: A. D. McKillop informs us that the article was reprinted in the *London Chronicle* (1761) and the *Court Miscellany* (1766) and that it 'was translated by Suard in the *Journal Etranger*, and struck the key-note for much later criticism'.[67]

The distinguishing feature of the sentimental novel is that it takes for its theme the impact of the world on sensibilities delicate enough to perceive the finest moral distinctions (Clarissa is 'exquisitely delicate', and Eloisa 'full of sensibility'). The subject of the sentimental novel is not moral action (which is the subject of *Tom Jones*) but moral discrimination: the important thing is not the doing of good deeds, but the right analysis of morally intricate and perplexing situations. A decision, of course, is always involved – the dramatic interest in a sentimental novel

[63] *Critical Review* XII (Sept. 1761) 204.   [64] Ibid. 205.
[65] Ibid. 207.   [66] Ibid. 208.
[67] *Samuel Richardson, Printer and Novelist* (Chapel Hill, 1936) 232.

is usually centred on the conflict of motives within the minds of the characters. Henry Mackenzie, writing in 1785 with an idea of the sentimental novel very similar to that presented in 1761 by the author of the article in the *Critical Review*, described this conflict as

> that contrast between one virtue or excellence and another, that war of duties which is to be found in many [novels, but] particularly in that species called the sentimental. These have chiefly been borrowed from our neighbours the French, whose style of manners, and the very powers of whose language, give them a great advantage in the delineation of that nicety, that subtility of feeling, those entanglements of delicacy, which are so much interwoven with the characters and conduct of the chief personages in many of their most celebrated novels.[68]

The main issue in a sentimental novel is the straightening out of 'those entanglements of delicacy': the problem with which the characters are faced can usually be reduced to that of coming to a correct moral evaluation of the situation in which they are placed, and then acting on it. Like Beckett in *Murder in the Cathedral*, they often have to fight and overcome the most subtle of all temptations – that 'last temptation' which is 'the greatest treason'

> To do the right deed for the wrong reason.

In most of the great sentimental stories – *The Portuguese Letters, La Princesse de Clèves, Clarissa, La Nouvelle Héloïse, Les Liaisons Dangereuses* and others – the climax is almost always the taking of a moral decision by the central character. *Le Princesse de Clèves* is typical: the climax of the novel is the decision of the Princess not to marry her lover, the Duc de Nemours, after her husband, to whom she has been consistently faithful, has died. The significance of this decision, which is private and comprehensible only to the Princess, is the 'point' of the novel: the rest of the story exists only to explain why she should have acted in this way and to demonstrate the value of what she has done. In the *Portuguese Letters*, the heroine,

[68] *Lounger* no. 20 (1785), in *The Works of Henry Mackenzie, Esq.* (Edinburgh, 1808) V 181.

Marianna, is involved in a similar struggle: a struggle the outcome of which is of importance primarily only to herself. She has
been deserted by her lover, and in the letters she sends him,
letters to which there is no reply, she expresses her passionate
sense of grief, longing, desolation and betrayal. At the same
time she ruthlessly analyses the situation in which she is placed,
forcing herself to face up to his selfishness and her gullibility:

> where's the Woman, that in my Place, would have done other-
> wise than I did? . . . We cannot easily bring ourselves to
> suspect the Faith of those we love . . . it was the Assiduity of
> your conversation that refin'd me; your Passion that inflam'd
> me; Your good humour that charm'd me; your Oaths and
> Vows that confirm'd me; but 'twas my own precipitate
> inclination that seduc'd me.[69]

Her deepest wound is her pride, her feeling that her *amour propre*
has not received the respect it deserves. In this she resembles
every sentimental heroine. She is revolted most by the thought
that she has given her love to one who has used her merely as a
prostitute. And it is her pride that finally saves her, that enables
her to decide to put his memory out of her mind without shame
or anger.

The resemblance of Marianna to Pamela and Clarissa, and to
Marivaux's Marianne, is obvious. In Richardson's novels it is not
the physical details of the stories that matter, the rapes and
attempted rapes, but the attitude of the characters towards these
things. No matter how hypocritical Pamela – and Richardson –
may seem, the point of the story is that Pamela and Mr B.
decide to marry because they love each other: this, fundamentally, is the moral decision they are forced to come to. In
Clarissa the rape that Lovelace succeeds in committing on the
body of his victim is insignificant in comparison to the rape upon
her spirit which Clarissa, by deciding not to marry him, refuses
to allow him to commit. The point of *Clarissa* and the real climax
of the novel, is the heroine's decision not to corrupt her integrity
by permitting the man who has humiliated her to claim her as
his wife.

One of the chief values of these novels is the way in which

[69] *Five Love-Letters from a Nun to a Cavalier.* Done out of French
into English [by Sir Roger L'Estrange] (London, 1678) 52.

they reexamine the basic human relationship of marriage, re-
assess the importance and power of love, and reaffirm the value
of individual dignity and freedom. And one feels that this kind
of revaluation could have been done only in the 'sentimental'
way, only through the presentation of that internal process of
moral exploration and discovery which one must go through
oneself before one can pretend to understand a situation fully
enough to evaluate it. The process of discovery is in itself a
process of evaluation: only through teasing out the full significance of a situation can one know what, in every sense of the
word, it does 'mean' to one.

Richardson has often been compared to Henry James for the
closeness with which he follows the finer movements of thought
and feeling within the minds of his characters; but it is in the
thoroughness and moral scrupulousness with which he works
out his themes that he resembles him most. In *Sir Charles
Grandison* this desire for completeness expends itself eventually
in the dreary chronicling of domestic trivia; but in *Clarissa* and
in the first part of *Pamela* one has the impression that Richardson
has been possessed, almost against his will, by a demon that will
not let him rest. Once he begins to let a situation worry him he
cannot leave it alone, no matter how painful and embarrassing
the process of investigation may be, until he has found out, both
for his own and for the reader's satisfaction, what its true nature
and significance are.

In this Sterne is almost the direct antithesis of Richardson.
Sterne is supremely self-conscious where Richardson seems often
only dimly aware of the direction in which his novel is taking
him; and while Richardson clings desperately to his faith in
man's ability to order and control life according to the conventional rules of prudent morality, to live, as Sir Charles Grandison
does, strictly according to principle, Sterne begins by assuming,
indeed insisting, that it is impossible ever fully to systematise
life, or even completely to understand it. Although the conclusions of his novels deny it, Richardson is forced by his own
artistic genius to acknowledge in them this same truth: indeed
the final result of *Clarissa* is to demonstrate tragically what
Tristram Shandy demonstrates comically: the ultimate inadequacy of systems, and the fact that belief in them is not
nearly so important as belief in the dignity and value of indi-

vidual human beings. Not only Richardson and Sterne, but indeed every sentimental novelist, makes this assertion: the simple lesson they teach is the necessity for love and toleration. The Shandys know this instinctively; the Harlowes have to be taught it; and the possibility of love, like a faint dream of paradise, haunts the bleak inferno which the Marquise de Merteuil and Valmont create through their scheming: 'Ah! Believe me, we are only happy through love,' writes Valmont to Danceny, in one of his last letters – and although the letter itself is part of an elaborate ruse one feels that Valmont, with the insight of a damned soul, is for once saying exactly what he means.

Although Sterne affects to despise the thoroughness with which someone like Richardson presents the lives of his characters, he shares with him the ability to capture the minutiae of experience: the world of Tristram and Yorick is predominantly a mental world – it is not so much what the characters in Sterne's novels do that is important, as the interpretations and evaluations they put upon their actions. Indeed the comedy in *Tristram Shandy* usually arises from the contrast between the completely different ways in which Toby and Walter interpret or respond to the same event. Their minds pursue parallel and unrelated courses: they agree merely in their love for each other, and in their belief that each of them has a right to look at the world in whatever way he chooses. '—For my own part, *Trim*,' says Toby, after the tragedy of Tristram's christening, 'though I can see little or no difference betwixt my nephew's being called *Tristram* or *Trismegistus* – yet as the thing sits so near my brother's heart, *Trim*, – I would freely have given a hundred pounds rather than it should have happened'.[70]

Yorick, in *A Sentimental Journey*, is at once the apotheosis of the sentimental character and a whimsical revelation of the inadequacies and superficialities inherent in the sentimental view of life. Like every sentimental hero or heroine he becomes involved in 'entanglements of delicacy', but the chains that ensnare Yorick, by comparison with those that weigh upon a Clarissa, a Julie or even a Marianne, are of the lightness and inconsequence of thistledown. He perplexes himself with the problem of how many sous to give a beggar; how many glances to give a *grisset*;

[70] *Tristram Shandy* 294 (IV, xviii).

and how many seconds he can with propriety give to the holding of a fair lady's hand; and in the tiny battles in each 'war of duties' provoked by these transient encounters he analyses with a wry amusement the shift and play of his own inconstant feelings. In this scrupulous concern with the most ephemeral moments of existence one can perhaps see, fined down and rarefied so that it is now a mere hint, a gentle insinuation, that 'Cervantic humour [which] arises from . . . describing silly and trifling Events, with the Circumstantial Pomp of great Ones',[71] and which, in *Tristram Shandy* is deployed in its full strength in the account of the meeting between Dr Slop and Obadiah in the muddy lane. It is a far cry from this piece of bucolic slapstick to the elegant comedy of Yorick's *Sentimental Journey*; but the ironic intention of both is the same: Yorick's nice concern over the corking pins is a comment – by implication at least – on false Grandisonian delicacy, just as Slop's tumble in the mire is a comment on false professional gravity.

But the triviality of the situations upon which the sentimental traveller has to bring such careful discrimination to bear illustrates in a quite unironic way an essential aspect of eighteenth-century sentimentalism: the equation of moral goodness with a highly developed sensibility. Yorick demonstrates that he is a good man by the sensitivity with which he responds to the most delicate nuances of feeling not only in himself but also in those he is with. He is what Chesterfield would have wished his son to be – a graceful adept in the exercise of those *leniores virtutes* which awaken not 'the respect and admiration of mankind', but 'their love and affection'.[72]

To act like a man of taste in matters of morality is a mark of high civilisation; and for many people in the eighteenth century the two went hand in hand: as Shaftesbury suggests, one cannot really be a man of taste without being moral, and one cannot be truly moral without being a man of taste.

> To philosophise, in a just significance is but to carry good-breeding a step higher. . . . The taste of beauty and the relish

[71] Letter to ————? [Summer 1759] *Letters*, ed. Curtis 77.
[72] Letter [Dec. 1749] to his son. *The Letters of Philip Dormer Stanhope, 4th Earl of Chesterfield*, ed. Bonamy Dobrée (London, 1932) IV 1472.

of what is decent just and amiable perfects the character of the
gentleman and the philosopher.[73]

The most attractive thing about this attitude is the way in
which ethical judgments were conceived as being related intrinsically to every other activity: one's response to a moral situation
was seen, both ideally and actually, as an expression of the whole
personality. One was expected to get the same pleasure and
satisfaction out of exercising one's moral taste as out of exercising one's taste for beauty – or for food or drink. And for this
simple hedonistic reason, if for no other, the moral taste was
considered to be worthy of refinement. The 'vertueuse et sage
volupté' of Rousseau's Julie expresses this ideal perfectly:

> La même délicatesse règne dans ses sentiments et dans ses
> organes. Elle étoit faite pour connoitre et goûter tous les
> plaisirs, et longtems elle n'aima si chèrement la vertu même
> que comme la plus douce des voluptés.[74]

But an undue emphasis on the need for refining the sensibilities
can lead to an unhealthy preoccupation with moral discrimination at the expense of moral action. The man of taste can become
a connoisseur and a voluptuary in matters of morality as well as
in matters of art or physical pleasure. The ideal degenerates into
that of possessing a 'delicate sensibility' – and the moral worth
of the sensibility increases proportionately with its delicacy.

The implications in the term, 'delicate sensibility', are twofold; that the sensibility is delicate suggests first that it can
respond to the finest of moral distinctions: a delicate sensibility
is a precise and sensitive moral barometer. But its delicacy implies
also that it is weak, that it is not strong enough to stand up to
the stresses and tensions of real life.[75] The implication is that the

[73] *Miscellaneous Reflections*, in *Characteristics*, ed. John M. Robertson (London, 1900) II 255–6.

[74] *La Nouvelle Héloïse*, ed. Daniel Mornet (Paris, 1925) IV 31.
Mornet's note on the contemporary attitude to this ethical voluptu-
ousness is illuminating. ('The same delicacy reigned in her sentiments
and in the organs of her body. She was made to know and taste every
pleasure, and for a long time she loved virtue no more dearly than
the sweetest of sensual delights.')

[75] Cf. William Empson's discussion of the shift in the meaning of
'delicate' (*The Structure of Complex Words* 44–5, 76–9). His amusing analysis of the moral, medical and social implications of the

possession of a delicate sensibility, while enabling one to appreciate more clearly than most people just what is right and wrong, tends to prevent one from doing anything about it. As Henry Mackenzie puts it, in the essay on novel writing from which I have already quoted,

> in morals, as in religion, there are not wanting instances of refined sentimentalists,[76] who are contented with talking of virtues which they never practice, who pay in words what they owe in actions; or, perhaps, what is fully as dangerous, who open their minds to impressions which never have any effect upon their conduct, but are considered as foreign to and distinct from it.[77]

The way in which this sentimentality developed is symptomatic of the weaknesses and inconsistencies in the social and moral theories of the enlightenment. It is a sign of the same hypocritical disease as Voltaire attacks in *Candide*: a disease generated by the gap that existed between the ideal vision of man as a benevolent, rational creature and the unromantic reality, a gap which, in the eyes of many, could never be bridged.

Despite the robust worldliness of his analysis of sentimentalism, it is Henry Mackenzie himself who provides the classic example of this moral defeatism in his two novels, *The Man of Feeling* and *The Man of the World*. Harley dies young because he cannot stand up to the strain of being a good and sensitive man in a harsh and evil world; Sir Thomas Sindall, the man of the world, also dies eventually, but in the years before the vengeance of those he has ruined catches up with him he enjoys a much better run for his money than the unhappy Harley. The problem of living the good life in a wicked world seemed insoluble to the young and idealistic Mackenzie: either one compromised one's principles and survived or one remained loyal to

---

Victorian Mama's pronouncement, 'You can't take Amelia for long walks, Mr. Jones; she's *delicate*', demonstrates that by the mid-nineteenth century the '*delicate* sensibility' had developed into the '*sickly* sensibility': 'the majesty of the [Matron's] utterance', he says 'was sufficient to turn the assertion of sickliness into some kind of moral praise' (p. 45). Amelia's 'delicacy' may seem far removed from the '*délicatesse*' of Julie: but the line of sentimental degeneration is unbroken.

[76] Note the use of 'refined'.   [77] *Works* V 183.

them and went under. The only other way out was to escape
from the artificialities of European civilisation and, like Annesley,
the man who finally kills Sindall, live in the wilds of the
American continent as a Noble Savage. The reward of blunting
one's sensibilities and forgetting one's scruples was worldly
success; the reward of being virtuous was worldly failure.
Writing to Richardson about the character of Grandison one of
his clerical correspondents remarked that

> your good man will be out of nature, if he is not persecuted:
> nay, he will be no very good man, if the world do not give him
> this testimony.[78]

Virtue, indeed, for the sentimental novelist, is almost always
virtue in distress.

That innocence may be corrupted by the world, and that the
fruits of experience can be bitter, are truths that men did not
have to wait until the eighteenth century to learn. The theme of
virtue in distress has always been a basic one in art and literature: pity is a feeling we can all enjoy. But the response both of
the novelist and his reader at this time to the theme seems to
have been slightly hysterical. Lady Bradshaigh, who emerges
from her letters to Richardson as an extremely capable, level-
headed and amiable woman, could still plead despairingly with
him to save Clarissa:

> Tears I would choose to shed for virtue in distress, but still
> would suffer to flow, in greater abundance, for unexpected
> turns of happiness . . . Therefore, Sir, after you have brought
> the divine Clarissa to the very brink of destruction, let me
> intreat (may I say, insist upon) a turn, that will make your
> almost despairing readers half mad with joy.[79]

As I have already suggested, the main reason for the emphasis
at this time on the theme of virtue in distress is that the
eighteenth century's conception of virtue was too ambitious.
According to the orthodox social, religious and philosophical
theories of the day – or, perhaps I should say, according to their
orthodox vulgarisations – virtue always received the reward it

[78] Letter from Rev. Mr Skelton, 10 May 1751. *Correspondence*,
ed. Barbauld V 210.
[79] Letter of 10 Oct. 1748. Ibid. IV 178–9.

deserved. In theory, at least, the virtuous man was always the happy and successful man; and since all men were reasonable, and capable therefore of perceiving the difference between good and evil, all men were capable of being virtuous and enjoying the rewards of virtue. How could it be otherwise in this best of all possible worlds? Leibniz's mystical vision of a logically perfect universe was all too easily translatable into that smugly complacent acceptance of things as they are which could accommodate amicably the theories that men were naturally benevolent and reasonable, that self-love and social were the same, and that slavery and poverty were inevitable and necessary. The ideal vision which the age had of itself was rational, liberal and humane – but in the context of the social and economic structure of contemporary society, it was impossibly optimistic.

The process of romantic disillusionment is one through which most individuals – perhaps most societies – have to pass. When idealism comes up against the obdurate facts of existence the temptation to retreat into pessimism or an easy cynicism – each a sentimental attitude – is always strong; and, as the eighteenth century moved towards its close this temptation became stronger and stronger. Even the romantic revival, in many ways a re-affirmation of faith in man, is in many others an acknowledgment of defeat: escapism came to be regarded by the poet not merely as an inevitable but as a valuable function of literature: consciously or unconsciously he yielded to the belief that it was safer to contemplate old, unhappy far-off things, where distance lent enchantment to the view, than to keep one's gaze fixed on the realities of contemporary life, which were equally unhappy, but embarrassingly close at hand.

The conflict between ideal and reality need not always lead to a retreat: Fielding, for instance, and his hero Tom Jones, exemplify a morality which, though perhaps unsubtle in some ways, is nonetheless strong, active and sensible; and Johnson's melancholia is outweighed by the ruggedness and nobility of the stoicism with which he kept it at bay. But virtue in the eighteenth century tended to be regarded more and more – especially by novelists – as something frail and delicate; something essentially passive and easily corrupted; something, above all, which needed protection. And if Tom Jones represents one eighteenth-century ideal of virtue, Uncle Toby and poor innocent Maria represent another. It is not fortuitous that Toby should be impotent and Maria mad; any more than that the death of Harley, the man of feeling, should be almost accidental. The central figure in the sentimental novel, the hero or the heroine, tends to be passive rather than active. While the picaroon, or the hero of a renaissance tragedy, attempts to shape the world and other people to his purpose, the sentimental hero is usually depicted as struggling to prevent other people from forcing him to do the things they want. What sentimental heroines like the Princesse de Clèves, the Portuguese Nun, Marianne, Clarissa and Julie value most is their personal integrity – they don't want love, they want respect – and in this insistence on their right not to *do* what they like but to *be* what they like they are at one with Walter and Uncle Toby. The sentimental heroine is prepared to go to almost any lengths to preserve her independence of spirit: Clarissa in fact pays the supreme penalty, a penalty exacted as much by her conventionally moral parents as by Lovelace, for daring to be true to herself.

Clarissa preserves her integrity, but she is, of course, defeated by the world: the virtue she symbolises is spiritually triumphant but materially weak – and it was the inherent weakness of virtue which people seemed to find more and more fascinating. Indeed Clarissa eventually came to be considered not sentimental enough, because she was too strong and self-assured a character to be truly pathetic. Thus, in her *Inquiry into those Kinds of Distress which excite agreeable Sensations*, Mrs Barbauld suggests that the one fault that may be found in *Clarissa* is that the character of the heroine

> is so inflexibly right . . . that she seems not to need that sympathy we should bestow upon one of a less elevated character.[80]

Earlier, Mrs Barbauld has observed

> that if an author would have us feel a strong degree of compassion, his characters must not be too perfect . . . Virtue . . . must therefore be mixed with something of helplessness and imperfection, with an excessive sensibility, or a simplicity

[80] *The Works of Anna Laetitia Barbauld* (London, 1825) II 224.

bordering on weakness, before it raises, in any great degree, either tenderness or familiar love.[81]

The notion that innocence is its own worst enemy is not peculiar to the sentimental novelist; but it is a notion which the sentimental novelist, particularly in the last decades of the eighteenth century, developed in a peculiarly morbid fashion. It is one thing to believe that 'lilies that fester smell far worse than weeds', and another to believe that the more beautiful the lily the more likely it is to go rotten. In the Shakespearian concept of tragedy it is not an excess of good qualities which brings about the downfall of a great man, but the presence of that 'dram of eale' which taints the whole personality, and leads him to exercise his talents in the wrong direction; for the sentimentalist however it is the good qualities themselves that leave the delicate and sensible character open to corruption. Mackenzie's description of the good Mr Annesly's children, Billy and Harriet, who are destined to become the victims of the villainous Sindall, the Man of the World, illustrates perfectly this sentimental attitude to virtue. 'Harriet was softness itself', easily moved to tears by 'the distress of a fellow creature' or 'some tale . . . of fictitious disaster'; Billy 'had a warmth of temper which the father often observed with mingled pleasure and regret; with pleasure, from considering the generosity and nobleness of sentiment it bespoke; with regret, from the foreboding of many inconveniences to which its youthful possessor might naturally be exposed'.[82] Annesly's responsibility was to educate without repressing unduly:

> To repress warmth of temerity, without extinguishing the generous principles from which it arose and to give firmness to sensibility where it bordered on weakness, without searing its feelings where they led to virtue, was the task he had marked out for his industry to accomplish . . . 'but here also,' said Annesly, 'it is to be remembered that no evil is so pernicious as that which grows in the soil from which good should have sprung'.[83]

[81] Ibid.
[82] *The Works of Henry Mackenzie, Esq.* (Edinburgh, 1808) I 277.
[83] Ibid. 282–3. James Boswell's account of his early life which he prepared for Jean-Jacques Rousseau in 1764 is cast in the same con-

By the end of the century the dangers of excessive sensibility had become a literary commonplace. Jane Austen parodies it in *Love and Friendship* and her other early novelettes; and she treats the theme seriously in *Sense and Sensibility*. The heroines of most of the sentimental novels of the last three decades of the eighteenth century are cut to the same pattern as Marianne Dashwood: the young women in Mrs Radcliffe's Gothic novels, for instance, suffer the terrors that lie in wait for them all the more keenly because of the delicacy of their constitutions; although, like Jane Austen, Mrs Radcliffe assumes, or tries to assume, an attitude of strict common sense towards the problems occasioned by having too sensitive a heart. But if, like Emily St Aubert, the heroine of *The Mysteries of Udolpho*, she maintains that sensibility is 'a quality, perhaps more to be feared than desired',[84] there can be no doubt that Mrs Radcliffe would, in the last resort, rather have been a martyr to sensibility than have lived the unexciting life of an ordinarily dull mortal.

Emily's father, M. St Aubert, like Mr Annesly, found that to be the parent of a sensitive child was a trying occupation: he soon came to the saddening conclusion that his Emily was of far too 'sensible' a disposition for her own good:

> while he watched the unfolding of her infant character, with anxious fondness, he endeavoured, with unremitting effort, to counteract those traits in her disposition which might here-after lead her from happiness. She had discovered in her early years uncommon delicacy of mind, warm affections, and ready benevolence; but with these was observable a degree of suscep-tibility too exquisite to admit of lasting peace. As she advanced in youth, this sensibility gave a pensive tone to her spirits,

---

ventional mould: 'I was born with a melancholy temperament. . . . Yet I do not regret that I am melancholy. It is the temperament of tender hearts, of noble souls. But such temperaments require a very careful education'. Although he promises Rousseau that he will see in him (Boswell) 'an extraordinary example of the effects of a bad education', he claims that at least from the age of eight to twelve things went reasonably well: 'I had a governor who was not without sentiment and sensibility' – presumably in the correct proportions. In *James Boswell: the Earlier Years*, by Frederick A. Pottle (London, 1966) I 2.

[84] *The Novels of Mrs. Ann Radcliffe*, in *Ballantyne's Novelists' Library* (London, 1824) X 350.

and a softness to her manner, which added grace to beauty, and rendered her a very interesting object to persons of congenial disposition.[85]

Emily, as it turns out, grows up to be much too cautious a young woman ever to let any person, no matter how congenial his disposition, play the sort of tricks upon her that Lovelace played on Clarissa, or Sir Thomas Sindall on the luckless Harriet Annesly. She does, however, run the risk of becoming a sentimentalist, and St Aubert devotes his last moments of life to warning his daughter against indulging in

> the pride of fine feeling, the romantic error of amiable minds. Those who really possess sensibility ought early to be taught that it is a dangerous quality, which is continually extracting the excess of misery or delight from every surrounding circumstance . . . Always remember how much more valuable is the strength of fortitude, than the grace of sensibility. . . . Remember too, that one act of beneficence, one act of real benevolence, is worth all the abstract sentiment in the world.[86]

In the novels of Mrs Radcliffe the distresses to which the virtuous are subjected are not, in the main, brought upon them by the fact that they are virtuous: the virtue and excessive sensibility of her heroines are used merely for the sake of heightening the horror and ugliness of the situations in which she places them. This, indeed, is the fundamental flaw in Mrs Radcliffe's novels, the thing that makes them in our sense basically sentimental.

On this point it is interesting to compare her stories with those

[85] Ibid. 225.

[86] Ibid. 259. The warning had by now become conventional. Adam Smith, in *The Theory of Moral Sentiments* (1759), had observed that: 'The man of the most exquisite humanity, is naturally the most capable of obtaining the highest degree of self-command. He may not, however, always have acquired it; and it frequently happens that he has not' (Vol. I, pt. III, ch. III). Hannah More makes the same point in her poem, *Sensibility* (1782), as does William Laurence Brown in his poetical *Essay on Sensibility* (1789). In fact the main subject of this lengthy 'Poem in Six Parts' is the question, 'whether sensibility, or the want of it, is, upon the whole, most productive of comfort and happiness in the course of life'. As the poet observes, it is a question which 'comes home to every feeling mind' (Preface).

other stories of terror and torture that were being written at the same time, the novels of the Marquis de Sade. Sade's theme is that distress is the only reward that the virtuous, especially the sentimentally virtuous, can ever hope to receive. 'Toujours est-il qu'un libertin est rarement un homme sensible', he says in *La Nouvelle Justine*, and adds in a footnote: 'et cela, par la seule raison que la sensibilité preuve la foiblesse, et le libertinage la force'.[87] His novels, *Justine, ou Les Malheurs de la Vertu* (1791) and the rewritten and vastly expanded version, *La Nouvelle Justine* (1797) were designed as systematic revelations of the falsity of the sentimental psychological and sociological theories of the eighteenth century. They are one of the most savage and sustained attacks ever made on social hypocrisy; and although they are long, repetitious, devoid of style and grace, and ultimately boring, the nightmarish and distorted vision which they give of man's inhumanity to man – or, as Sade might say, man's *humanity* to man – is unforgettable. His portrait of the human race is a grotesque caricature: but like all good caricature it expresses certain truths which could not be expressed so vividly in any other way. It is true, as the moral theorists of the enlightenment pointed out, that man can be sympathetic, benevolent, reasonable and altruistic; it is also true, as the Terror, which Sade, a supporter of the Revolution, barely survived, was to demonstrate, that man can be irrationally cruel and selfish: the one is as natural as the other. Sterne's picture of the simple affection and respect that Trim and Uncle Toby have for each other is a revelation – unsentimental and completely convincing – of one aspect of eighteenth-century life; Sade's grimly detailed and apparently interminable account of the acts of cruelty, greed and bestiality committed by the rich and the powerful is another; and, although it is presented in terms of nightmare and fantasy, it too, like the gently comic vision of Shandy Hall, has its roots in reality.

Nowhere else in the literature of the eighteenth century is sentimentality subjected to such a merciless and unrelenting attack. This is not surprising: Sade, though not the monster he is

[87] *La Nouvelle Justine, ou Les Malheurs de la Vertu* (en Hollande, 1797) I 149 ('We always find that a libertine is rarely a sensitive man – and that for the single reason that sensibility is a sign of weakness and libertinism a sign of power.')

generally imagined to be, was not exactly a normal man: only someone capable of an extremely unusual degree of detachment from himself and other people would have been able to conceive a figure so consistently merciless and selfish as Juliette or St Fond. Sade's 'madness' – though not his literary genius – is of the same order as that of Swift and Blake. Most writers are much more deeply involved with the human race than satirists and visionaries such as these. Indeed the involvement of writers such as Sterne and Richardson and Laclos is probably a necessary condition of their being *novelists*, of their being able to create rounded and individual characters, rather than flat allegorical symbols or distorted and exaggerated caricatures: Walter Shandy, Lovelace and Valmont are human beings, Gulliver and St Fond are not.

Richardson was deeply committed to the conventional ideals of the world he was writing about, which was also the world he was writing for. Ostensibly he wanted to write stories that were sentimental in every sense: in the conclusions of his novels poetic justice is dispensed with scrupulous exactness, and the theme of them all is that virtue is rewarded if not on earth at least in heaven. Some of his characters – Goodman Andrews, for instance, or the old Welsh knight, Sir Rowland Meredith, in *Grandison* – are sentimentalised almost completely; others, like Pamela herself, are seen now with the eye of a sentimentalist, and now with the eye of a dispassionate and realistic reporter. Sterne is so self-conscious and sophisticated that one can scarcely compare his occasional lapses into sentimentality with those of Richardson; and it has become fashionable indeed in recent years to maintain that Sterne is never really sentimental at all – that he is always fully aware of what he is doing. Perhaps: but whatever the *intention* of something like his description of Maria in A *Sentimental Journey*, the effect of the scene, especially if it is taken in isolation, has every appearance of sentimentality (and since Sterne was the victim of the sentimental anthologist, it often *was* taken in isolation). When Tristram meets Maria the company of her goat, as E. N. Dilworth observes, reduces the maudlin to the farcical; but in the fragile Boucher sketch of her encounter with Yorick, the goat, significantly enough, has been replaced by a dog. And for those who would emphasise the hardness of Sterne's head rather than the softness of his heart, there is always the problem of explaining away the embarrassingly lachrymose *Journal to Eliza*.

All this is merely to say that Sterne and Richardson are sentimental novelists in every sense of the word 'sentimental'. They can be called sentimental because of their interest in the 'sentiments' of their characters – their thoughts and feelings, and, in particular, their moral responses to particular situations – rather than their actions; because of the moral purposes which inform their work; because of the themes with which they are concerned – the theme of virtue in distress, and the theme of the conflict between the free (and essentially moral) individual, the independent sensibility, and the forces of convention, 'the world'; and also because of that emotional excess and self-indulgence of which they, like their degenerate imitators and successors, both seem at times to be guilty. But although Richardson and Sterne are, to a varying degree, involved in the sentimentalities of their own age, their greatness as novelists depends on the way in which they expose, criticise and evaluate the very sorts of sentimentalism to which they are themselves most attracted. It depends, in fact, on the extent to which they can be described as anti-sentimental.

In the opening pages of this inquiry I referred to the way in which Rousseau, Richardson and Sterne had been grouped together by the author of *Le Voyageur sentimental* as tutelary deities of the cult of sensibility. A less likely trinity could be formed by placing Richardson, Sterne and Sade together. The conjunction may seem arbitrary: but these writers do in fact have something in common. In this case however, it is not their sentimentalism but their anti-sentimentalism which they share.

It may seem paradoxical to describe Richardson as an 'anti-sentimentalist'; but whether he was conscious of it or not he was profoundly disturbed by the 'sentimental' assumptions embodied in many of the most conventional moral attitudes of his society. *Clarissa* is almost as much an attack on the moral ideal typified by the heroine as a defence of it; Richardson, like Milton, writes much of the time as if he is a member of the devil's party. The devil in his case is Lovelace, and Lovelace is a thoroughly 'sadistic' character. His sadism does not consist so much in his cruelty as in the motives that lie behind it. His cruelty is partly an expression of frustration and impotence, as most cruelty is; but it is also the outward expression of a radical and fundamentally reasonable hatred of that sort of hypocrisy which the smugly conventional Harlowes represent. Lovelace is a libertine; and so, at another level, is Pamela. Sterne, in his own way is also a libertine – a rather deliberate one in fact, since he was a member of the society of Demoniacs who gathered annually at Crazy Castle for a carousal at which the conversation, if nothing else, was Rabelaisian.

One cannot lay too much weight on links which may be coincidental, but it is not without significance that Sterne, by belonging to the Demoniacs, was a corresponding brother of the much more genuinely devilish Medmenham fraternity.[88] Diabolism and libertinism for these rather self-conscious rakes was to a great extent nothing but a huge and elaborate joke. But it cannot be dismissed so lightly as this: 'libertine' is a most complex word, the philosophical, social and political connotations of which are just as important as its more obvious sexual ones. The libertine, no matter how sentimental he may be in some ways, is, at least by conviction, the arch enemy of all forms of sentimentality. Sexual libertinism, in short, is the physical expression of a sceptical and critical attitude to life, an attitude which, taken to extremes, becomes anarchic and nihilistic. Sterne wore his libertine notions, as he wore everything, with a light and faintly mocking air; for Richardson they were an incubus that he would have been glad to escape from – Lovelace is his own Grand Inquisitor, and he torments his creator with a truly Jesuitical relentlessness. For Sade liberty is everything: he is the complete sceptic – and in his uncompromising materialism, his ruthless and logical opposition to every form of superstition, faith and wishful thinking, there is something genuinely Satanic.

[88] Betty Kemp in *Sir Francis Dashwood: An Eighteenth-Century Independent* (London and New York, 1967) 131–6, argues plausibly that there is little factual basis for the legend of the monks of Medmenham. Most reports of their supposed orgies and blasphemies seem to be founded on an account given in 1765 by Charles Johnstone, a man fanatically opposed to Wilkes, in his satirical novel *Chrysal, or The Adventures of a Guinea*. Nonetheless it is difficult to believe that there was not even a small fire to justify Johnstone's smoke; and Wilkes certainly had the not unjustified reputation of being both a sexual and politcial libertarian – a libertine in the fullest sense of the word.

But if he is the devil incarnate, he is the devil returned to plague an age that had attempted to argue him out of existence. If he does nothing else Sade succeeds in demonstrating with appalling thoroughness the dreary reality of evil. That he should have done so at a time when men were proclaiming with such idealistic fervour the sentimental doctrine of the brotherhood of man is perhaps what makes him really significant.

III

The theme of all Sade's work is virtue in distress – *les malheurs de la vertu* – a theme which, of course, he treats in his own highly idiosyncratic way. In one form or another this is the theme of all sentimental fiction – giving the word 'sentimental' the very broad definition which I have attempted to establish earlier in this study. But in the sense in which the word is understood today Sade can scarcely be called a sentimental novelist – nor, for that matter, can Choderlos de Laclos nor Jane Austen; and it is only by qualifying the term very carefully that we can apply it in any justly meaningful way to Laurence Sterne and Samuel Richardson. Yet it is clear that all these novelists belong in some sense to the sentimental literary tradition; a tradition which also includes writers whose work is obviously sentimental in the twentieth-century sense of the word. And there are real and important connections and similarities between the work of the unsentimental and the sentimental members of the movement: *Le Voyageur sentimental* and *A Sentimental Journey* are in some sense the same *kind* of book; Clarissa, Emily St Aubert and Justine belong to a group from which Moll Flanders, Roxana and Sophia Western are excluded. Thus while it is useful and meaningful to speak of sentimentalism both as a literary tradition and as a much wider intellectual, ideological and cultural movement in the civilisation of eighteenth-century Europe, it can in some ways be confusing to speak of the sentimental novel as a genre. *Clarissa*, for instance, is a centrally significant document in that cluster of ideas which constitute sentimentalism – but it is quite clearly not, in one very important sense of the word, a sentimental novel.

For this reason it may be helpful to borrow E. A. Baker's term, 'the novel of sentiment' and slightly enlarge its terms of reference. Baker uses the term in a simply historical way: in his analysis the novel of sentiment precedes the novel of sensibility. But there would be considerable advantage, it seems to me, if, in certain contexts, we could also use 'novel of sentiment' to describe works produced late in the eighteenth and early in the nineteenth century – *Les Liaisons Dangereuses*, for instance, or the novels of Jane Austen. These are intimately and vitally related to the whole sentimental tradition, but like *Clarissa* and some of the earlier French novels I have mentioned, their fundamental realism makes the application to them of 'sentimental' in the modern sense quite misleading. 'Novel of sentiment' can also in certain circumstances legitimately be extended to cover much more recent fiction – the novels of James, Joyce, Woolf, Proust and Beckett, for instance (to cite only the most obvious examples), which are concerned predominantly with the inner life of the individual. In this they resemble the novels of sentiment of the eighteenth century; and within the developing tradition of the novel they are indeed lineally connected with them – although, of course, there are also many immediate factors in nineteenth- and twentieth-century literature and society which have led to the concern shown by novelists with isolated, introspective and alienated characters and to the emergence of the stream of consciousness and other related experimental techniques.

'The sentimental novel', however, is a term too well established in the histories of literature to be abandoned, and, despite its ambiguousness and equivocality, it is also too useful. Indeed both from necessity and choice I have employed it often myself throughout this study to describe novels which it is my ultimate concern to show are not sentimental in the sense that the word is understood today – novels like *Clarissa*, *Tristram Shandy*, *A Sentimental Journey*, *Werther*, *Les Liaisons Dangereuses*, and others. The fundamental realism of these works demands that we have when we need it another term available which while not obscuring their involvement with sentimentalism will at the same time allow us to suggest their lack of sentimentality. 'The novel of sentiment' supplies the need, suggesting as it does both the psychological veracity, the emphasis on thought and feeling, on the inner life, which characterises these novels, and their moral seriousness. The fantastic narratives of the Marquis de

Sade cannot be called 'novels of sentiment' in this sense – for although they reflect their author's inner life the characters that fill them are for the most part mechanical symbols with very little real individuality. But Sade is, of only in a negative and corrective way, inextricably part of the sentimental tradition; and he is certainly morally serious – indeed it is this that makes him permanently interesting and significant. 'You must read him for the sentiment' – Johnson's remark applies in the end almost as aptly to Sade as it does to Richardson. And it applies even more fittingly, of course, to all those other authors whose works, when we wish to speak accurately and with justice, we should call novels of sentiment.

6

The Sentimental Tradition

My purpose so far has been twofold: firstly to give some account of eighteenth-century sentimentalism in general and secondly to indicate in particular the way in which the sentimental novel is related to this large, diffuse and complex set of ideas. I have suggested that it may be useful to use the term 'novel of sentiment' to describe those sentimental novels which are more realistic than sentimental in the modern sense of the term; and I have attempted to suggest what some of the distinguishing characteristics of this genre may be.

Sentimentality of one sort or another is to be found in every human society, but the sentimentalism of the eighteenth century is of particular interest to us for a number of reasons. In the first place we are, whether we like it or not, its inheritors: the moral ideals of modern secular humanism and the political ideals both of liberal democracy and of revolutionary radicalism were to a large extent conceived and formulated in the eighteenth century, and they are essentially sentimental – in at least one of the senses of that complex word. In the second place it is extremely interesting that although sentimentality has always existed, the word to describe this particular human condition did not come into being until the eighteenth century. I do not think that the appearance of the word at just this time should be taken as evidence that people in the eighteenth century were in general more sentimental than people in any other age. But they were undoubtedly more sentimental about certain things. And some of the objects of their most excessive feelings were things that were associated with the *word* 'sentimental'. They were, for instance, sentimental about morality, and they were sentimental about feeling: in short, they were, or they became, sentimental about eighteenth-century sentimentalism itself.

Sentimentality as we understand the term today is essentially a means of retreating from or protecting oneself against the unpleasant aspects of reality. We all indulge in it from time to time, and it may take many forms. It is always, to some extent, a compensation for impotence. If we encounter in life a problem that seems insoluble, we are apt to make up for our helplessness by indulging in the emotions that the problem has generated. The act of concentrating on these emotions, and of giving them a value in themselves, tends to take the mind away from the situation that has initially generated them. In Leslie Stephen's phrase, one can make 'a luxury of grief'.[1] One can also make a luxury of hope, or of rage or violence. The sentimental optimist is one who uses his ideal vision of the potential goodness of man not as a spur to action, but as a comforting illusion: he excuses his own ineffectiveness to himself by maintaining that men are much better than in fact they are. The pessimist, on the other hand, takes refuge in the belief that all men are villains at bottom. The man of action – the revolutionary – is often guilty of a similar sort of sentimentality, when violence and anger become ends in themselves, rather than means of achieving something.

It is perhaps worth noting briefly that all these various types of sentimentalism and sentimentality have manifested themselves with increasing clarity in contemporary literature and society during the last twenty years – particularly in the United States, where the tensions and problems of western civilisation seem to make themselves felt more urgently and more forcefully than anywhere else. One of the most striking features of the American scene – and to an increasing extent of the international scene – during this period has been the emergence of a new social group which is characterised both by its revulsion from the corporate state and its refusal, on the whole, to oppose it in any of the conventional political or revolutionary ways. This group which is youthful and dissenting (or at least manages to preserve the stance of youth and dissidence) is also articulate and well-publicised: its underground newspapers, its posters, novels, poetry, films, songs, music and drugs constitute a large, dynamic, heterogeneous and complicated cultural phenomenon which society is still in the process of trying to understand and come to terms with.

When this whole complex movement, the 'counter-culture', is

[1] *History of English Thought in the Eighteenth Century* (London, 1902) II 436.

set against the sentimentalism of the eighteenth century certain similarities and connections immediately become apparent, especially if we look particularly at the literature of dissent. To take two examples: *Howl*, by Allen Ginsberg, and *The Catcher in the Rye* by J. D. Salinger. Both works were published in the fifties – *Howl* in 1956 and *The Catcher in the Rye* in 1951 – and each may be regarded as important documents in the development of the ideas and the ideology of the beat generation and the hippies and the yippies who have followed them. Ginsberg is accepted internationally as a leading spokesman for dissent, especially in its non-violent, passive aspects, and the popularity and influence of *The Catcher in the Rye* among adolescents in the fifties have been widely acknowledged. Jerry Rubin, for instance, one of the founding fathers of the yippies, when describing his all-American high school days, mentions only *one* book – Salinger's novel:

> I went to the kind of high school where you had to pass a test to get *in*.
> I graduated in the bottom half of the class . . .
> I had short, short, short hair.
> I dug *Catcher in the Rye*.
> I didn't have pimples.[2]

Ginsberg's poem is more important as an expression of an attitude, a mood, than as an influence. The attitude is summed up in the title – it is a howl of anguish, despair and impotence in the face of Moloch, Ginsberg's symbol of the materialistic, violent, impersonal American state. It is saved from maudlin self-pity by Ginsberg's sense of the absurd, his resilience, his good humour, and by the genuine power and specificity with which he evokes the image of his America:

> Moloch the incomprehensible prison! Moloch the crossbone soulless jail-house and Congress of Sorrows! Moloch whose buildings are judgement! Moloch the vast stone of war! Moloch the stunned governments!
> . . . . .
> Moloch! Moloch! Robot apartments! Invisible suburbs! skeleton treasures! blind capitals! demonic industries! spectral

[2] *Do it! Scenarios of the Revolution* (New York, 1970) 12.

nations! invincible madhouses! granite cocks! monstrous
bombs!
They broke their backs lifting Moloch to Heaven! Pavements,
trees, radios, tons! Lifting the city to Heaven which exists
and is everywhere about us.

But despite the energy of this denunciation the basic mood in
Howl is outrage, not so much at the horribleness of society as at
the way in which it has destroyed the innocent and sensitive:
the whole poem is an expansion of and comment on the
Wertherish first line:

I saw the best minds of my generation destroyed by madness,
starving hysterical naked . . .

The Catcher in the Rye is a more ambiguous and elusive work,
and one with a much broader appeal than Ginsberg's anarchic
and sexually uninhibited statement. Because of its theme, its
structure, and the questions it raises it is impossible to resist the
temptation to describe Salinger's novel as the *Sentimental
Journey* of its day. Holden Caulfield, like Parson Yorick, is preoccupied with the problem of emotional honesty, of distinguishing between the fake and the real, between false or dissimulated
and genuine feeling. Like Yorick he travels, running away from
school, and passing through a number of situations which test
both his own and other people's honesty and integrity; and as
with Yorick the situations usually involve either love (or sex) or
money or a combination of the two. He even has an encounter
with a prostitute where, like Yorick, he ends up paying 'as many
a poor soul has *paid* before [him] for an act he *could* not do, or
think of'. Like Yorick he is the victim of an impotence that is
more than sexual: although he dreams of being generous and
helping people – of being the catcher in the rye who saves the
children – he finds it impossible to move without compromising
his integrity. And the pressures on him are far greater than the
pressures on Yorick: Holden Caulfield's journey is no quiet pursuit of the heart in search of nature, it is a flight from school,
from society, from his family and finally from himself, a flight
which leads him to a nervous breakdown and the hospital in
which he is supposedly writing his story. As in *A Sentimental
Journey* it is the style – sharp, ironic, tender, colloquial – which

holds the potentially mawkish emotionalism of *The Catcher in the Rye* in check. But the book still raises the question of whether it is or is not self-indulgent and self-pitying; and it is significant that Salinger's later work has increasingly attracted from critics the comment that it is 'sentimental'. (That Holden Caulfield should be writing his confession as 'therapy' is not without significance. Allen Ginsberg's *Howl* is an epistle to Carl Solomon in the sanatorium for the mentally ill, Rocklands. *One Flew over the Cuckoo's Nest* by the great advocate of the salvific promise of LSD, Ken Kesey, the novel which embodies the mood of the sixties, as *Catcher in the Rye* embodies the mood of the fifties, is set in an asylum – an institution which we finally come to realise breaks minds instead of healing them, an institution which expresses in its most sinister and oppressive form the impersonal and depersonalising power of the technocratic corporate state. For the contemporary man of feeling the twentieth-century world is not so much evil as insane. And the mark of its insanity is its persecution of the 'best minds', the way in which it either falsely accuses them of being mad, or in fact drives them into madness.)

In *The Greening of America* which, like Jerry Rubin's *Do It!*, (though from a very different standpoint) is an attempt to give a comprehensive account of 'the movement', Charles A. Reich observes that 'it is little more than twenty years since the first members of the new generation were born. And it is only that long since, in Holden Caulfield . . . we heard their first voice'.[3] And to anyone who has been looking at eighteenth-century sentimentalism the voice sounds remarkably familiar: 'Consciousness III [Reich's term for what might be called the *sensibility* of the new generation] starts with self . . . the individual self is the only true reality . . . The first commandment is: "Thou shalt not do violence to thyself" '. But, he goes on, 'to start from self does not mean to be selfish. It means to start from premises based on human life and the rest of nature, rather than premises that are the artificial products of the Corporate State, such as power or status . . . Consciousness III postulates the absolute worth of every human being – every self.'[4]

It is not only in its emphasis on the needs of the individual,

---

[3] *The Greening of America* (London, 1971) 289.   [4] Ibid. 166.

the right of everyone to 'do his own thing', that the new consciousness (to adopt Reich's terminology) strikes one as sentimental. It also assumes an enthusiastic and optimistic view of man's benevolence – 'Given an abundance of material goods, the possibilities of a human community are finally made real, for it is now possible', asserts Reich, 'to believe in the goodness of man'.[5] And it has a touching belief in the power of love and the force of example: under slogans such as 'Superzap them all with love' hippie demonstrators make the peace sign at baton-wielding cops and put flowers in the muzzles of soldiers' rifles. And they do more than this: at their most positive the dropouts from 'straight' American society offer an 'alternative life-style' (the jargon, unfortunately, seems inescapable) which in the things it emphasises is unquestionably valuable as an example and, in the context of the problems facing the human race in the latter half of the twentieth century, extremely significant. If the disease ridden pads of the heroin addicts in Haight-Ashbury represent one possible end of the hippie road, the rural communes now growing up all over America represent another. The Voltairian admonition to cultivate one's garden is being accepted by many of these latter day Candides with a practicality and common sense that would have been admired and understood in the eighteenth century. Publications like the encyclopaedic *Whole Earth Catalog* and *The Mother Earth News*, for instance, exhibit a notable blend of idealism and pragmatism. They express a lively and intelligent concern with the crucial ecological problems of pollution and over population, together with a belief that if these problems are ever to be solved it can only be through the efforts of individual human beings, through a radical change of consciousness within man himself. They are much less starry-eyed about the ease with which this will happen, or is happening, than Reich is. People like Stewart Brand, leader of the team who edited most of the *Catalogs*, and John and Jane Shuttleworth, who are the driving force behind *The Mother Earth News*, know that there is a direct and essential relationship between the number of callouses on the palms and the greenness of the land. Among their patron saints are not only Thoreau and Kropotkin, but also – and more directly – Buckminster Fuller and Ralph Nader. *The Mother Earth News* in particular often reads like a

[5] Ibid. 260.

blend of *Walden* and *Popular Mechanics*. The epigraph to the farewell message of *The Last Whole Earth Catalog*, entitled 'How to do a Whole Earth Catalog', effectively suggests just how qualified in this area the romanticism of the counter-culture has become: 'The masked man left behind a silver bullet. The people said, "We'd rather have a scribbled diagram", and they shot him with his silver bullet. Here's our scribbled diagram.'

Even the new sod-busters and commune-building home-steaders, however, agree with the acid-heads and yippies in one thing: the modern industrial corporate state is evil, inhuman, mechanical and inefficient, and in order to preserve one's humanity one must escape from it – or use it without letting it use you. Sir Charles Grandison was able to ' [live] to himself and his own heart, rather than to the opinion of the world', and still maintain a fairly comfortable relationship with the society of which he was a member. But those who wish 'to live to themselves and their own hearts' today can no longer do this: increasingly it seems to many that no compromise is possible. The pressures exerted by the state are felt to be so powerful and pervasive that one of the strongest motivations operating in 'the new consciousness' has become the urge simply to withdraw, to 'turn on, tune in, drop out', as Timothy Leary, the one-time Harvard psychologist who found his vocation in preaching the virtues of LSD, memorably phrased it. And this is reflected in some of the more colourful forms in which the urge to escape manifests itself. The veneration of the American Indian, for instance, which has become an increasingly prominent feature of the hippie movement, finds its expression not only in the organisation of communes into tribes and families, but also in the costume – beads, bells, fringes, paint, head-bands – adopted by the hippie vagabonds of the streets and highways. The white indians of Venice or Greenwich Village are involved in an elaborate game of make-believe, a self-conscious attempt to act out the myth of romantic primitivism, to recreate in the mechanised wilderness of modern America the sentimental dream of the noble savage. At another extreme the Weathermen are attempting to act out the much more dangerous myth of romantic revolution. Each can be seen as a gesture of sentimental despair; both the pot-smoking Washington Square Indian and the young anarchist blowing up yet another branch of the Bank of America are dramatically expressing their realisation that although they hate 'Amerika', they are powerless to change it.

And yet although the counter-culture may be born of despair the feelings and attitudes which seem most prominently to characterise it are benevolent, enthusiastic and optimistic. *Hair*, for instance, 'the American tribal love-rock musical', with its celebration of communal, polymorphous, perverse and miscegenous promiscuity ('Black, white, yellow, red/Copulate in a king-size bed'), its evangelistic appeals to legalise pot, outlaw pollution and take off all your clothes, and its antipathy to war and authoritarianism generally, is a cheerful – and innocent – piece of theatre. It is also remarkably sentimental – both in its moral fervour and its emphasis on feeling. As one unusually acerbic London critic commented, 'it is not the blasphemy or the obscenity or the nakedness that shocks . . . [it is] the wholesomeness, the suffocating worthiness, the relentless naivety of it all'.[6] Not surprisingly *Hair* (which is also an extremely lively and pleasantly noisy production) has been a resounding theatrical success: unlike the much more radical *Che*, which also began (and ended) off-Broadway. *Che*, from all accounts, may well have deserved to fail for its simple dramatic deficiencies. But it is worth observing that while the public and the 'authorities' eventually found the revolutionary message of *Hair* safe and acceptable, they found the sexual and political anarchism of *Che* disgusting or incomprehensible: not only did the play fail, but those associated with its production were prosecuted.

Cheerful optimism is also the dominant note in *The Greening of America* – although the optimism is at the same time accompanied by a romantically apocalyptic sense of gloom and terror. If the world is to be saved it will only just be saved in the nick of time. *The Greening of America*, like *Hair*, offers itself as a 'revolutionary' work, and like the musical it has achieved a remarkable popular success, especially in the United States where it was a best-seller for a number of weeks. It has also aroused considerable opposition from a majority of serious reviewers and critics, together with a certain amount of qualified approval accompanied by a recognition that the book, whatever the ultimate validity of its insights, is a cultural phenomenon of some importance. As one commentator observes, 'the most interesting

[6] Milton Shulman in the *Evening Standard* 30 Sept. 1968.

thing about this book is the tremendous interest it has stirred'.[7]
'If the book is froth', another critic, Michael Harrington, remarks, adapting a metaphor from Lenin, it is 'a significant
froth'.[8] And the measure of this significance is reflected in the
liveliness and the level of the discussion initiated by its publication. The anthology of reviews and articles brought out under
the title, *The Con III Controversy*, in June 1971 (less than a year
after the first appearance of *Greening* in *The New Yorker*) is a
mixed but surprising weighty bag, containing comments from
people such as Herbert Marcuse, John Kenneth Galbraith,
Nathan Glazer and Dwight MacDonald, cheek by jowl with
statements from the editor of *Rolling Stone*, the rock critic from
the *New Yorker*, and one of the editors of *Rags*, presumably a
fashion journal.

Reich offers an extremely rosy vision of the future and at the
same time suggests that the transition from the present mess to
the imminent utopian solution will be magically easy. These are
the aspects of *The Greening of America* which have attracted
the most antagonistic and scathing comments. But his account
of what is wrong with the present situation – or rather of why
some people (predominantly the college educated WASPs) feel
that it is wrong – is much more sober and shrewd. Indeed Reich's
analysis of why the middle class, liberally minded, educated
American finds living in his corporate state increasingly painful
and uncomfortable is the best thing in the book: if he has done
nothing else he has succeeded in articulating a widespread
malaise.

He has also articulated a widespread hope – the hope that
revolution is possible and that it can be achieved peacefully and
without pain. One of the Beatles' hit records of 1967, *All you
need is Love*, prophetically expressed the same hope. It begins
with a quotation from the opening bars of that well-known
revolutionary anthem, the *Marseillaise*; but this almost immediately modulates into the melody of the Beatles' song itself. 'All
you need is love' is also Charles Reich's utopian and magical
panacea:

[7] Charles Ford, 'Reich and the Romantics', *The Con III Controversy: the Critics look at The Greening of America*, ed. Philip
Nobile (New York, 1971) 91.
[8] 'The Defoliation of Charles Reich', *The Con III Controversy* 178.

There is a revolution coming. It will not be like revolutions of
the past. It will originate with the individual and with culture,
and it will change the political structure only as its final act.
It will not require violence to succeed, and it cannot be successfully resisted by violence. It is now spreading with amazing
rapidity, and already our laws, institutions and social structure
are changing in consequence. It promises a higher reason, a
more human community and a new and liberated individual . . .[9]

Nobody likes the present situation – so everybody must want to
change it. But you can't really upset the corporate state: the
machine is too powerful. Therefore you change yourselves – and
then the machine will become the servant, not the master, of
man. Once we are all 'turned on', as the young have been
turned on, we shall be transformed into Consciousness IIIs: 'Now
all we have to do is close our eyes and imagine that everyone has
become a Consciousness III: the Corporate State vanishes.'[10]
Bliss was it in that dawn to be alive, But to be young was very
heaven . . .

Not everything in *The Greening of America* is so fatuous,
and there is much to be optimistic about in the United States,
especially in the idealism of its youth. But Reich's book is dis-
quietingly sentimental in the most pejorative sense of the word:
its optimism becomes finally so all-encompassing that one feels
it can have been achieved only by a deliberate refusal to contemplate squarely the very problems it is supposed to deal with. Its
optimism, which gives the appearance of being positive, turns
out, on closer examination, to be the mask for a thoroughly
sentimental withdrawal from a situation which is too puzzling,
too disturbing and too difficult to consider honestly.[11] Although
Reich acknowledges the horrors of the corporate state and the
ugliness which increasingly characterises so much of contemporary American life he manages to convey no sense of having
immediately experienced them. Violence, poverty, urban decay,

[9] *The Greening of America* 1.   [10] Ibid. 224.
[11] In the context of my general argument the language of Marcuse's
comment is interesting: 'His analysis of the hippie sub-culture is
sensitive – though again much too sensitive – sentimental sublima-
tion' ('Charles Reich as Revolutionary Ostrich', *The Con III
Controversy* 17).

pollution, organised crime, political corruption, inter-racial tensions – these are words, not realities, in Reich's greening America.
Hard drugs present no problem, the Mafia rates a passing mention, the assassinations of the Kennedy brothers and Martin
Luther King are superficial irrelevancies, and Hell's Angels lie
down together in harmony and love with all the other happy,
innocent inhabitants of the paradisal supermarkets of California
– a world 'of gleaming opulence and richness'. 'Nineteen sixty-
eight was the year of Chicago. Nineteen sixty-nine was the year
of Woodstock. That speaks of the distance we have come, and
the speed with which we are travelling.' And nineteen-seventy
was the year of Kent State, the Manson family murders, the
Angela Davis/Soledad brothers case, *Easy Rider* and *Gimme
Shelter* – and that speaks of the distance which separates Reich's
fantasy world of flower children from reality. The most disturbing feature of Reich's fantasy is his complete refusal to acknowledge the possibility that individual human beings may somehow,
at some level, be responsible for the evils of society. And this
refusal becomes all the more damaging when it is borne in mind
that the spear-head of Reich's revolution is the individual who,
blessed with the new wisdom of Consciousness III, chooses to
realise himself in an ethically responsible way and so – perhaps
without intending it – transform society. But in Reich's view
things have not gone wrong because some individuals have acted
badly or unwisely or stupidly – it is simply that the machine is
out of control. In Reich's world it is the machine, the corporate
state, technology, that drops atom bombs, runs slave-labour
camps, sprays people with napalm, turns on gas ovens, makes
slums, pulls the trigger of the policeman's pistol – or the
criminal's. As one reviewer has observed, 'It is impossible to
come away from his book disliking anybody.'[12] One does not
have to be a doomsday pessimist to disagree with Reich: one
merely has to observe that man and society are infinitely more
complex than he is willing to allow – and that one aspect of
man's complexity is his capacity to choose deliberately and
apparently spontaneously to do what he believes to be evil. And
this choice is often exercised in a deliberate parody of that course
of good, humane, benevolent behaviour which man, according

[12] L. J. Clancy, 'Revolution without Guns: Thoughts on the
Counter-Culture', *Meanjin Quarterly*, XXX (1971) 249.

to the naïve sentimentalist, if given the freedom, will choose to follow.

To choose to drop out is to assert one's right to act freely – and Reich is obviously correct in seeing this as the ideal of the new consciousness. But he completely fails to realise that it can be extraordinarily difficult and dangerous to act freely, and that the dream of freedom may go sour (as the brilliant film *Easy Rider* so movingly demonstrates); and that those who choose to opt out from American society may not necessarily follow the course of gentle withdrawal. Black Power is as charismatic a slogan as Flower Power, and one that people are prepared to die for; the Hell's Angels are as much a reality as manta-chanting gurus; and the Manson family grew like a malignant parodic cancer in the west-coast hippie world of love-ins, communes, and complete permissiveness. And these phenomena – like so many aspects of the counter-culture in general (including *The Greening of America*) – seem to be more important for what they symbolise than for what they are in themselves.

The Hell's Angels and the other outlaw motorcycle clubs of America's West Coast (and their imitators in other parts of the world) offer a particularly clear cut example of this. Although they came into existence more or less of their own accord and in answer to the needs of the depressed suburban society from which their members are mostly drawn, they rapidly acquired a national, not to say international symbolic prominence as an image of violent, undirected libertinism – an image in which rebellion, sex, freedom, power and man's mastery of the machine are uniquely blended. As Hunter S. Thompson has demonstrated in his study of these people, this image to begin with was built up by the press: 'the Hell's Angels as they exist today were virtually created by *Time*, *Newsweek* and the *New York Times*'.[13] But the image (which the Hell's Angels have tried their best to live up to) would have been brought into being, Thompson argues, only because it answered some obscure but deeply felt communal need: 'the main reason the Angels were such good copy is that they were acting out the day-dreams of millions of losers who don't wear any defiant insignia and who don't know how to be outlaws . . . They command a fascination, however reluctant, that borders on psychic masturbation.'[14] And the

[13] *Hell's Angels* (Harmondsworth, 1967) 42–3.   [14] Ibid. 273.

fascination is the same as that exercised by the Sadistic fantasy of complete freedom, absolute and unfettered rebellion. Like Sade's bands of criminals the Angels and their imitators use ritual defilement (with faeces, urine and menstrual blood) in the initiation of their members and gang rape in the initiation of their women followers; and they have a general interest in communal and often 'perverse' sexual behaviour. An account of some of their activities – even more of some of their *supposed* activities – reads like a synopsis of one of the milder episodes in *Justine*. And they act out their symbolic role with results that are sometimes disastrous. It was somehow cruelly and ironically fitting that the murder which turned the Altamont Rock Concert into an obscene parody of the idyllic Woodstock festival should have been carried out – on camera – by a Hell's Angel. The film in which this appears, *Gimme Shelter*, was not intended to be an answer to or comment on the simple and enthusiastic optimism of Woodstock; but inevitably – and rightly – this is how it has been received and interpreted.

Even more fascinating and disturbing are Charles Manson and his family, for not only did they bring Sade's anti-sentimental fantasies to life by 'dropping out' and creating their own utterly libertine world in which every imaginable act, including murder, was made possible, but, like Sade they saw themselves (albeit in a confused and fumbling way) as critics of society, as exposing by the honesty of their actions the hypocrisies of the corporate state. The Manson family, like the accused in many recent political trials in the United States, used the courtroom as a theatre; and during the long ritual drama of their trial repeatedly made two points: a society as *institutionally* violent and murderous as the United States had no right to punish them for what they had done;[15] and their guilt, if they were guilty, was something in which every member of society was involved. It would be easy to dismiss Manson as nothing more than a semi-literate, criminal madman who used the clichés of the counter-culture to

[15] '"Killing eight people is just business as usual, right, Sadie?" prosecutor Vincent T. Bugliosi asked [Susan Atkins] on cross-examination. ". . . Eight bodies are no big thing to you?"

"Well, are they?" asked the pale, dark-haired young woman. "Are 1 million dead because of napalm, because of your justice a big thing? It doesn't seem to be to you all."'

Los Angeles Times 12 Feb. 1971.

justify his and his followers' insanely cruel and selfish actions. But although this is true it would be a mistake to see it as the whole truth. The Manson family, terrible, pitiable and confused though they may be, insist on being acknowledged as human beings, not as monstrous aberrations. When the judge passed sentence on one of the Manson women, Patricia Krenwinkel, she commented: 'You have just judged yourselves.' In the context of the My Lai trials, the first of which had just been concluded, the observation does not seem completely inappropriate.[16]

The Greening of America and the trials of the Manson family may seem peculiarly contemporary and peculiarly American phenomena – and in a sense they are. But the polarities they represent and the ways in which they are imaged and conceptualised are also intimately related to those complexes of sentimental and anti-sentimental ideas which first clearly emerged in the eighteenth century. The counter-culture – like the corporate state – is a child of the enlightenment, and its myths and nightmares, like the myths and nightmares of that earlier age, are embodied in its art.

They are also sustained by art and self-advertisement: the hippie and the beatnik are almost as much creations of the media, inventions of the press, television, film and also certain well-publicised writers and poets, as are the Hell's Angels. The hippie is an image of ineffective and often distressed virtue; full of love and tenderness, but quite powerless to express his benevolence in meaningful social action. The Hell's Angels (and in a more shocking way, the Manson family) present an image of naked, amoral, personal power – an image which in its implications is

---

[16] A recent comment by Lilian Roxon, an Australian journalist who lived in New York and who made a special study of pop culture – especially its music – highlights the significance of the Manson case:

It's become a sort of parlour game to work out exactly when the sixties died. When the speed freaks replaced the flower-children in Haight-Ashbury? When a man was stabbed to death by a Hell's Angel at a Rolling Stones concert?

For a lot of people the end came with Charles Manson's trial. His life-style was in many ways just too close to the sixties dream for comfort. It took every sixties fantasy to its logical conclusion and there was no escaping that.

    – 'Press here for a Happy Ending', *Sydney Morning Herald*
27 Nov. 1971.

anti-sentimental. But both can induce a sentimental and emotionally self-indulgent response in the 'straight' citizen who condemns equally the behaviour of the hippie and the outlaw while
vicariously enjoying it. Truman Capote's *In Cold Blood* and the
reports of the Manson trial are the gothic novels of our day[17] –
just as our voyageurs sentimentals are the beatnik travellers in
novels like *Catcher in the Rye* and Kerouac's *On the Road*, or
the dropout wanderers in films like *Easy Rider* and *Five Easy
Pieces*: impotent rebels who preserve their integrity, and in
particular their capacity to *feel*, by either travelling physically
across the face of America or else by 'taking a trip', remaining
perpetually on the move, on drugs through the inner world of
their own psyches. This is not to say that such works are necessarily sentimental in the pejorative sense – some of those I have
mentioned are works of great artistic integrity, complex, realistic
and substantial renderings of the contemporary human condition. But they deal with both the ideals of our day and their
sentimental vulgarisations; and even while they criticise them
help to keep them alive.

The same, of course, can be said of the eighteenth-century
novel of sentiment. The best examples of the genre are impressive literary works of art in their own right, and worth examining simply from this point of view. But they assume a new
dimension of meaning when set in the context of the sentimentalism of their own day; and they take on an added interest
for the modern reader because of the way in which they can be
seen to prefigure certain important elements in both the life and
the literature of our own time. The fashionable social and literary
sentimentalities of America (and to some extent Europe) in the
nineteen sixties and seventies are not merely analogous to what
was capturing the public taste two hundred years ago, but part
of a continuing tradition. Ginsberg, Kerouac and Reich all look
back to and acknowledge their descent from Whitman; and
Whitman (despite his assertion that he is 'no sentimentalist') is
pre-eminently the celebrant of Nature, Freedom and the Democratic Sensibility. A more Rousseauistic poet it would be difficult
to imagine: his major poetic achievement is a confession – indeed

---

[17] During his trial Manson published a column, 'Memo from
Purgatory', in one of the most substantial of the underground papers,
the weekly *Los Angeles Free Press*.

his work as a whole could well bear the title of his most representative production, *Song of Myself.*

But there are other and perhaps more significant ways in
which modern literature can be related to the sentimental
literature of the eighteenth century. The theme of virtue in
distress, for instance, and the figure of the powerless but well-
intentioned observer, the helpless man of sentiment, have an
immediate contemporary eighteenth-century relevance: the
image of the suffering heroine at the mercy both of her own
delicate sensibilities and the cruel world is a potent symbol of
moral uneasiness and despair. But its significance extends beyond
the period in which it was initially conceived. In the eighteenth-
century novel of sentiment we hear sounded clearly for the first
time the theme of alienation, a theme which has been one of the
most dominant in European and American literature for the last
two hundred years. The sentimental traveller, like the central
characters in many of the novels of Melville, James, Joyce,
Faulkner and others, is – to borrow a most perceptive phrase
from Leslie Fiedler – an 'impotent voyeur', a protagonist who
witnesses and suffers all but can do nothing. 'What [the blind]
Tiresias *sees*', according to the author of *The Waste Land*, 'in
fact, is the substance of the poem'. What the impotent pseudo-
author mentally experiences – recollects, imagines, invents – is
the substance of *Tristram Shandy*. This is not the sort of analogy,
I admit, which can be made to bear too much weight; but in the
novel of sentiment as in the work of the great romantic and post-
romantic poets we see reflected a growing sense of isolation, an
awareness of the gulf which can separate the sensitive and
intelligent individual human being from his society, from the
world of action.

At one level this can express itself in self-pitying and escapist
fantasies; at another, the withdrawal from the world can lead to
a concentration on the inner life, on *sentiment* in the fullest
sense of the word, which is richly creative and transforming.
The best of the eighteenth-century novels of sentiment are the
product of this process, major and enduringly meaningful works
of art. And even some of the lesser and more truly sentimental
examples of the genre have a historical interest which makes
them worth examining. It is to the discussion of some of these
novels that the second part of this work is devoted.

PART TWO

Some Novels of Sentiment

I

Clarissa: The Sentimental Tragedy

In the fiction of the eighteenth century *Clarissa* occupies a peculiarly central place. Such critics as concerned themselves with the novel – usually novelists themselves, like Fielding and Diderot – freely acknowledged the genius displayed in *Clarissa*; and the pattern Richardson established in this and his other books, particularly *Sir Charles Grandison*, was widely imitated by scores of lesser writers. Even when his popularity began to decline his effect on the form he had helped to establish could still be discerned: if it is debatable whether he can be called the greatest novelist of his age there can be no doubt that he was the most influential. Moreover his works were enjoyed and admired by an unusually wide and varied group of people, including some who would have looked on the reading of fiction in general as a frivolous and possibly sinful occupation. Richard Griffin, for instance, writing of life in relatively humble circumstances towards the end of the eighteenth century, has recorded how *Pamela*, the first novel he ever read, was introduced into the family by his grandmother:

> She (good woman) was no novel-reader – she would not have read one for the world – but how could she ever imagine that a book was one which bore such a title as 'Pamela, or Virtue Rewarded'. . . . She believed every word of it, as she did her Bible: and in the winter evenings . . . she would read aloud to the listening family, page after page, with the most supreme satisfaction . . .[1]

Clarissa, no doubt, did not have quite the same breadth of appeal; but when Griffin's testimony is set beside Diderot's extravagant and well known assertion that Richardson's works deserved to

[1] *Specimens of the Novelists and Romancers* 1st American from 2nd Edinburgh ed. (New York, 1831) II 43. Quoted by McKillop, *Samuel Richardson* 86.

stand on the same shelf as those of Moses, Homer, Sophocles and Euripides, we get some notion of the extent of his fame and influence. His prolixity, his sentimentality and his inverted snobbery were criticised from the beginning, but he never lacked readers or imitators. He dominates the literature of his age as does no other novelist. It is, I think, highly significant that amongst those who admired his achievement and learnt from his example we must include two novelists who in most ways are utterly dissimilar – Jane Austen and the Marquis de Sade.[2]

Why did Richardson's novels, and in particular *Clarissa*, his greatest work, enjoy this special status? The explanation is to be found first of all in his realism, his moral seriousness, and the dramatic intensity and immediacy which he attained through the use of the epistolary form. But these are not the most important reasons: what distinguishes *Clarissa* is its thematic complexity, its range of social and moral significance, and the way in which the various elements in the work are brought together into a single coherent, concentrated action. The climax of the story is the rape of Clarissa by Lovelace. This in itself does not make Richardson's novel unusual: rape and attempted rape were stock situations in the eighteenth-century novel – to such an extent that George Colman, in the Prologue to his farce *Polly Honeycombe*, produced in 1760, was able to sum up the popular fiction of the day as follows:

And then so *sentimental* is the Stile,
So chaste, yet so bewitching all the while!
Plot, and elopement, passion, rape, and rapture,
The total sum of ev'ry dear – dear – Chapter.[3]

[2] In *De la Littérature* (1800) Mme de Staël claims that apart from *La Nouvelle Héloïse* all French novels are imitations of the English. 'They were the first who ventured to believe that the representation of private feelings was enough to interest the mind and heart of man ... [They] transformed novels into works of morality in which obscure virtues and destinies can find grounds for exaltation. . .' (*Madame de Staël on Politics, Literature and National Character*, trans. and ed. Morroe Berger, New York, 1965, 193–4). Among English novelists she singles out Richardson and Fielding for special comment. Sade follows the same pattern in his *Idée sur les Romans* published in the same year by way of introduction to his collection of *novelle*, *Les Crimes de l'Amour*.

[3] Prologue to *Polly Honeycombe*, A *Dramatick Novel of One Act*

What distinguishes *Clarissa* is not merely that it contains only one rape, but that the rape itself is the most significant, the most widely meaningful in the whole of eighteenth-century literature. Lovelace's violation of Clarissa and her subsequent rejection of his offer to marry her are the culminating incidents in a remarkably complicated conflict, a conflict which is much more than a simple sexual struggle between a man and a woman. It is a struggle between the symbolic and ultimately heroic representatives of different social classes, different moral and intellectual attitudes, different visions of life; a struggle which naturally and easily assumes mythical and ideological proportions. Clarissa is the feminine embodiment of the sentimental virtues and ideals: she believes in man's innate benevolence and in the right of the individual to follow the promptings of his own heart. She is also a woman of exquisite sensibility and, beneath her reserve, one who is capable of deep sexual passion. The trials to which she is subjected first by her family and then by Lovelace are thus not merely a test of her own personal toughness and integrity, they are also a test, almost casuistic in its thoroughness, of the moral attitudes she represents.

Clarissa, however, is not an allegory, an eighteenth-century morality play. It is a novel, and like all great novels its strength lies in its characters. Clarissa and Lovelace are not flat symbolic figures, they are complex, contradictory, living individuals; and the conflict in which they and Clarissa's family are involved is fought out as much within the secret recesses of their own hearts as it is on the open field of battle. The confinements and tortures to which Clarissa is subjected have an authentic physical reality – locked doors, secret houses, disguised persecutors, fierce wardresses, and so on – but they are to a large extent terrifying only because Clarissa herself permits them to be. She half-creates the nightmare world she lives in: it is significant that once Lovelace has in fact raped her his power over her and the power of his criminal associates magically vanishes.

Clarissa and Lovelace, indeed, provide a classic example of the sort of situation which has been so wittily analysed by the

---

(London, 1760). 'A novel for my money!' says Polly. 'Lord, Lord, my stupid Papa has no taste. He has no notion of humour, and character, and the sensibility of delicate feeling' (p. 2).

psychologist Eric Berne in his *Games People Play*. They are perfectly matched partners in a highly involved eighteenth-century version of 'Rapo'; although, to be fair to Clarissa, it must be admitted that she is genuinely tricked into entering the game, and that she is forced to keep on playing long after she wants to cry halt. But there is an element of sub-conscious acquiescence in her relationship with Lovelace which gives it a peculiar sado-masochistic force. It is highly significant that, at the very last moment, she gives in: 'I remember, I pleaded for mercy. I remember that I said I *would be his – Indeed I would be his* – to obtain his mercy. But no mercy found I.'[4] It is too late for her to become his mistress, however: the rape must continue. And, at a very profound level this is also what Clarissa desires: she wants Lovelace to be not only her lover but also the one who punishes her for her independence and unconventionality. Despite her determination to preserve her integrity, she feels (quite consciously) that, as a dutiful daughter she should obey her father, and (far less consciously) that, as a woman she should submit to Lovelace, or at least willingly become his sexual partner. If she is to preserve her virtue she knows that she must suffer for it: her sort of virtue tested in this sort of situation must inevitably be distressed, though ultimately triumphant. Lovelace is the victim of a similar set of conflicts. In raping Clarissa he half-realises that he is seeking his own destruction; and once the violation has taken place he accepts Clarissa and her family as instruments of vengeance: the torturer now becomes the victim, indeed he almost welcomes the reversal of roles. Each of the lovers is a rebel against social conventions – not necessarily the same conventions – and each ultimately accepts the right of society to impose its justified penalties. There is a sense in which each can be said not merely to acquiesce in punishment but to invite it.

The world of *Clarissa* is thus very much a mental world. As Coleridge observed, Richardson's story has a dream-like quality. It is the first great psychological novel, with a strong element of fantasy in it, especially in its structure, although the detail is so naturalistic that this is not immediately apparent. And to describe it as phychological is merely another way of saying that it is a novel of sentiment.

[4] *Clarissa* V 264 (Everyman III 371).

It is above all a novel. Richardson was the first English writer to demonstrate that an extended piece of naturalistic prose fiction could be a major work of art. *Clarissa* is by no means a faultless production, but it is technically remarkably sophisticated. Much of the power of the book no doubt is generated by elements in it of which Richardson himself was perhaps not fully aware. But in general he had a very good understanding of what he was doing. *Clarissa* is a highly accomplished technical achievement. And in *Clarissa*, as in all genuine works of art, technique and meaning are in the end inseparable: a close examination of the one inevitably leads to a deeper understanding of the other.

Richardson's technical mastery manifests itself with particular force and clarity in the opening sequences of the novel, those which deal with the events in the Harlowe household that precede Clarissa's elopement with Lovelace. At first sight this section may seem disproportionately lengthy; and some of Richardson's first readers complained that here 'the Story moved too slowly', and that far too much space was taken up by the altercations between Clarissa and her family. 'But', Richardson argues in his *Postscript*, '. . . those altercations are the Foundation of the whole, and therefore a necessary part of the work.' And if the account seems unusually 'circumstantial and minute' this is justified because it preserves 'that Air of Probability, which is necessary to be maintained in a Story designed to represent real Life'.[5]

Richardson's argument is valid. To appreciate just how valid it is, however, it is necessary to understand the extent and nature of the difficulties which he had set himself to overcome in this extensive prelude to the main action. That he did overcome them, and overcome them with such success, is a measure of his sheer craftsmanship as a novelist. Richardson's handling of the exposition of his story is masterly; and it is because the groundwork is laid so firmly here that the powerful emotions generated by the subsequent action and the wider significances it is made to bear seem so eminently justified. The sentimentalism of *Clarissa* always has a solidly realistic foundation.

In his Preface to the first edition Richardson states that a main purpose of the novel is

[5] *Clarissa* 4th ed. (1751) VII 367–8. Reprinted in my *'Clarissa': Preface, Hints of Prefaces and Postscript*, Augustan Repr. Soc., 1964.

To caution Parents against the *Undue* Exertion of their natural
Authority over their Children, in the great Article of Marriage:

And Children against preferring a Man of Pleasure to a
Man of Probity, upon that dangerous, but too commonly
received Notion. *That a Reformed Rake makes the best Husband.*[6]

Clarissa is a tragedy with a moral. And the tragedy occurs first
because the family try to force Clarissa to marry Solmes: second,
because Clarissa commits the original mistake of conducting a
clandestine correspondence with Lovelace, and then elopes with
him. But Clarissa is supposed to be an unusually virtuous and
intelligent girl, and her parents are supposed to be people who,
until this occasion, have acted with reasonable kindness and
good sense. Richardson's problem is to make his reader understand how a girl of Clarissa's reserved and modest nature should
find herself in the extraordinary situation she does – and preserve
throughout her integrity – and also how her family could bring
themselves to act with such appalling selfishness, cruelty and
stupidity. Richardson does make us understand these things; and
what is more he makes us accept and believe in a state of affairs,
a series of events, which on the face of it, is rather incredible.

The basis of Richardson's success lies in the painstakingly
detailed thoroughness with which he worked out the situation
within the Harlowe family, and all its ramifications – emotional,
financial and social; a situation which needs only Lovelace's
entrance upon the scene for it to develop in the way it does.

Richardson had originally intended to call the novel *The
Lady's Legacy*. The root of the trouble in the Harlowe family is
the decision by Clarissa's grandfather to bestow the bulk of his
estate on her, rather than on his son (Clarissa's father) or his
grandson (Clarissa's brother, James). The will is mentioned in
Anne Howe's first letter to Clarissa, which is also the first letter
in the book – and it is of basic importance.

The strongest emotion in *Clarissa* is lust – not surprisingly in
a novel that has a rape as its climactic incident. But it is not
sexual lust which primarily motivates the characters in this

---

[5] *Clarissa* 4th ed. (1751) VII 367–8. Reprinted in Brissenden,
'*Clarissa*'.

novel, it is the lust for power. In the Harlowe family this expresses itself most clearly in the lust for money – in Lovelace in the lust for sexual domination (Lovelace's desire for Clarissa is by no means a simple sexual one: it is more important for him to humiliate her than it is for him to possess and enjoy her physically – sex is the means by which he demonstrates his power over other people). Clarissa, through her simple desire to live her own life, to be true to her own sense of justice, her refusal to allow herself to be *used* by others, frustrates, stands in the way of, the desires and designs both of her family and of Lovelace.

The Harlowe family are in an extremely interesting social position. They have a great deal of money, although their rise to wealth has been relatively recent. They are *nouveaux riches* – but they are on the verge of moving out of this class into the real establishment. Political power depends for them largely on the ownership of land – social power, social prestige (and, to some extent, political power also) on becoming part of the aristocracy, on getting a title. Both can be attained through marriage. Clarissa, because she is not only the daughter of wealthy parents but also wealthy in her own right, is thus an attractive prize, and a most important piece in the complicated game of social-climbing chess played by the ambitious members of her family. Because of her financial independence she is, however, difficult to manage; and because she has given control of the estate she has inherited into the hands of her father she is particularly vulnerable to family pressure – the more so because she has a strong sense of filial piety. Clarissa really believes (as Richardson did) in the fifth commandment: to disobey her father's lawful orders in her eyes is a sin. The question, of course, is, 'what is lawful?' It was generally believed that parents had the right to forbid a daughter to marry a prospective husband whom they considered unsuitable, but that they did not have the right to force a daughter to marry a man whom she disliked. All sorts of pressures, of course, could be brought to bear on reluctant daughters – especially on a girl, like Clarissa, who was known to take her filial duties very seriously.

The situation is further complicated by the particular position in the family hierarchy occupied by Clarissa's brother, James. The historian Christopher Hill has revealed that owing 'to technical legal changes' which took place in the mid-seventeenth century the father became in effect life-tenant of the estate. The eldest son came to occupy a unique position of authority; and the estate, the family property, acquired greater importance than the individual owner.[7]

This situation is exaggerated in the Harlowe family because the father, a strong-willed man, is ill, and his wife, a weak but well-meaning woman, is powerless to restrain her son. It is given further dramatic force by the energetic characterisation of the son James: a brutal, selfish, vulgar and arrogant young man, who is perfectly capable of twisting his sister's arm in a fit of childish rage, but quite unable to behave like a gentleman in his quarrel with Lovelace. Taken out of the context of the family quarrel he is a grotesque caricature of the blustering young *parvenu*; but within the walls of Harlowe Place he is a thoroughly nasty and all too human bully.

The Harlowes, as Clarissa tells her friend Anne Howe, have long had 'the darling view . . . of *raising a family* as it is called . . . a view too frequently it seems entertained by families which having great substance, cannot be satisfied without Rank and Title'.[8] The aim is to get James a peerage – either through marrying him into the nobility, or through making him so wealthy that he can buy his way in. And the whole family is united in this aim, including the uncles, who are childless, and so can concentrate all their wealth and their ambitions on young James.

This careful scheme is unfortunately upset by two things: by Clarissa's character, and by an accident. Both, as befits a tragedy, have an ironical quality. Clarissa, without deliberately attempting to do so, makes her grandfather so fond of her that he bequeaths his estate to her instead of to her brother. This arouses the envy and finally the hatred of her brother and sister. Her good nature is her downfall. The accident occurs when Lord M., Lovelace's well-intentioned but rather stupid uncle, introduces him to the Harlowe family as a suitor to Bella instead of to Clarissa. Bella is the elder sister, and so has a right to first choice; but this right would normally have been waived if Lovelace had approached Clarissa, in whom he was really interested, in the

[7] 'Clarissa Harlowe and her Times', *Essays in Criticism* V (1955) 315.
[8] *Clarissa* I 70 (Everyman I 53).

beginning. He extracts himself from the embarrassing situation by cleverly proposing to Bella in such a way that she feels she ought to refuse him – or at least temporise. When he then transfers his attentions to Clarissa (as technically he now has the right to), this inflames Bella against her sister, and also revives an old enmity between brother James and Lovelace.

The situation is worsened when Clarissa now refuses to marry an alternative suitor, Mr Solmes. Solmes is no aristocrat and almost no gentleman – but he is embarrassingly rich, and he is prepared to abandon in favour of the Harlowes any commitments he may have to members of his own family in order to marry Clarissa. The Harlowes have no right to force Clarissa to marry Solmes (who is personally repulsive) but Lovelace has annoyed them so much that they lose all sense of proportion. Also, having chosen to feel aristocratically insulted by the Harlowes' behaviour towards him – particularly that of James – Lovelace secretly aggravates the whole position by spreading scandalous stories about himself and rumours that he is about to carry off Clarissa by force. His abduction of the lady is entered upon as much in a spirit of mischief as of revenge, and his desire to humiliate the Harlowes does not at first involve Clarissa. One of the ironic and tragic complications of the action as it develops after the elopement is that Lovelace, the more he genuinely and deeply falls in love with Clarissa, the more he feels driven to humiliate her. The rape was no part of his original scheme at all.

Clarissa's beauty as well as her goodness thus ironically contributes to her unhappiness. Two further elements in her character, each in its way admirable, play their part also. The first is, what for want of a better word, must be called her toughness. No one – not her family, nor Lovelace, nor even Clarissa herself – realises that she is the sort of person who can be pushed so far and no further, that she actually grows stronger through resisting unjust pressure. The growth of this steel-spring resistance in the girl's character is one of the most fascinating threads of development in the novel. The other is her sentimentality – almost in the modern sense of the word: her wish to believe the best rather than the worst of people. This is an amiable fault, but a dangerous one. Clarissa just cannot imagine the depths of cruelty to which her family, whom she has always thought to have loved her (partly, of course, because she believes members of families *ought* to love each other) can descend; and she has no conception of the sophisticated, premeditated, self-delighting villainy in which Lovelace indulges. This is another most important factor in the situation. Lovelace's almost childish delight in plotting, his deep commitment to revenge, the lengths to which he is prepared to go – these are all rather improbable and unpredictable but by no means impossible. He is an Iago-like character, with a genuinely diabolic air. Ultimately he becomes like a man possessed.

The final element in this complicated and involved set of relationships is the genuine love which grows between Lovelace and Clarissa, and which each, for various reasons, attempts to stifle and destroy. This, however, is really the motivating force of the middle section of the novel.

These, then, set out very briefly, are the main features of the situation in which Richardson places his characters at the beginning of the novel. It is unusually complex; but at the same time it has been planned with remarkable care and thoroughness. Richardson displays the attention to detail one expects in the writer of a detective story. And the purpose of the whole intricate design is to force Clarissa and her family further and further apart, so that she can be driven first into the arms of Lovelace and finally completely onto her own resources. The climax of the whole book is Clarissa's violation and then her triumph over Lovelace, her family and the world. 'It is all but one Story, with one Design', as one of Richardson's friends, defending the tragic conclusion, wrote: 'and the making the lady fortunate in the End, would have varied the Fact, and undermined his Design.'[9] Richardson's eyes, as he moved slowly through the seven volumes of his masterpiece, were set firmly on this predetermined conclusion. Thus although the writing is copious and often diffuse in *Clarissa*, there is little that can fairly be called superfluous. Every incident, every letter, is related to the main issue: every step the characters take leads them inevitably towards the central act of violation and the final glorification of the heroine.

Richardson's subsidiary aim in the first section of the novel is to get Clarissa out of the garden gate and into Lovelace's chariot, with her father's curse echoing after her – on the road at once to ruin and to triumph. His aim is to achieve this, and at the same

[9] Joseph Spence. In Brissenden, *'Clarissa'* 10.

time to show us how and why it happened, and in particular to enable us to understand the depth, violence and bitterness of the passions involved. Because he has laid the groundwork of their development so firmly, these feelings acquire a strong and irresistible life of their own. As a result, although the action moves slowly, whenever anything does happen it has an immediate and far-reaching effect. The scenes of increasingly angry argument between Clarissa and other members of her family become more and more powerful because we know in such detail what lies behind them.

The tension builds up gradually but relentlessly. In scene after scene of agonisingly circular and repetitive argument Clarissa's resistance to the plan to marry her to Solmes grows harder. As it does the true motives of her supposedly loving family begin to reveal themselves. None of them – incredible as it may seem – has the compassion, the courage, or the strength to help her. Guilty and ashamed of what they now find themselves forced to do, and frightened of going into her presence alone because of her power to arouse their pity, they band together like a lynching mob. They even go to the extent of signing a document to bind themselves to their purpose. And at this point in the novel the conventional paraphernalia of letters and papers is transformed into an integral part of the action. Forbidden to talk to anybody, Clarissa is forced to communicate with the rest of the Harlowe household by letter.

The spectacle of the Harlowe family furiously exchanging letters under the one roof with the daughter they have confined to her chamber has perhaps more than an air of madness about it. But it is the sort of madness which bitter and irresoluble family conflicts often generate. And the atmosphere which gradually builds up in Harlowe Place is most convincingly claustrophobic and oppressive. For Clarissa herself the most terrifying figure is the one with whom she has least immediate contact – her father. Her brother James storms and shouts at her, and physically maltreats her – roughly dragging her about the room, for instance, and letting her fall flat on her face – but he cannot frighten her as the mere thought of her father can. As I have remarked elsewhere, although Clarissa rarely sees him, '[her] father is a figure of tremendous psychological force . . . she receives his commands like distant thunderings from Mount

Sinai, and the curse he hurls after her as she flees with Lovelace haunts her to her deathbed'.[10]

To the besieged Clarissa, Lovelace, like Anne Howe, comes to represent sanity and reason, the fresh air of the world outside the Harlowe hot-house. But no hope could be more tragically deceptive than the hope Lovelace offers her. When she places herself in his protection she leaves the world of reality and steps into a bewildering and cruel maze of trickery and illusion. One of the greatest ironies in the novel is that Lovelace, the man who worships reason above all else, should be the master (and eventually the victim) of lies and deception. But this is merely one of the paradoxical elements in the tragic situation for which Richardson has been preparing with such care: the elopement of Clarissa with Lovelace, the painful and tangled growth of their love, and her final violation.

The most impressive section of *Clarissa* is that dealing with the events from the elopement to the rape and Clarissa's escape from Mrs Sinclair's house. Although this is long drawn out (it occupies Volume II and more than half of Volume III in the Everyman four volume edition), it is continuously interesting and often exciting and moving. The general ideas with which Richardson is concerned are here explored in a most searching and subtle way, the characters of Lovelace and Clarissa, and the complexities of their relationship, are realised with unusual vividness, detail and dramatic intensity. Moreover, it is through the emotional involvement of these two people, through their passionate and tortured responses to each other, that the intellectual or philosophical concerns of the novel are most forcefully presented and investigated. Richardson, like all great novelists, raises, and compels himself to answer, the question: what is man? In particular how does the real nature of man accord with the conventional notions we have of it? Is man innately good – or innately depraved? What do we mean by good and evil? How far do we understand our own or other people's motives? These are the issues which are examined – often with painful honesty – in *Clarissa*. And they are raised through the clash of two radically different personalities.

Clarissa represents one eighteenth-century ideal of feminine – indeed, human – excellence. She is intelligent, sensitive – she

[10] *Samuel Richardson* (London, 1965) 28.

has 'a feeling heart' – and conscientiously moral. She is
Christian, of course, and she generally takes an optimistic view
of things. She assumes that man is naturally benevolent, and that
given the chance he will behave unselfishly rather than selfishly.
She trusts people. She believes that parents naturally love their
children, and that children should be dutiful to parents, wives to
husbands. She also believes that any sexual relationship other
than that of marriage is sinful and must lead to unhappiness,
that conventional sexual morality is more important than love.
She believes, in short, in the enlightened, Christian, protestant
view of what the world ought to be like – and, at the same time,
acts on the assumption that the ideal bears a fairly close
resemblance to the reality. Richardson himself – at least in one
aspect of his personality – shared these views.

Lovelace, on the other hand, is a sceptic. He believes that man
is innately selfish, an intelligent animal who cloaks his savagery,
lusts and cruelty beneath the conventions of morality. He trusts
no one. Most people, in his view, are hypocrites, frightened to
acknowledge the emotional realities of the situations they are in,
terrified to admit that, in their inmost hearts, they are sexually
attracted to some people, and hate and despise others. He is a
man of reason, and a highly intelligent one. He is an ambiguous
character, by no means entirely a villain. Like Clarissa he acts
according to principle, and his principles are not altogether
despicable. He values intellectual honesty almost more than anything else; and many of the views he advances on politics, social
morality, marriage and related matters, though stated cynically,
are basically sensible. He, in fact, continually, by both words
and actions, shows up the hypocrisy, cruelty and selfishness of
the Harlowe family for what they are. He is a complex and
powerful figure; and Richardson is as deeply involved in him as
he is in Clarissa. As one critic, Brian Downs, has said, Richardson in all his work is preoccupied with 'the divided mind';[11] and
the conflict between Lovelace and Clarissa is the fictional body-
ing forth of a profound and ultimately irresoluble conflict within
Richardson's own heart. This conflict is echoed within the
personalities of the two characters: Clarissa is not pure white nor
Lovelace pure black – they, too, have 'divided minds', distorted
and troubled, battling not only externally with each other, but

[11] *Richardson* (1928) (London, 1969) 128.

also internally, as it were, with their own private fears and hopes, doubts and beliefs.

The dominating motive in the world as it is portrayed by Richardson is lust – sexual lust, lust for money and possession, but above all lust for power. 'Who loves not power?'[12] asks Clarissa, resignedly, as she attempts to analyse the motives and actions of the rest of her family. Beneath the polite façade of conventional behaviour human beings are as ruthless as any other animal: if they are forced into the position in which they have to fight for their lives, or in which their greed, their avarice, their lust, or their desire for domination over other people are aroused, it is the law of the jungle, and not the law of love – of benevolence and 'humanity' – which prevails. 'There is more of the savage in human nature than we are commonly aware of,'[13] says Lovelace. The only thing that prevents the ordinary person from behaving with complete selfishness is that he is denied the opportunities. As Lovelace, again, declares:

> Not a Sovereign on earth, if he be not a *good man*, and if he be of a warlike temper, but must do a thousand times more mischief than I. And why? Because he has it in his *power* to do more.[14]

This could perhaps be dismissed as simply part of the general rationalistic, Hobbesian philosophy that Lovelace has inherited from the libertines of Restoration drama, were it not for the way in which it can be paralleled by statements from most of the other characters in the novel. Where Lovelace talks of sovereigns, his servant talks of 'poor plane' people:

> We common folkes have our joys, and plese your Honner, lick as our betters have; and if we sometimes be snubbed, we can find our underlings to snub them agen: And if not, we can git a Wife mayhap, and snub her: So are Masters some how or other oursells.[15]

Anne Howe makes exactly the same point, only with a little more sadistic subtlety, when she defends her love of teasing

[12] *Clarissa* I 71 (Everyman I 54).
[13] Ibid. II 228 (Everyman II 247).
[14] Ibid. IV 158 (Everyman II 494).
[15] Ibid. III 86 (Everyman II 146).

Hickman. She reminds Clarissa that since this is the only opportunity she can ever have of exercising her power over a man, she
is making the most of it:

> This is my Time, you know, since it will be no more to *my*
> credit, than to *his*, to give myself those airs when I am mar-
> ried. He has a joy when I am pleased with him, that he would
> not know, but for the pain my displeasure gives him.
>
> . . . If I do not make Hickman quake now-and-then, he will
> endeavour to make me fear. All the animals in the creation
> are more or less in a state of hostility with each other. . . .
> I remember, that I was once so enraged at a game-chicken that
> was continually pecking at another (a poor humble one, as I
> thought him) that I had the offender caught, and without
> more ado, in a *Pet of Humanity*, wrung his neck off. What
> followed this execution? Why that other grew insolent, as
> soon as *his* insulter was gone, and was continually pecking at
> one or two under *him*. Peck and be hanged, said I – I might as
> well have preserved the first; for I see it is the *nature of the
> beast*.[16]

'The nature of the beast' – the phrase has a Hobbesian ring,
and like Hobbes Richardson sees the nasty brutish nature of the
beast operating in every human relationship. There can be no
love, he believed, without fear. The closest of friends in Richardson's world never forget that they must always be rivals in some
things at least – if it is only in the attempt to be virtuous. The
ideal friendship of Anne Howe and Clarissa is founded on the
understanding that each has a duty 'freely to *give* reproof, and
thankfully to *receive* it, as occasions arise'.[17] This is based on the
view that the best – if not the only – way of making people good
is to shame them into it: Anne Howe confesses to her friend that
she fears her almost as much as she loves her.[18] All of Richardson's characters – even the most admirable of them, delight in
'raillying' each other – teasing in a way which is often childishly
cruel and priggish.

Against the sombre background of *Clarissa* images of cruelty
appear and reappear like a pattern of scarlet thread. Lovelace is

[16] Ibid. III 69–70 (Everyman II 134).
[17] Ibid. III 63 (Everyman II 130).
[18] Ibid. III 66 (Everyman II 132).

continually justifying his action by referring to the way in which man mistreats not only his fellows but also the lesser animals. Cruelty to birds in particular seems to fascinate him: the image of Clarissa as the captive bird occurs several times, and he seems to see something very significant in the way in which human beings make use of birds simply as a source of pleasure for themselves:

> How usual a thing is it for women as well as men, without the least remorse, to ensnare, to cage, and torment, and even with burning knitting-needles to put out their eyes of the poor feather'd songster.[19]

It is in the long closing sections of the novel that the pattern of cruelty stands out most vividly: as Clarissa gradually sinks towards her peaceful death Lovelace, trapped in the hell of his own devising, becomes the tormented victim not only of his own remorse, but also of the almost gloating reproaches of Belford, suddenly grown priggish and self-righteous. As he waits upon the rack for news of the woman he is unable to see or to help, his frustrated love, hatred and despair explode in violent and painful tirades against the world, against himself, and against his friend:

> Confound thee for a malicious devil! I wish thou wert a post-horse, and I upon the back of thee! How would I whip and spur, and harrow up thy clumsy sides, till I made thee a ready-roasted, ready-flayed, mess of dog's meat; all the hounds in the county howling after thee as I drove thee, to wait my dismounting, in order to devour thee peace-meal; life still throbbing in each churned mouthful!
>
> Give this fellow the sequel of thy tormenting scribble . . . Every cushion or chair I shall sit upon, the bed I shall lie down upon (if I go to bed) till he return, will be stuffed with bolt-upright awls, bodkins, corking-pins and packing-needles: Already I can fansy, that to pink my body like my mind, I need only to be put into a hogshead stuck full of steel-pointed spikes, and rolled down a hill three times as high as the Monument.[20]

[19] Ibid. III 228 (Everyman II 247).
[20] Ibid. V 363–4 (Everyman III 451).

This is not pretty, but it is unforgettable. It stays in the mind like the torture machine in Kafka's *Penal Settlement*, or Svidrigailov's vision of hell in *Crime and Punishment*. It is grotesque and exaggerated but not improbable. And this is why the picture of humanity presented in *Clarissa* is so bleak and depressing. It is a distorted picture – but the terrible thing is that the distortion does not seem an impossible one. Lovelace's behaviour, extravagant and self-defeating though it may be, does not seem implausible; and the Harlowes are all too real. As Douglas Jefferson has said, the Harlowes are 'just ordinary mean, unattractive people, made monstrous by special circumstances'.[21] *Clarissa* is such a horrifying book because it suggests that, if the circumstances are special enough, there are very few of us who would not become monstrous too.

There *are* good people in the world, of course: Clarissa is presented as an example. She represents, moreover, the idealistic side of human nature: she refuses to think the worst of people until she is actually forced to, and she continues to believe that the virtuous, simply by the power of their virtue, can survive and triumph over a wicked world. But circumstances conspire cruelly against her – as they conspire against everyone else in the novel – to test this comfortable belief in every possible way. It is Clarissa herself who gives us the saddest vision of humanity in the novel, a vision she finds almost too painful to endure:

> I wish it could please God to take me to his mercy! – I can meet with none here – What a world is this! The good we hope for, so strangely mixed, that one knows not what to wish for! And one half of mankind tormenting the other, and being tormented themselves in tormenting![22]

At one level her death is not so much the triumph that Richardson wishes it to be as an admission that the notion of the absolute power of moral excellence cannot be maintained. The idealist must compromise his ideals with the reality of the situation in which he finds himself in order to survive. Clarissa is literally too good for this world. At another level her death is the last of her sentimental attempts to evade, to refuse to acknowledge, the

[21] Introduction to *Eighteenth-Century Prose, 1700–1780* (London, 1956) xxiii.
[22] *Clarissa* I 346 (Everyman I 265).

sexual realities of her relationship with Lovelace. It is the climax of a series of fainting fits, the vapours, weeping and rage: fits into which (to be fair to her) Lovelace has forced her.

The action of *Clarissa* demonstrates that although Richardson wants to believe, as the sub-title to *Pamela* puts it, in 'Virtue Rewarded', his view of human nature is fundamentally pessimistic. But the theme of *Clarissa* is not simply that there is evil in the hearts of men: it is more complex than this. In his Preface to the fourth edition of *Clarissa* Richardson gives as the first of his intentions in writing the novel: 'To warn the inconsiderate and thoughtless of the one sex against the base arts and designs of specious contrivers of the other.' At the sexual level the theme is the old one – so easily sentimentalised – of virtue in danger: 'Do not trust him, gentle lady'. But the theme is much wider than this: the sexual encounter between Lovelace and Clarissa is merely the focus for a general uneasiness and disquiet about the human condition. It is not just sexual virtue which is always in danger, but virtue in the most general sense – the notion (philosophically speaking) of absolute virtue is constantly threatened by experience, just as the man of goodwill, prepared to trust to the generous impulses of others, is continually in danger of having this trust abused. This danger in the field of morality is merely a specific example of a more general problem, the problem of certainty in knowledge of anything. The lesson *Clarissa* seems to teach is that nothing, except perhaps the inner voice of conscience, is ever what it seems. People are not to be trusted; expressions of love, affection, loyalty can never be taken at their face value; respectability, 'middle class morality', is a mask which society assumes to disguise the real nature of the beast. Ultimately the individual is alone: in the last resort all you can depend upon is yourself – or God. As Clarissa says in her will, 'I am nobody's'.

If this is the truth it is a very uncomfortable truth to live with. It is extremely unsettling to be made to realise, suddenly and without warning, that something you have believed to be the case is in fact radically different. Richardson continually subjects his characters – and thus himself and his readers – to shocks of this kind. The situations in which Clarissa is placed become progressively disillusioning, and the process is often painful and terrifying. Richardson's novels often take on a nightmarish character: the most disturbing scenes are those in which the mask is dropped, when an apparently friendly or harmless figure changes before one's eyes into the terrifying shape of the enemy one fears and hates the most. The obsessive delight which Richardson's villains take in disguise, and in revealing their true identity at the right moment, is part of this more general pattern of disillusionment which runs throughout the novels.

It can be seen in *Pamela*, where Mr B. twice dresses up as a maidservant in order to try to overcome Pamela by force. The trick is childish, but there is a moment of real terror in the second attempt when he reveals himself. Pamela thinks that she is sharing a bed with Nan, the other maid, but begins to feel suspicious of the way 'she' is behaving:

> Said I, is the Wench mad! Why, how now, Confidence? thinking still it had been *Nan*. But he kissed me with a frightful Vehemence; and then his Voice broke upon me like a Clap of Thunder.[23]

More subtly terrifying than this, however, is the incident at the inn when Pamela is being taken to Mr B.'s country retreat by his brutal housekeeper, the vile Mrs Jewkes. Pamela seizes a moment when she is alone with the woman who owns the inn to seek her help:

> I said, I am a poor unhappy young Body that wants your Advice and Assistance, and you seem to be a good sort of Gentlewoman, that would assist an oppressed innocent Person. Yes, Madam, said she, I hope you guess right, and I have the happiness to know something of the Matter before you speak. Pray call my Sister *Jewkes* . . .[24]

This is pure nightmare, and in *Clarissa* it occurs again and again. The elopement itself provides the pattern: Clarissa, seeking to escape from the intolerable situation within her family, places herself in the hands of a man who is determined to ruin her much more ruthlessly than her family are. The most terrifying feature of this situation is her dawning realisation that the whole thing has been arranged. To the reader, who knows more fully than she what is going on, it makes her position genuinely

[23] *Pamela* I 272.   [24] Ibid. I 90.

pathetic and frightening. When looked at in cold blood, Lovelace's power and energy in plotting and scheming, the way in which he can organise people and get them (often without their realising it) to further his plans, are rather incredible. Within the context of the novel, however, while we are actually reading it, he becomes a convincing and disturbing figure. And that Clarissa should place her trust in him, of all people, is ironic in the extreme.

Once Clarissa has committed herself into the hands of this insanely ingenious plotter, she is trapped in an almost incredible Chinese box of illusions. Nothing is what it seems to be, none of the people Lovelace introduces her to – with the exception of Belford and one or two minor characters – has his or her right name, or can be trusted. Mrs Sinclair, the supposedly respectable Scots widow, is a bawd, and the young ladies of her establishment are prostitutes. Her house – a symbol of the whole situation, with its inner building hidden from the street by the outer one – is not only a high class brothel, but it is not even in the area where Lovelace leads Clarissa to believe it to be. And he has arranged beforehand that Dorcas (not her real name of course), the 'artful Servant at the Vile house', shall pretend to be illiterate so that, unsuspected, she can take copies for him of Clarissa's correspondence. Once Lovelace has got Clarissa to London, and into Sinclair's establishment, everything takes on the unreal yet hyper-real atmosphere of a dream. Basically it is fantastic and incredible; but the people in it are so solidly and convincingly presented that, despite ourselves, we are compelled to believe in what is happening.

The section of the novel which deals with the events in London is dominated by Lovelace; and it has a remarkable richness and complexity of tone and texture. This is partly because of Lovelace's own character – a most involved, self-tortured, but at the same time lively and energetic one – and partly because of the complicated, almost self-contradictory manner in which the action develops. The novel here is at its most dramatic – and since dramatic interest is generally created and sustained through conflict, this is not surprising: conflict at every level is the essential characteristic of the situation Richardson is presenting. Nothing is allowed to develop simply, freely and in a straight line, as it were – everything is at cross purposes, events and people continually cut across each other sharply and jarringly. Moreover the outcome of the courses of action initiated, planned and executed by the characters is usually the reverse of what they have intended. This imbues the whole passage with a strongly ironic flavour.

Nowhere is this more apparent than in the relationship between the two lovers. As Lovelace observes, with wry humour, to Belford: 'I imagined, for a long while, that we were born to make each other happy: but, quite the contrary; we really seem sent to plague each other.'[25] Lovelace, of course, creates more than half the difficulties himself – he is determined to make Clarissa yield herself to him physically before they marry. His motives for this are complex: he genuinely wants to prove that love, not convention, is the basis of the relationship, he wants to assert his masculine superiority, he wants to humble the proud Harlowes – and deepest of all, he wants to punish himself. Like all sadists he is drawn almost as much by the desire to inflict pain on himself as by the urge to make others suffer. For whatever the reasons, he perpetually encourages Clarissa and then frightens her and antagonises her. She, for her part, refuses to acknowledge (at least on the surface) the element of physical desire in the relationship. Yet, at the same time, she is drawn, against her will, towards this man who torments and loves her. The relationship is fraught with guilt, fear and self-accusation. Improbable though it may be, it is sustained by the strength and vitality of the conflicting emotions it symbolically represents.

One of the most ironic aspects of the situation is that the means by which Lovelace brings Clarissa to trust him and finally to declare her love for him are such that they must, of their very nature, make the realisation of this love completely impossible. Lovelace's great plot becomes finally a trap not for Clarissa, but for himself – a most ingeniously painful way of punishing *himself* for his life of sexual freedom. Lovelace despite all his libertine rationality is, at the deepest level, a man haunted by sexual guilt. In this, he is (like Mr B.) a rather improbable rake. Lovelace is burdened, beneath his gay, free, aristocratic exterior, with the puritanical conscience of his creator.

For whatever the reasons, Lovelace is a most complex character, and the events in which he is involved have, as a result, the

[25] *Clarissa* III 261 (Everyman II 270).

tragically ironic characteristic of being perpetually and painfully self-defeating. Nowhere is this more obvious than in his most dazzling piece of strategy, the introduction of Captain Tomlinson. Just when Clarissa is becoming most suspicious, a respectable gentleman appears on the scene, who purports to be an emissary from her uncle. His mission is to bring about a reconciliation between Clarissa and her family. Nothing could delight and comfort the poor, harassed girl more. She is ready to forgive Lovelace, to overlook his tricks and deceptions (the situation, up to now, has perhaps warranted them), and she is even, at last, prepared to begin to allow herself to love him.

But Tomlinson is not what he seems: his real name is Patrick MacDonald, and he is a criminal acquaintance of Lovelace – the whole affair is a monstrous fraud. The scenes between Clarissa, Lovelace and Tomlinson thus have an extraordinarily ironic quality. Lovelace is to be pitied almost as much as Clarissa, for he is now thoroughly entangled in his own devices. Even if he could persuade Clarissa later on into an honourable marriage, the quite unforgivable truth would eventually have to come out, and any chance of Clarissa's finally loving him would be lost for ever. '*If I had never valued him*', she says to Tomlinson, '*he never would have had it in his power to insult me*; nor could I, if I had never regarded him, have *taken to heart as I do* the insult (execrable as it was), so undeservedly, so ungratefully given.'[26] It is a measure of the power of these scenes, that we feel (as we should) that Lovelace's deception of Clarissa in this way, is far more villainous than the physical violation which occurs later. Tomlinson gradually assumes the guise of a Mephistophelian familiar whom Lovelace will never be able to disown or escape from.

And Lovelace realises what he is doing but is unable to stop himself. 'Why had not this scene a real foundation?' he cries in half-mocking despair after he has described a particularly warm and affectionate encounter between himself, Clarissa and Tomlinson.

Do not despise me, Jack, for my inconsistency – In no two Letters perhaps agreeing with myself – Who expects consistency in men of our character? – But I am mad with Love –

[26] Ibid.

Fired by Revenge – Puzzled with my own devices – My Invention is my curse – My Pride my punishment – Drawn five or six ways at once, can *she* possibly be so unhappy as I? – Oh, why, why, was this woman so divinely excellent?[27]

At the purely dramatic level the deception of Clarissa by Lovelace and the gradual process of disillusionment through which she has to pass are at once moving, horrifying and fascinating. And the most interesting aspect of the way in which the situation develops is that it is at once deceptive *and* disillusioning: the more thoroughly Lovelace deceives her, the more powerful the illusion *he* creates, the less powerful become the illusions by which Clarissa has sustained her life – her belief in herself and other people. Lovelace brings into existence a horrible parody of the world in which Clarissa places her faith, gets her to accept it, and then destroys it. Thus at the symbolic or poetic level this dual process of deception and revelation provides a surreal analogue, a cruel parallel, of the painful process of self-discovery and disillusionment about other people that first her family and then Lovelace force Clarissa to go through.

Whether Richardson realises it or not, Mrs Sinclair is really Mrs Harlowe in another form – the nightmare version of the mother figure (significantly she becomes *physically* more brutal, repulsive and frightening as the book goes on). Mrs Harlowe, by conniving at the scheme to sell her daughter to Solmes, exhibits the morality of a whore-monger. And when Lovelace, at Hampstead, suddenly throws off the disguise which he has assumed of a benevolent old gentleman, his gesture echoes the behaviour of Mr Harlowe, and symbolically demonstrates the whole pattern of deceit and cruelty which he and the Harlowes have practised on Clarissa, and which Richardson fears we all practise on each other. The book abounds in those persona beloved by the psychoanalyst: father-figures and mother-figures, figures who, as in dreams, suddenly and terrifyingly change from friend to enemy. It is this which gives the book its peculiar intensity, and Lovelace his unique interest as a character.

Lovelace is in some ways an artificial character, a 'fancy piece' as Mrs Barbauld calls him, but nonetheless he comes to life in a most vigorous and independent way. And as the novel unfolds

[27] Ibid. IV 114 (Everyman II 460).

he exercises, both as symbol and suffering individual, a growing power and fascination over the reader. Richardson gives a brilliant picture of an acute, subtle, intelligent and inordinately proud man, torn between a longing to be loved and a desire to be feared, keenly aware of the pain he is causing the woman whom, in his perverted way, he loves, yet so delighted by his own ingenuity and cleverness that he cannot abandon the schemes he has invented. The schemes, indeed, give him more satisfaction than their accomplishment. 'I have ever had more pleasure in my contrivances than in the end of them,' he tells his agent, Joseph Leman. 'I am no sensual man; but a man of spirit – One woman is like another . . . In coursing all the sport is made by the winding Hare. A barn-door Chick is better eating.'[28] Nothing could be more purely sadistic. As Simone de Beauvoir remarks in her essay on Sade, 'Sadistic crime can never be adequate to its animating purpose. The victim is never more than a symbol . . . That is why the Bishop in *The 120 Days of Sodom* "never committed a crime without immediately conceiving a second".'[29] And Lovelace, like Sade, is a man fascinated by the *idea* of evil: the thought of temptation in itself is enough to excite him. He wants all fruits to be forbidden. At first, when his initial stratagems succeed so brilliantly, he is infectiously pleased with himself; but as he gradually begins to realise the true character of the woman he has entangled himself with, his very ingenuity becomes a torment to him.

And in Clarissa herself, of course, he chooses the perfect punishment. She *is* unusually reserved – a rather stiff, prudish young woman. 'Dear creature!' he exclaims in admiring and puzzled despair, 'Did she never romp? Did she never, from girlhood to now, hoyden?'[30] Had Clarissa been an ordinary woman she would either have succumbed to Lovelace or have left him. But her uncompromising rectitude, plus her deep and growing passion for the man, force him either to rape her or to marry her. And fate frustrates every attempt Lovelace makes to

[28] Ibid. III 88 (Everyman II 147).
[29] 'Must We Burn Sade?', in *The Marquis de Sade: The 120 Days of Sodom and Other Writings* (New York, 1966) 32 ['Faut-il brûler Sade?', originally published in *Les Temps Modernes* Dec. 1951–Jan. 1952].
[30] *Clarissa* IV 15 (Everyman II 383).

take the honourable course. There are times when he deliberately and teasingly works Clarissa up to the point of expecting a proposal, only to disappoint her hopes in some way; but there are also occasions when he is within an ace of throwing himself at her feet, or she of accepting him wholeheartedly, when something unaccountably goes wrong.

Lovelace's function in the allegorical scheme of the novel is complicated and even contradictory. At one level, he represents the ultimate logical extension of the eminently reasonable assumptions by which Clarissa can justify her opposition to her family. He has the intelligence and honesty to see through the Harlowes' pretentious hypocrisy. But Clarissa, when she is with him, supports her family and refuses to admit to him that they were in the wrong. She thus places herself in the ironic position of supporting the very attitudes and beliefs which, in the early part of the novel, she herself has been attacking, and which have in effect driven her into Lovelace's arms. The rape then is in part at least a violation not merely of Clarissa but also of the conventional values which she and her family represent: 'It is the most violent expression of that hatred of middle-class hypocrisy and materialism by which so much of the novel is animated'.[31] And the attack is pressed home in an unexpected way by Clarissa's refusal after the assault to marry her seducer. When she cries out to Lovelace: '*The man who has been the villain to me you have been, shall never make me his wife,*'[32] she is in effect acknowledging the rape, and flaunting it in the face of Lovelace and her own family; and she is also, of course, making them acknowledge it before the world. The rape has occurred because Clarissa has trusted those whom convention asserts ought to be trusted – her family, her friends and her lover. Now she is left with nothing but her belief in her own personal integrity. She has been forced to abandon most of the comfortable illusions which we normally cling to, and accept the full reality of the situation: and this she does with honesty and courage.

And so too, to do him justice, does Lovelace. In the first long letter he writes to Belford after the rape he admits that what he has done to Clarissa is unforgivable. And the terms in which he admits this are, significantly, *sentimental*: if what he has done is

[31] R. F. Brissenden, *Samuel Richardson* (London, 1965) 27.
[32] *Clarissa* V 75 (Everyman III 222).

wrong, it is wrong not so much because of the nature of the act
itself as because of what it means to Clarissa.

> But people's extravagant notions of things alter not *facts*,
> Belford: And, when all's done, Miss Clarissa Harlowe has but
> run the fate of a thousand others of her Sex – Only that they
> did not set such a romantic value upon what they call their
> *Honour*; that's all.
>
> And yet I will allow thee this – That if a person sets a high
> value upon anything, be it ever such a trifle in itself, or in the
> eye of others, the robbing of that person of it is *not* a trifle to
> *him*. Take the matter in this light, I own I have done wrong,
> great wrong, to this admirable creature.[33]

At the level of moral theory, then, the movement of the action,
the significance of the climax is clear. At the level of human
passion it is more confused, but just as forceful. Lovelace's determination to rape Clarissa, to humble her before he marries her,
is also a savage assertion of that superiority which convention
has always assigned to the male – and to which marriage, of
course, is a threat. The rape Clarissa suffers at his hands can be
regarded as a punishment meted out to her by the aggrieved
masculinity which Lovelace represents. Clarissa is an independent
woman – but she is also a prude and a sentimentalist so far as
sex is concerned – and convention, in the form of the unconven-
tional Lovelace, punishes her on both counts: for daring to rebel,
to defy her respectable family, and also for failing to respond to
the sexual realities of the situation in which she places herself.
At a deep and primitive level there is a sense in which Clarissa
both asks and deserves to be raped.

But if the rape is almost a natural consequence of Clarissa's
puritanical attempt to deny the existence of sexual desire, it is
at the same time a confession of Lovelace's impotence. What he
really wants, as he confesses pathetically time and again, is that
Clarissa should love him for himself. As a *lover*, however, in the
full sense of the word, he is a pathetic failure. He continually
destroys and undermines the trust and affection which normally
accompany the growth of physical desire. The only way in
which he can make Clarissa confess that she loves him is by the
extraordinary and devious method of causing himself pain – he

[33] Ibid. V 47 (Everyman III 199).

takes ipecacuanha, and makes himself physically ill. Lovelace in fact battles with himself as strenuously to deny love – tenderness and affection – as Clarissa does to deny her own physical desires. With an almost religious ardour Lovelace confirms and strengthens his flagging determination to subdue his mistress before allowing himself to love her: to make her fear him before allowing her to love him: to force her to acknowledge that superiority which he feels is his by right. But the grand culmination of Lovelace's brilliant plotting is a failure on all counts, a completely hollow victory. In the first place he has to drug her into insensibility, so that it can be regarded as a token rape only; in the second, the result of the assault is not to make Clarissa love him, but to confirm her hatred and contempt for him.

It is a sad and sorry story. Yet one of the morals to be drawn from it is that life without love is impossible: in a negative and perverse but yet profoundly moving way it demonstrates both the truth and the falsity of the sentimental assertion that man is by nature a benevolent creature. Lovelace provides a scarifying comment on the complacent assumption that all men are naturally good – but at the same time he presents a pathetic picture of a man struggling against his better feelings. 'What *Sensibilities*', says Clarissa to him, 'must thou have suppressed! – What a dreadful . . . hardness of heart must thine be; who canst be capable of such emotions as sometimes thou hast shown; and of such sentiments as sometimes have flowed from thy lips; yet canst have so far overcome them all, as to be able to act as thou hast acted . . .'[34]

The shocking thing, so far as certain eighteenth-century conventional beliefs were concerned, is that the better feelings are defeated. Until the final act of violation Clarissa just cannot believe that Lovelace or any civilised man, could be completely and deliberately cruel and selfish: in her delirium after the rape, she confesses to Lovelace that at first she had found him attractive:

At first, I saw something in your Air and Person that displeased me not. . . . You acted not ignobly by my passionate Brother. Every-body said you were brave: Every-body said you were generous. A *brave* man, I thought, could not be a *base*

[34] Ibid. IV 391 (Everyman III 152).

man: A *generous* man could not, I believed, be *ungenerous*, where he acknowledge *obligation.* . . . You seemed frank as well as generous: Frankness and Generosity ever attracted me: Whoever kept up those appearances, I judged of their hearts by my own . . .[35]

Clarissa is made to suffer a terrible disillusionment – and it is a disillusionment with the widest social implications. Her story is a comment on the facile assumption that man is naturally a rational and benevolent creature. It provides, in sharply focused human terms, through the sufferings of two firmly realised individuals, a tragic revelation of the insufficiency and one-sidedness of the sentimental picture of man; but at the same time, Lovelace, the pitiable, perverted and impotent villain, demonstrates the value and importance of the sentimental ideal, of the hope that man can realise his potentialities for altruism, generosity and honesty, of the necessity for believing in the sanctity of the individual.

In his examination of the conventional moral assumptions of his age Richardson spares neither himself nor his characters. What we might call the theoretical or dialectical exhaustiveness of the novel is matched by the complexity and depth of the feelings aroused in the characters involved in this moral drama. Once Richardson has established his situation he is committed to working it through to its tragic conclusion. It is this which gives the novel an organic life and integrity which makes all its limitations, severe though some of them may be, seem in the last resort irrelevant. *Clarissa* is a great novel, and its greatness lies in the rigour, the unremitting thoroughness and the compassion with which the sentimental ideal is tested against the reality of man's nature.

[35] Ibid. V 58 (Everyman III 208).

2

The Sentimental Comedy:
Tristram Shandy

In his *Comprehensive Etymological Dictionary of the English Language*, first published in 1967, Dr Ernest Klein notes that the word 'sentimental' was 'coined by the English clergyman and novelist, Laurence Sterne (1713–68) in 1767 (in the title of his *Sentimental Journey*)'. The statement is riddled with inaccuracies. 'Sentimental' first appears in Sterne's writings not in 1767 but 1759,[1] in Volume I of *Tristram Shandy*; *A Sentimental Journey* was published in 1768 not 1767; and the word in any case had been in existence for some years before Sterne used it. It is understandable, however, that the myth that 'sentimental' was invented by Laurence Sterne should still be perpetuated almost two hundred years after his death. So far as the sentimentalism of the eighteenth century is concerned he is a central figure.

He is also an enigmatic one. From the beginning he has puzzled and irritated people almost as much as he has delighted them. While he has never lacked enthusiastic and discerning admirers there has also always been a group of intelligent and perceptive readers who have found both the man and his books if not altogether unbearable at least absurd and pretentious. 'Mere *amusers* are never respected', said Walter Bagehot a century ago, writing about Sterne and one of his most savage critics, Thackeray.[2] And it is clear that for certain sensibilities the fact that such an irreverent and bawdy amuser should be taken seriously is infuriating. F. R. Leavis, for instance, contemptuously dismisses Sterne's work from his 'great tradition' as 'irresponsible (and nasty) trifling'.[3]

---

[1] For a discussion of the theory that Sterne may have used the word in 1739–40 see above p. 98.
[2] *Literary Studies* (London, 1911) II 121.
[3] *The Great Tradition* (London, 1948) 2 note 2.

But Sterne obstinately refuses to be dismissed. Not only are *Tristram Shandy* and *A Sentimental Journey* still widely read but they are perhaps better understood in some ways today than at any time since they first appeared. His 'trifling', rightly interpreted, is the play of a complex and sensitive intelligence which is fascinated by the paradoxes of existence. He is not a philosopher, but the problems which excite his interest – communication, meaning, identity, time – are philosophical problems. And his approach to them seems curiously modern: he clearly belongs, in one aspect of his writing, with the perpetual avant-garde of literature, with Joyce, Beckett, Nabokov, Ionesco, Borges and the wilder guerrilla groups like concrete poets and dadaists.

At the same time he is a highly traditional writer – often most so when he appears to be most revolutionary. The way in which he plays with the physical structure of the book, for instance – displacing chapters and prefaces, scattering black, marbled and blank pages throughout the text, transforming the dash into a unique system of punctuation – seems both original and prophetic: it obviously prefigures the attempt of William Burroughs to produce the 'cut-up' novel. Yet as Wayne C. Booth has demonstrated, a great many of the comic techniques which may seem at first sight to be of Sterne's own invention are part of a tradition of parody and playfulness which had been growing up within the novel itself, and which also looks back to the older traditions of learned wit and dramatic rhetoric.[4] It is quite possible that there is not one of Sterne's tricks and methods – from asterisks and marbled pages to dislocated chapters and disordered time schemes – which cannot be paralleled in the work of earlier writers. But the important thing, of course, is that the amalgam of all these rather trite and mechanical fooleries which Sterne produces is peculiarly his own – a unique fictive mode, with its own organic vitality.

Like almost every other aspect of Sterne's work it reveals his fascination with the general problem of communication. Sterne possessed a quite unusually heightened awareness of the way in which the means and forms of expression condition not only *how* we communicate with each other but also *what* is communicated. One of the basic jokes in *Tristram Shandy* resides in

[4] 'The Self-conscious Narrator in Comic Fiction before *Tristram Shandy*', PMLA LXVII (1952) 163–85.

the paradox that the very act of writing his biography must prevent Tristram from ever concluding it:

> I am this month one whole year older than I was this time twelve-month; and having got, as you perceive, almost into the middle of my fourth volume – and no farther than to my first day's life – 'tis demonstrative that I have three hundred and sixty-four days more life to write just now, than when I first set out; . . . – I shall never overtake myself – whipp'd and driven to the last pinch, at the worst I shall have one day the start of my pen – and one day is enough for two volumes – and two volumes will be enough for one year.[5]

Sterne, it is clear, would have had no difficulty in understanding Marshall McLuhan: both as a physical thing and as a process in which Tristram and his creator are involved, *Tristram Shandy* is a beautifully apt and quite conscious demonstration of the doctrine that 'the medium is the message'.[6] And Sterne's message is essentially *sentimental* – as he understood, or came to understand, that elusive and complex term.

This may seem a rather obvious thing to say but nonetheless it is worth saying, for sentimentalism is much more than the theme or subject of *Tristram Shandy* and *A Sentimental Journey* – it is their animating spirit. It was Sterne's innate genius for creating characters and endowing them with life which made him a novelist; but the mode in which this genius worked, the forms of thought and feeling in which it chose to express itself, were essentially sentimental – in the non-pejorative sense of the word. What transforms *Tristram Shandy* from an exercise in learned satire or dramatic rhetoric or obscure bawdry into a novel is primarily its sentimentalism.

When Sterne began to write the history *ab ovo* of Tristram Shandy, Gentleman, however, it seems fairly clear that he did not realise he was going to produce a *novel*. Like Richardson,

[5] *Tristram Shandy* 285–6 (IV, xiii).

[6] In his widely ranging and suggestive article, 'Sterne and the Delineation of the Modern Novel', in *The Winged Skull* ed. Arthur H. Cash and John M. Stedmond (Kent State, U.P., 1971) 21–41, Robert Gorham Davis observes that '*Tristram Shandy* demonstrates more fully and translucently the basic ontology of the novel, the sense of what the novel really is and does, as we have come to understand it . . . than any single modern novel you can mention' (p. 23).

who 'slid into' the writing of *Pamela*, he discovered that he was a novelist only after he had become fully engaged in the writing of his book. The point at which this occurs (as I have attempted to demonstrate in detail elsewhere[7]) can be located with some accuracy: *Tristram Shandy* only becomes a novel towards the end of Volume I when Toby and Walter quite clearly undergo a creative transformation from Scriblerian humours into living characters – and this transformation coincides, significantly enough, with the emergence of sentimentalism as a major theme. Up till this point they seem to have existed in Sterne's imagination primarily as caricatures, puppet figures from the world of learned satire. Once he sets them really talking with each other, however, the novel comes to life, energised and animated by the comic bond of love and misunderstanding by which the two brothers are united.

There seems little doubt that Sterne's original intention had been simply to produce a bawdy and irreverent satire on pedantry and humbug in the tradition of Rabelais, Swift and Pope, with a strong local flavour – something after the style of his slight but embarrassingly successful lampoon, *The History of a Good Warm Watchcoat*, in which he had cleverly sent up some of the big-wigs involved in the ecclesiastical politics of York. His immediate ambition, we can fairly safely assume, was to produce the *Memoirs of a Yorkshire Martinus Scriblerus*. But Sterne, like Richardson, almost immediately burst the bonds of the conventions within which his work had found its immediate inspiration: *Tristram Shandy* is greater than *Scriblerus* for the same reason as *Pamela* is greater than *The Family Instructor* – because it is a *novel*. That is to say, it is a work of fiction presenting, or telling the story of, convincing and lifelike characters: behind the elaborate façade of *Tristram Shandy* there lies a real world.

It cannot be denied, however, that at one level at least, there appears to be a conflict between the inner life of the novel and its outer form. The way in which Tristram tells his story is, in itself, continually frustrating and irritating. We are always being whisked away from the parlour at Shandy Hall or the bowling green on some wild digressive goose chase at the very moment when we feel that we are at last going to be given the

7 '"Trusting to Almighty God": Another Look at the Composition of *Tristram Shandy*', *The Winged Skull* 258–69.

chance to get to know Walter and Uncle Toby and Trim and
my mother. But we never do really get to know them: they
remain amongst the most tantalising and elusive characters in all
fiction. Yet in a paradoxical fashion the obliqueness and in-
completeness of the way in which Sterne presents the Shandy
world ultimately reinforces the reader's impression of its reality.
As Coleridge (one of Sterne's shrewdest critics) observes, 'the
digressive spirit [is] not wantonness but the *very form* of his
genius, the connection is given by the continuity of the characters'.[8]

But although Sterne's method of presenting the Shandys ultimately strengthens our sense of their reality it frustrates our
attempt to involve ourselves with them. We are never allowed
to identify ourselves with the people in the novels of Sterne as
we seem to be able to do with the characters created by other
novelists. This is thoroughly in keeping, however, with the
spirit of the book, for the way in which Sterne frustrates the
desires of the reader to get closer to his characters is in essence
equivalent to the way in which these characters are themselves
perpetually failing to communicate with each other. The comedy
of the Shandy brothers arises from the fact that it is their hobby-
horses, the things they would most dearly love to explain to each
other, which always obstruct their attempts to establish that
intellectual *rapport* which they both desire. And, significantly
enough, it is Tristram's own hobby-horse which prevents him
from telling his story to us in the normal way: it is his superb
self-confidence that he and only he knows how to tell his own
story that leads him on such a madly erratic course: 'What a rate
have I gone on at', he exclaims, half-way through the book, in
bewildered self-admiration, 'curvetting and frisking it away,
two up and two down for four volumes together, without looking
once behind, or even on one side of me, to see whom I trod
upon! . . . – up one lane – down another, through this turn-pike
– over that, as if the arch-jockey of jockeys had got behind me.'[9]

Yet, in spite of their hobby-horses, Walter and Toby are able
to make some contact with each other; and in spite of all
Tristram's disruptive curvetting and frisking the reader receives

[8] *Coleridge's Miscellaneous Criticism*, ed. Thomas Middleton Raysor
(London, 1936) 126 (Lecture IX: '*Wit and Humour*').
[9] *Tristram Shandy* 298 (IV, xx).

a vivid and enduring impression of the Shandy world. On the face of it this may seem paradoxical. Perhaps it is – but it is nonetheless true. And it is with the truth and mystery of this paradox that Sterne is most deeply concerned.

Somehow meaning is established, somehow communication occurs. Stated in the most general terms, what Sterne is preoccupied with are the attempts which every man must make, first to discover a meaning in or to impose a meaning on the apparently insensate and unordered universe of things into which we are born, and next to communicate this meaning to his fellow human creatures. We all need to make both the world and our own personal lives significant in some way to ourselves, and we all need to be able to make ourselves understood to other people. As John Traugott has said, 'Given any vagary of existence, every man will create his own rhetoric.'[10] But as the tangles that Walter and Uncle Toby get themselves into demonstrate, no rhetoric, no interpretation is ever perfect.

The theme of Sterne's work, looked at in a slightly different way, might be described as the comedy of human imperfection – or human limitation. At the lowest level this comedy plays itself out in the struggle between man, conscious and intelligent, and the unconscious material universe. We are all, like Tristram himself, the 'sport of small accidents';[11] sash-windows, like the rain, can fall on the just as well as the unjust, and time is the servant of no man: no matter how hard he tries, Tristram, from the very nature of things, will never be able to make his nose grow straight – or finish his own biography. At a higher level, both of irony and pathos, the comedy of human limitations displays itself in the conflict between man and his own nature. Not only are we all victims from time to time of the quirks of fate or chance, but we are also, often unconsciously, the victims of our human constitution, and of our own attempts to act deliberately and intelligently in a contingent and senseless universe. Mr Shandy invites the disasters in which he becomes involved because he tries too hard to make life meaningful, and to control the world. He is the comic symbol of mankind perpetually entangling itself in its own devices, confounding itself in its

[10] *Tristram Shandy's World: Sterne's Philosophical Rhetoric* (Berkeley and Los Angeles, 1954) 112.
[11] *Tristram Shandy* 166 (III, viii).

efforts to establish order and significance in what William James was to describe as the 'big blooming buzzing confusion' of existence.

The effort, of course, is not always unsuccessful: by the exercise of reason and judgment we are able not only to make sense out of things but also to control them; and by the use of language we are able to communicate with each other. But there comes a point at which reason and logic – the power to systematise and order things and ideas – seems to break down. Richardson was preoccupied with the problems which arise when our efforts to systematise our moral and social life begin to falter: his heroines are examples of the special individual human case against which all absolute principles of morality must eventually be tested. Sterne too was aware of this particular moral difficulty, but he saw it merely as one aspect of the general problem of human existence. The Shandys are symbols of man's gallant but never completely successful attempt to grapple intelligently and reasonably both with the unpredictable universe of things and also with his own irrationality. Walter is unable to protect his infant son from such contingencies as Susannah's faulty memory, and Trim's zeal in making artillery – and he is equally unable to conduct a rational discourse with his wife: try as he might he is unable to turn her into 'a woman of science':

> she went out of the world at last without knowing whether it turned *round*, or stood *still*. – My father had officiously told her above a thousand times which way it was, – but she always forgot.[12]

It is in the sphere of human relations – of what, in a more limited sense, Richardson termed 'relative duties' – that Sterne finds the greatest material for comedy and pathos. It is not Walter's and Toby's whims in themselves which are ridiculous and pathetic but the way in which the exercise of their fancies impinges on the people with whom they live (in its own way *Tristram Shandy* is as great a novel of family life as *Clarissa*). The great problem of living in society is that of understanding other people and of getting them to understand us; and it is in just this aspect of living that our human limitations are most

[12] Ibid. 472 (VI, xxxix).

apparent and most frustrating. 'If the fixure of *Monus's* glass, in the human breast . . . had taken place', says Tristram as he hunts for some way of conveying the essential character of Uncle Toby to the reader, '. . . nothing more would have been wanting, in order to have taken a man's character, but to have taken a chair and gone softly, as you would to a dioptrical bee-hive, and look'd in, – view'd the soul stark naked . . .'[13] But we can neither view nor display the soul stark naked – 'our minds shine not through the body, but are wrapt up here in a dark covering of uncrystalized flesh and blood'[14] – and it is often when we are most anxious that they should shine forth that the dark covering is most obscure. As Coleridge acutely observes, Walter's character exhibits 'a craving for sympathy in exact proportion to the oddity and unsympathizability'.[15]

Sympathy is exactly the right word, for it is in sympathy that Sterne sees the solution – or, at least, the partial solution – to the perplexities and sad confusion of life. Thus if the theme of *Tristram Shandy* (and to a large extent of *A Sentimental Journey*) can be stated as the comedy of human limitations, the books themselves may be regarded as a positive demonstration of the way in which these limitations may be, in part at least, transcended. Against the isolating and socially disruptive force of the hobby-horse and the ruling passion Sterne sets the power of sympathy: man is saved from the loneliness to which he is confined, through his inability to communicate exactly his own thoughts and feelings and to understand exactly those of other men, by his capacity for sympathetic imagination, his ability to put himself in the other person's place, and to picture to himself his joys and sorrows. Thus, although Walter is a character who discourages the sympathy he needs, he is not deprived of it. Toby does not pretend to understand his brother's speculative flights and philosophical prejudices – but he *does* understand that the enjoyment of them is necessary to his brother's happiness. Out of the affection which they have for each other, and out of their own good nature, the brothers are prepared not simply to tolerate but to sympathise with each other's idiosyncrasies.

Sterne's sentimentalism, his advocacy of the virtues of sensi-

---

[13] *Ibid.* 74 (I, xxiii).
[14] *Ibid.* 75 (I, xxiii).
[15] *Coleridge's Miscellaneous Criticism*, ed. Raysor 124.

tivity, tact and tolerance – of respect for that personal integrity which Clarissa Harlowe had eventually to sacrifice her life to protect – can thus be seen as an integral part of what is fundamentally an ironic and sceptical attitude to life. And the way in which the brothers' love for each other enables them to surmount the barrier of intellectual incomprehension which separates them is a positive demonstration of the power of the cardinal sentimental virtue – sympathy. Whether Sterne intended it or not, *Tristram Shandy* may be read as an illustration and verification of sentimentalism – of the psychological and moral theories advanced and developed by Shaftesbury, Hume and Adam Smith.

But the greatness of *Tristram Shandy* resides primarily not in its philosophical implications but in its fictive, its novelistic qualities. Sterne may have originally intended his book to be an exercise in 'philosophical' satire, a farce of Scriblerian humours, but he could not prevent himself from becoming interested in his humours as individual human beings: his caricatures develop into characters. That this should have happened is an incidental illustration of one of the main themes of the novel – the ultimate superiority of the individual to the system: Walter Shandy's attainment of human stature, his emergence as a unique and living personality, is a comment on the notion that people can never be finally typed and labelled. This is the point which all anti-pedantic wit makes, although in satire of the Scriblerian sort the emphasis is usually placed more on the failure of grandiose schemes of classification than on the ultimate indefinability, the positive intrinsic value, of the individual personality.

The emergence of the characters in *Tristram Shandy* came about because Sterne, like Richardson, possessed unknown to himself the genius of a novelist, a genius which the writing of *Tristram Shandy* released. In particular, he possessed the genius of a *sentimental* novelist, that is to say a novelist who is more interested in the analysis of character and situation than in simply telling a story. Indeed every novelist who is more than a mere story teller or reporter must be to some extent a man of sentiment. James, Proust, Joyce, Virginia Woolf, Samuel Beckett – these could all be described as sentimental novelists: they are interested in the individuality of their characters; they examine states of mind – sentiments – rather than simple actions; and they are all concerned with the inner moral significances of the situations in which they place or discover their characters. Joyce, indeed, is remarkably like Sterne in many ways. His work exhibits similarly sceptical fascination with schemes of thought and belief, with man's attempts to construct some bridge of logic and reason across 'the incertitude of the void'.[16] At the same time he demonstrates the tragi-comic inability of men to communicate by language and logic alone. Both *Tristram Shandy* and *Ulysses* could carry the sentimental sub-title, *'or the Power of Sympathy'* – it is sympathy which brings Stephen and Bloom together just as it enables the Shandy brothers to love, and, at one level, understand each other.[17] The emergence of the characters in *Tristram Shandy* can thus be seen in one way as a demonstration of the triumph of sentimentalism in the world of learned satire.

The characters do not establish themselves firmly, I have suggested, before chapter xxi of Volume I. Here Walter and Toby really begin to talk to each other, and here for the first time we learn that Uncle Toby (previously and uniquely referred to as Mr Toby Shandy) has a military past and is also, partly as a result of a wound sustained on active service, a man of 'a most extream and unparallel'd modesty of nature'. The fictive rather than the satirical pattern in the book now assumes a predominant position. Some signs of this coming ascendancy can be discerned in earlier chapters. Walter, for instance, though not I think seen clearly by Sterne, begins to assert himself as a character sooner than Toby. Signs of this can be observed in chapter xvi, in the account we are given of his impatient and angry fretting on the way back from London, out of patience with his wife for the 'vile trick' which either deliberately or through weakness, she had put upon him. The way in which he teases Mrs Shandy with satirical descriptions of the foolish figure

[16] *Ulysses* (London, 1937) 658.
[17] Joyce acknowledged an affinity between what he was trying to do in *Finnegans Wake* and what Sterne had achieved in *Tristram Shandy*. In *Finnegans Wake*, he told Eugene Jolas, 'I am trying to build many planes of narrative with a single aesthetic purpose. Did you ever read Laurence Sterne?' And the broken sentence which concludes *Finnegans Wake* was perhaps suggested by the similar non-conclusion of *A Sentimental Journey*. See 'Sterne and the Delineation of the Modern Novel', by Robert Gorham Davis, in *The Winged Skull* 21–41.

they will cut in church the next Sunday, and the way he syllogises with himself 'for a stage or two together' on the word 'weakness' are both characteristic and amusing. But the telling touch, the one stroke which really brings the whole passage to life, is the greengages:

> what vexed him more than every thing else was the provoking time of the year, – which, as I told you, was towards the end of *September*, when his wall-fruit, and green gages especially, in which he was very curious, were just ready for pulling: – 'Had he been whistled up to *London*, upon a *Tom Fool's* errand in any other month of the whole year, he should not have said three words about it.'[18]

The greengages, like the hinge on the parlour door which was never oiled, and the thread-paper which Walter uses to mark his place in Slawkenbergius, is one of those minute, but precise, touches of domestic detail that do so much to bring the Shandy world to life. In their own way they are more effective than a whole page of that exact and detailed description which the nineteenth-century realists taught us to regard as necessary in a novel. The things which Sterne introduces into his picture of life at Shandy Hall are often, in themselves, slight and trivial; but they are usually of great importance in the lives of the characters. It is not the squeaking hinge in itself which is important, but the effect which this trifle has on Walter's mind – just as the winding of the clock takes on an added significance because of the train of associations which it sets up in the mind of Mrs Shandy. In his awareness of things such as these and of the part which they can play in a person's life Sterne reveals how closely he himself approximates to one aspect of the ideal pattern of the man of sentiment, for he reveals himself here as one who is remarkably conscious of the way in which things which are of trifling importance in the eyes of the world may, for certain individuals, be the cause of misery or happiness. He reveals himself, that is to say, as one who is tactfully and sensitively – or sentimentally – aware of the foibles of others. Sterne's insistence that a man's hobby-horse, his ruling passion, may have its origins in a mere bagatelle, though not originally or

[18] *Tristram Shandy* 41 (I, xvi).

exclusively sentimental, is completely in harmony with the sentimental attitude to life.[19]

A concern primarily with character rather than action is, as I have already suggested, a distinguishing feature of the sentimental novelist. It may be useful, therefore, at this point to have a closer look at the way in which Sterne presents his characters. His methods are interesting in themselves; and also in some ways remarkably original. Basically his technique is historic: we are never allowed to forget that we are being told *about* Walter and Toby by someone who once knew them. But as he becomes more interested in his characters his presentation of them tends to become more dramatic. The way in which the two methods, the historic and the dramatic, are blended, leads to great complexity of tone. The members of the Shandy household are distanced from us in time: they are remembered. They are also, however, continually being brought into vivid close-up: we hear their voices, we see them in action – we follow the odd cross-currents of Walter's stream of thought, and catch the infection of Toby's excitement and delight in his mimic battlefield. They both exist – as does the whole Shandy household – very plausibly as *remembered* persons. The hobby-horse, the ruling passion, is naturally most important; but Sterne seems to be conscious of it in a very spontaneous, unforced way:

> My father was never able to give the history of this distemper, – without the remedy along with it.
>
> 'Was I an absolute prince', he would say, pulling up his breeches with both his hands, as he rose from his arm-chair, 'I would appoint able judges at every avenue of my metropolis, who should take cognizance of every fool's business who came there ...'[20]

The thing to note here is the apparent exactness of the memory: a habitual remark is remembered with a typical action.

[19] Cf. Hannah More in her *Sensibility, A Poetical Epistle* (1782):
Since trifles make the sum of human things,
And half our misery from our foibles springs;
Since life's best joys consist in peace and ease,
And few can save or serve, but all may please:
Oh! let th'ungentle spirit learn from hence,
A small unkindness is a great offence.

[20] *Tristram Shandy* 46 (I, xviii).

The use of 'he would say', the imperfect tense of the verb, is a common practice with Sterne in describing the doings of the Shandys: it suggests the continuing pattern of their lives – a pattern in which Walter Shandy waxed eloquent every time the parlour door squeaked open, but never found the time to oil it; in which Uncle Toby blushed regularly at the mention of Dinah and the coachman; and in which the winding of the clock and the despatching of some other little family concernments were dutifully accomplished on the first Sunday night in every month. Sterne usually accompanies his account of some habitual action with a precise and vivid memory of a particular occurrence – often, as in the very first chapter, of a particular occurrence which in some way disturbs the established routine. The moments he remembers are not always so disturbing as Mrs Shandy's untimely inquiry about the family time-piece: usually the habitual pattern cross-fades so gently into the particular instance that it is difficult to say where one begins and the other leaves off.

A particularly fine example of this technique (though less subtle than some) occurs in the concluding three paragraphs of chapter xxiv, Volume III. Two particular incidents are recounted: the breaking of the Dutch drawbridge across the ditch by Corporal Trim and Bridget, and the coughing fit brought on in Walter by the smoke from Toby's pipe. These are set, however, in the context of the innumerable remembered occasions on which Walter would tease Toby about his military hobby and would get him to tell in his innocent way the story of Trim's accident:

– Well, – but dear Toby! my father would say, do tell us seriously how this affair of the bridge happened. – How can you teaze me so much about it? my uncle Toby would reply, – I have told it you twenty times, word for word as Trim told it me. – Prithee, how was it then, corporal? my father would cry, turning to Trim. – It was a mere misfortune, an' please your honour, – I was shewing Mrs. Bridget our fortifications, and in going too near the edge of the fosse, I unfortunately slipp'd in. – Very well Trim! my father would cry, – (smiling mysteriously, and giving a nod, – but without interrupting him) – and being link'd fast, an' please your honour, arm in arm with Mrs. Bridget, I dragg'd her after me, by means of which she fell backwards soss against the bridge, – and *Trim's* foot, (my uncle *Toby* would cry, taking the story out of his mouth) getting into the cuvette, he tumbled full against the bridge too. – It was a thousand to one, my uncle *Toby* would add, that the poor fellow did not break his leg. – Ay truly! my father would say, – a limb is soon broke, brother *Toby*, in such encounters. – And so, an' please your honour, the bridge, which your honour knows was a very slight one, was broke down betwixt us, and splintered all to pieces.

At other times, but especially when my uncle *Toby* was so unfortunate as to say a syllable about cannons, bombs or petards, – my father would exhaust all the stores of his eloquence (which indeed were very great) in a panegyric upon the BATTERING-RAMS of the ancients, – the VINEA which *Alexander* made use of at the siege of *Tyre*. – He would tell my uncle *Toby* of the CATAPULTAE of the *Syrians* which threw such monstrous stones so many hundred feet, and shook the strongest bulwarks from their very foundation; – he would go on and describe the wonderful mechanism of the BALLISTA, which *Marcellinus* makes so much rout about, – the terrible effects of the PYRABOLI, – which cast fire, – the danger of the TEREBRA and SCORPIO, which cast javelins. – But what are these, he would say, to the destructive machinery of corporal *Trim*? – Believe me, brother *Toby*, no bridge, or bastion, or sally port that ever was constructed in this world, can hold out against such artillery.

My uncle *Toby* would never attempt any defence against the force of this ridicule, but that of redoubling the vehemence of smoaking his pipe; in doing which, he raised so dense a vapour one night after supper, that it set my father, who was a little phthisical, into a suffocating fit of violent coughing: my uncle *Toby* leap'd up without feeling the pain upon his groin, – and, with infinite pity, stood beside his brother's chair, tapping his back with one hand, and holding his head with the other, and from time to time, wiping his eyes with a clean cambrick handkerchief, which he pull'd out of his pocket. – The affectionate and endearing manner in which my uncle *Toby* did these little offices, – cut my father thro' his reins, for the pain he had just been giving him. – May my brains be knock'd out with a battering ram or a catapulta, I care not which, quoth my father to himself, – if ever I insult this worthy soul more.[21]

The main effect of this combination of the general and the particular is to add greatly to our sense of the historical reality of the Shandy world. Not until Conrad, I think, do we get such a complex use of temporal distancing, such a subtle blending and distinction of the manifold levels of memory. The effect Sterne achieves is different from that continuous, cinematic impression of immediacy, of perpetual presentness, that the reader receives from the post-Jamesian novel. The illusion of immediate, dramatic reality is created only sporadically in *Tristram Shandy* (though fairly continuously in *A Sentimental Journey*, since Yorick himself is the observer of almost all the scenes he records); but the sense of historical reality – the feeling that the Shandy world did once exist – steadily grows stronger as one moves through the book.

In his attempt to present such a many-sided, diverse image of the Shandy household Sterne is aided as much as anything by the nervous flexibility and suppleness of his style – a manner of writing, rapid, allusive and fluent, which enables him to skip from the parlour at Shandy Hall 'some millions of miles into the very heart of the planetary system',[22] or from the immediate present – 'this very rainy day, *March* 26, 1759 . . . betwixt the hours of nine and ten in the morning'[23] – back to the night, thirty-one years previously when Tristram was born, without once breaking the vital thread of continuity. Consider, for instance, in the following passage, the easy way in which Sterne shifts from the general description of Mr Shandy's arguments and way of thinking to the brief, dramatic sketch of the frustrated natural philosopher, a vivid and unpretentiously realistic illustration which focuses the mood of the whole passage:

Amongst the many and excellent reasons, with which my father had urged my mother to accept of Dr. *Slop*'s assistance preferably to that of the old woman, – there was one of a very singular nature; which, when he had done arguing the matter with her as a Christian, and came to argue it over again with

[21] Ibid. 210–12 (III, xxiv).
[22] Ibid. 72 (I, xxii).   [23] Ibid. 64 (I, xxi).

her as a philosopher, he had put his whole strength to, depending indeed upon it as his sheet anchor. – It failed him; tho' from no defect in the argument itself; but that, do what he could, he was not able for his soul to make her comprehend the drift of it. – Cursed luck! – said he to himself, one afternoon, as he walk'd out of the room, after he had been stating it for an hour and a half to her, to no manner of purpose; – cursed luck! said he, biting his lip as he shut the door, – for a man to be master of one of the finest chains of reasoning in nature, – and have a wife at the same time with such a headpiece, that he cannot hang up a single inference within side of it, to save his soul from destruction.[24]

The details in this sketch are only lightly touched on, but they are precise and vivid. The cumulative effect of this swift, impressionistic way of writing is to convince the reader imperceptibly but unmistakably of the reality of the people Tristram is remembering (the one flaw in the convention – the fact that Tristram himself could never have witnessed most of the scenes he 'remembers' – is at no stage mentioned, and so does not worry us: besides, the *general* impression he creates is the quite plausible one of a memory not of particular events but of habitual ways of behaviour in the household of which he was a member). Even more important in creating this effect than the reality of the details is the attitude which Tristram – or even Sterne himself – displays towards his characters. It is quite clear that Tristram himself unhesitatingly believes in the existence of the people about whom he is writing. He exhibits no surprise in his discussion of their eccentricities: he describes his father's odd notions with little or no comment on their oddity, and this, together with the fact that Walter's strange theories arouse passions which are not at all strange or peculiar, confirms the illusion of his actual existence.

Sterne initially conceived Walter Shandy as a stock figure of fun – a pedantic humour. But he was too interested in individual people to be purely or for long a satirist. Martinus Scriblerus is, in himself, ridiculous: most of Walter's ideas are as ridiculous as those of Scriblerus, but Walter himself is not: he has dignity. As a man, an individual, he is more important than the fantastic

[24] Ibid. 146–7 (II, xix).

scaffoldings of magic and science which he erects around himself. He is comic and pathetic – but he is always admirable: he respects other people. And it is because he believes, just as strongly as Sterne himself, that the individual personality is intrinsically valuable that he demands our respect and admiration. His insistence on preparing 'scientifically' for the birth of Tristram is pedantic and laughable – but the assumptions on which he grounds his subtle 'chain of reasoning', and the courage and honesty with which he clings to them, are unassailable.

My father set out upon the strength of these two following axioms:

First, That an ounce of a man's own wit, was worth a tun of other peoples; and,

Secondly, (Which, by the bye, was the ground-work of the first axiom, – tho' it comes last) That every man's wit must come from every man's own soul, – and no other body's.[25]

The emergence of Walter Shandy as a rounded and vital personality from the husks of the Scriblerian convention is the measure of Sterne's genius as a novelist. He is far more important than the more immediately lovable Toby. And the way in which he develops symbolises the central theme of the novel: the superiority of the individual to the system. Walter – and Toby – are both more important than their hobby-horses. It is Sterne's realisation of this, and his hatred of those who go careering through life completely unaware of other people – unaware, even, that they are mounted on a hobby-horse – that provides the original and unfailing source of both his wit and his pathos. Like Richardson's preoccupation with the conflict between the individual and the moral law, it acts as the thread around which the process of fictive crystallisation may begin. And although the tradition in which Walter Shandy was conceived seems at first sight to have no connection with eighteenth-century sentimentalism, Walter can be regarded as a sentimental figure. His virtues – independence of judgment, a preoccupation with the finer points of thought and feeling – are the sentimental virtues. The fact that his delight in subtle theorising and rhapsodic flights of speculation seems sometimes to make him oblivious to other people prevents him from being a thorough

[25] Ibid. 147 (II, xix).

sentimentalist; but he is much more conscious of the feelings of others than Scriblerus is: much as he loves theory, Walter, in the last resort, always admits that the happiness of other people should not be sacrificed for the sake of a principle. It is his senti-mentality – his awareness of the value of the feelings not only of himself, but also of other people – which, together with his inconsistencies and his sense of humour, transforms Walter Shandy from a pedantic puppet into a living individual.

As I have already suggested, one of the most important factors in the development of the characters in *Tristram Shandy* was the attitude of Sterne himself – or of the narrator, Tristram – towards them. It is difficult to say just how conscious Sterne was of his attitude, or even whether he was aware that he had an 'attitude' at all. But in one essential, indeed almost revolutionary, respect, Sterne's attitude towards the people in his novel is different from that displayed by a great many of the novelists who had preceded him towards the characters in theirs. The difference is that fundamentally Sterne did not look upon his characters as created fictions, puppets to be moved about as he, their creator, willed, but as people existing in their own right. Richardson, it is interesting to note, looked at his characters in much the same way – and, I believe, for much the same reason: because he did not set out to write a conventional novel in the first place. When Sterne began to write *Tristram Shandy*, he claimed that he was going to confine himself 'neither to [Horace's] rules, nor to any man's rules that ever lived'.[26] He certainly did not intend to confine himself to the conventions of the novel as it then was. Thus when his characters began to come to life, he began to write about them as Tristram might have done had they been real people. He was helped in this, of course, by the fact that from the beginning of the book Tristram himself is a completely lively, credible and likeable character. Tristram's charm, his amiability, displays itself in his affectionate tolerance and accept-ance of his father's and his uncle's eccentricities; and this in itself plays a considerable part in confirming the air of reality which the whole Shandy world wears. It is also worth noting that Tristram's attitude is, in one sense of the word, essentially senti-mental: his civilised tolerance of other people is a positive display of the active functioning of the sentimental ideal.

[26] Ibid. 8 (I, iv).

Although it is to his unconventionality (as a novelist) that Sterne, as much as anything, owes his fresh and uncomplicated attitude towards his characters, it is, paradoxically enough, when he appears to be most conventional – that is, when Tristram appears in the by now almost hackneyed role of the self-conscious narrator – that this attitude stands out most clearly. Wayne C. Booth has shown how this device had already been developed and played with in the novels of Cervantes, Scarron, Furetière, Marivaux, and later Fielding and some minor novelists in England.[27] In *Don Quixote*, *Le Romant Comique*, *Le Roman Bourgeois*, *Pharsamon*, *Tom Jones*, and other less important novels, the narrator becomes a personality in his own right. He comments on the action of the story, on the plot, on the charac- ters, on himself and on his problems as a writer. Sometimes the characters even comment on the narrator – Sancho Panza, in the second part of *Don Quixote*, expresses his surprise that somehow the adventures of himself and his master have been recorded and published in a book – the writer, he tells Don Quixote, has even included 'many things that pass'd betwixt no-body but us two, which I was amaz'd to hear, and could not for my soul imagine, how the Devil he that set 'em down cou'd come by the Know- ledge of 'em'.[28] Don Quixote's reply that he 'must be some Sage Inchanter', comforts Sancho Panza; but it does not really solve the problem. Other writers, notably Furetière, Marivaux and a whole group of minor novelists who aped Fielding's tricks of editorial intrusion in the 1750s, achieved several comic effects by having the narrator demonstrate his control of the fictional events and the fictional characters he is creating. 'It is now in my power to form here a Heroine that shall be stollen away, as often as I have a mind to write Volumns,'[29] says Furetière; Marivaux, in *Pharsamon*, puts his characters to bed, then gets them up again to carry on their performance for the reader – 'Up! Up! –

---

[27] 'The Self-Conscious Narrator in Comic Fiction before *Tristram Shandy*', PMLA LXVIL (1952) 163–85.

[28] *The History of the Renowned Don Quixote de la Mancha*, publish'd by the late Mr. Motteux . . . Revis'd a-new . . . by Mr. Ozell (London, 1743) 28. Cf. *The Adventures of Don Quixote*, trans. J. M. Cohen (Harmondsworth, 1950) 484.

[29] *Scarron's City Romance* [*Le Roman Bourgeois*] (London, 1671) 19. Quoted by W. C. Booth, 'The Self-conscious Narrator in Comic Fiction before *Tristram Shandy*', PMLA LXVII (1952) 168.

I am instantly obey'd ... They have slept till they are sober; but find themselves a little tir'd'.[30]

Now it is obvious not only that *Tristram Shandy* was conceived in this particular literary tradition, but also that, as Mr Booth has emphasised, Sterne carries the device of the self-conscious narrator to further and more ridiculous lengths than had any of his predecessors. It is also clear that the device of the self-conscious – the *rhetorical* – narrator, when properly used (as Fielding and Sterne use it) can be extremely valuable: it gives the author an opportunity of controlling and directing the thoughts and feelings of his readers, and also of establishing and preserving a useful detachment between himself and the reader on the one hand and the characters on the other. It has, however, one grave disadvantage: if it is employed injudiciously, if the editor intrudes tactlessly, he can dispel in a moment that illusion of life, that sense of continuity which Coleridge recognises as one of the fundamental and essential qualities in a novel or a drama. Fielding is sometimes guilty of this maladroitness – and Thackeray is a constant offender. But, with the possible – though doubtful – exception of his treatment of the death of Yorick, *Sterne never is.*

This, it seems to me, is the one vital difference which separates Tristram's methods of narration from those of all preceding comic story tellers: although his methods are crazy and whimsical in the extreme, they are never such as may suggest that either the characters or the events he is describing are nothing but invented fictions. One cannot say this for Furetière, Marivaux (in *Pharsamon*) or even, on occasion, Fielding. Either consciously or unconsciously, Sterne solved the problem that had been bothering novelists ever since the novel began to distinguish itself from biography and history (both genuine and, as in the case of Defoe's fictitious narratives, spurious); the problem of how to convince the reader that the characters are real and the story true. Sterne's whimsy is never the sort of whimsy which can result in an alteration in the lives of the characters in his book, or in an alteration in the nature of the events in which they are involved – *it can result only in an alteration in the manner in which these lives and these events are presented.* His method of describing the Shandy world is apparently disordered, chaotic,

[30] *Pharsamond* (London, 1750) II 117. Quoted by Booth, op. cit. 173.

unpredictable – but that world itself is as solid and immutable as our own. *Within the confines of the novel Sterne (or Sterne/ Tristram) never suggests that his characters are fictions.* This assumption that his characters are real people is perhaps the most unselfconscious, and, so far as the technique of the novel is concerned, the most important thing Sterne does.

The most striking illustrations of the way in which Sterne – or Tristram – regards his characters, occur in those moments when Tristram is playing the conventional role of the comic narrator most assiduously. The comic narrators in the novels of Furetière and Marivaux (in *Pharsamon* – not, of course, *Marianne*) represent themselves as being in full control of the lives and destinies of their characters. But the Shandys lead such a life of their own that Tristram represents himself as being almost completely at their mercy. Thus, when Walter and Uncle Toby fall asleep, Tristram exclaims with relief: '– All my heroes are off my hands; – 'tis the first time I have had a moment to spare, – and I'll make use of it, and write my preface'.[31] The significant thing is that Tristram has to wait until they fall asleep of their own accord: he can neither wake them up nor put them to sleep. Similarly, when the two brothers are coming down the stairs, Tristram appears to be even less able to control them:

> Is it not a shame to make two chapters of what passed in going down one pair of stairs? for we are got no farther yet than to the first landing, and there are fifteen more steps down to the bottom; and for aught I know, as my father and my uncle *Toby* are in a talking humour, there may be as many chapters as steps; – let that be as it will, Sir, I can no more help it than my destiny . . .[32]

And when he sends for a critic to help him 'to get my father and my uncle *Toby* off the stairs, and to put them to bed',[33] the solution to his problem is not the solution one would offer if one were dealing with puppets:

> – So then, friend! you have got my father and my uncle *Toby* off the stairs, and seen them to bed? – And how did you manage it? – You dropp'd a curtain at the stairs foot – I

[31] *Tristram Shandy* 192 (III, xx).
[32] Ibid. 281 (IV, x). [33] Ibid. 285 (IV, xiii).

thought you had no other way for it – Here's a crown for your trouble.[34]

The obvious implication is that behind the curtain the Shandys are carrying on with their own independent life: the dropping of the curtain merely hides them from Tristram's and the reader's view – Tristram no longer has the responsibility of telling us what they are doing.

Ultimately all, or almost all, the comic devices in *Tristram Shandy* have the effect of intensifying the belief of the reader in the Shandy world – not so much because Sterne deliberately set out to do this, but because the Shandys assumed a life of their own. They lived for Sterne, and all his devices in some way reflect and reveal this life. Even the digressions and disruptions, though often arbitrary, are not mechanical (as they are, for instance in *A Tale of a Tub*, and in minor novels like *Charlotte Summers*), they are organic. And one of the most important causes of the organic unity of *Tristram Shandy* is Sterne's subordination of the narrator to the characters and to the situation. Tristram must be regarded as part of the Shandy world, not as something detached from and superior to it. Mr Booth sees Tristram as a force holding the apparently disintegrating Shandy world together. It would be more accurate, I feel, to see Tristram as a force who disrupts nothing but his own impressions of a world which is itself not chaotic or crazy at all. And it must be recognised at the same time that Tristram, by the very fact of his own distinctive personality, is able in a paradoxical way to impose some sort of unity on the material which he seems to be disorganising.

Yet 'impose' is not quite the right word to use, for part of the comedy of Tristram arises from his being the victim of the story and the characters he is supposed to control. Like Uncle Toby, he is a comically impotent figure – betrayed continually, as are all the Shandys, by his own erratic nature, and frustrated by the vagaries of chance and fortune. Tristram's impotence reveals itself most clearly in the complete helplessness which he exhibits in the face of life, and in the face of his own particular system of trying to represent it. His intentions are simple: to give an account of his own life and opinions. But life – anyone's life – is

---

[34] Ibid. 286–7 (IV, xiii).

so complicated, and there are so many aspects of it, that Tristram soon realises the task of fulfilling his original purpose to be an almost impossible one.

> Could a historiographer drive on his history, as a muleteer drives on his mule, – straight forward . . . – he might venture to foretell you to an hour when he should get to his journey's end; – but the thing is, morally speaking, impossible: For, if he is a man of the least spirit, he will have fifty deviations from a straight line to make with this or that party as he goes along . . . there are archives at every stage to be look'd into, and rolls, records, documents, and endless genealogies, which justice ever and anon calls him back to stay the reading of: – In short, there is no end of it; – for my own part, I declare I have been at it these six weeks, making all the speed I possibly could, – and am not yet born. . .[35]

Tristram's inability to complete his own biography, or even to get it properly under way, is, like his father's failure to beget him and rear him in a 'scientific' manner, yet another example of that theme of human limitation and imperfection which runs not only through *Tristram Shandy* but also through *A Sentimental Journey*. Sterne was preoccupied, one might almost say obsessed, with the problem of impotence. His heroes are all failures in one way or another; they all conform to the basic sentimental pattern of being both virtuous and distressed. But for the most part Sterne's presentation of them is not in itself sentimental. He is usually more interested in the comic rather than the pathetic aspects of the situations in which they find themselves. Tristram, Yorick and Uncle Toby do not simply fade away in a mist of tears as the Man of Feeling does. Yorick (in *A Sentimental Journey*) perhaps tends to sentimentalise at times – but most obviously only in those situations in which it is impossible for him to be actively benevolent. Maria of Moulines, for instance, is, in the full sense of the word, *helpless* – no one can do anything to assist her. She can demand nothing from the world *but* sympathy – and this is all that Yorick gives her:

> Adieu, poor luckless maiden! – imbibe the oil and wine which the compassion of a stranger, as he journieth on his way, now

[35] Ibid. 36–7 (I, xiv).

pours into thy wounds – the being who has twice bruised thee can only bind them up forever.[36]

This, unquestionably, is the typical sentimental situation in its purest form – everyone is virtuous, everyone is distressed, everyone is helpless. Maria, indeed, is so 'disordered' that she can scarcely be said even to understand the extent of Yorick's compassion. His spontaneous sympathy expends itself without thought of reward on the uncomprehending world: the feeling can therefore be savoured and evaluated simply for its own sake.

Such completely sentimental scenes occur rarely in Sterne's work; and when they do his delicate control of language and his superb sense of timing save him from becoming mawkish. And usually the pathos is tempered with wit and humour. The situations may be sentimental, but the presentation of them is not: sentiment in Sterne is always held in check by irony; and it is this which gives his work its unique complexity of tone.

But the conventionally sentimental situation clearly held an unusual fascination for Sterne. One reason for this was his preoccupation with impotence – particularly sexual impotence. A large proportion of the sexual wit – and the sexual fantasy – in *Tristram Shandy* is concerned with one form or another of impotence. Impotence is not always the direct theme: in sexual, as in other matters, the main targets for Sterne's satire and ridicule are, as with all satirists, affectation and hypocrisy, and much of the bawdry in *Tristram Shandy* arises out of Sterne's ironic but not altogether unsympathetic attitude towards affectation and hypocrisy in sexual matters – that is towards the sentimental *attitude* to love. Sterne had very few illusions about the real nature of 'that tender and delicious sentiment, which ever mixes in friendship, where there is a difference of sex'.[37] The story of Corporal Trim and the fair Beguine – like the story of his brother Tom and the Jew's widow – contains in it 'the essence of all the love-romances which ever have been wrote since the beginning of the world', and, as Uncle Toby learns to his sorrow, there is only one cause for the widow Wadman's 'compassionate' interest in his wounds, and that is her 'humanity': a word which Trim writes carefully in large letters, and which he explains to his master in a manner that is quite

---

[36] *A Sentimental Journey* 276.   [37] *Tristram Shandy* 49 (I, xviii).

unsentimental. The scene in which Trim finally opens Uncle Toby's eyes is, one might add, one of the most delicately yet most firmly drawn in the whole book: it exhibits to perfection that blend of humour and pathos which is uniquely Sterne's – it is at once witty, amusing and in its simplicity much more moving than the obviously set pieces of sentimental rhetoric, the descriptions of Maria, the caged starling, the dying prisoner and the like. The conclusion is particularly fine:

> My uncle Toby gave a long whistle – but in a note which could scarce be heard across the table.
> The Corporal had advanced too far to retire – in three words he told the rest –
> My uncle Toby laid down his pipe as gently upon the fender, as if it had been spun from the unravellings of a spider's web –
> – Let us go to my brother Shandy's, said he.[38]

The significance of Uncle Toby as a symbol not only of goodness, but also of impotence, is not always recognised. He is impotent, of course, in more ways than one: he is much more dependent on other people than Walter is, for instance. Walter's response to the cruel blows of chance is to fall back on his own inner resources – he philosophises on the unhappy lot of man, and detaches himself from his troubles by attempting to consider them sub specie aeternitatis. But Toby needs the support of other people, both in his sorrows and his joys (the bowling green would not have been half so much fun without Trim). Nor is it usually recognised just how much Toby's goodness depends on his impotence – although Sterne tries to make it clear that there are very good physical reasons for Uncle Toby's modesty.

Sterne's attitude to at least one aspect of the sort of sentimental virtue represented by Uncle Toby is demonstrated very clearly in his description of the poor hack which Parson Yorick had to ride. Yorick's horse, Tristram tells us, was

> full brother to Rosinante . . . – except that I do not remember 'tis any where said, that Rosinante was broken winded; and that, moreover, Rosinante, as is the happiness of most Spanish horses, fat or lean, – was undoubtedly a horse at all points.

[38] Ibid. 643 (IX, xxxi).

I know very well that the HERO's horse was a horse of chaste
deportment, which may have given grounds for a contrary
opinion: But it is as certain at the same time, that *Rosinante's*
continency (as may be demonstrated from the adventure of
the *Yanguesian* carriers) proceeded from no bodily defect or
cause whatsoever, but from the temperance and orderly current of his blood. – And let me tell you, Madame, there is a
great deal of very good chastity in the world, in behalf of
which you could not say any more for your life.[39]

The affair of the Yanguesian carriers in fact demonstrates something rather different. Rosinante, it is true, is both a horse at all
points and (usually) a horse of chaste deportment: Sancho
believed that

he was so mild and so little lustful a beast that all the mares in
the pastures of Cordova would not provoke him to any impro-
priety. But on this occasion, he was taken with the desire to
disport himself with the lady mares . . . But they, apparently,
preferred the pastures, and gave him such a welcome with
their hooves and teeth that in a very short while they had
broken his girths and left him stripped of his saddle and
naked.[40]

Although this adventure witnesses both to Rosinante's virility
and to the normal temperance and orderly current of his blood,
it also proves that, on this occasion at least, he was chaste because he could not get what he wanted – 'and there is a great
deal of very good chastity in the world in behalf of which you
could not say more'. One could certainly say not much more for
Uncle Toby's chastity. One can say much more for his good
nature – but it is important to realise that Uncle Toby's virtue
stems to a certain extent from the fact that he is powerless either
to harm or to help anybody. It is true that, within his physical
and financial means, he is benevolent and generous enough: he
is kind alike to flies, to servants and to children. But although a
naturally good and lovable man, he is at the same time extraordinarily passive and even in some ways limited. Although an

[39] Ibid. 18 (I, x).
[40] *The Adventures of Don Quixote*, trans. J. M. Cohen (Harmondsworth, 1950) 112.

admirable character he is also a pathetic one: and it is because Sterne realises that he is limited and therefore pitiable that Uncle Toby is saved from being a figure who is, in the modern sense of the word, sentimental. He conforms in many ways to a senti-mental pattern – the pattern of the good old man, the venerable but powerless father-figure (it is not without significance that he is an uncle); but Sterne does not allow his admiration and affec-tion for Uncle Toby to stifle his common sense. Uncle Toby's sentimentalism is not only presented, but evaluated. It is, of course, impossible to realise the full force of this evaluation if one sentimentalises *Tristram Shandy* by bowdlerising it as one reads.[41]

Sterne's comparison between Yorick's horse – or, rather, geld-ing – and Rosinante plays a very trivial part in the novel as a whole. It is interesting nonetheless that Yorick, a symbol, like Uncle Toby, of impotent virtue, should ride an impotent horse; and even more interesting that the comparison of this poor jade with Rosinante should be found, when investigated, to involve a situation of comic impotence of the true Shandy sort. The fact that one has only to scratch the surface of the novel to discover this recurring theme of impotence and frustration, demonstrates more clearly perhaps than anything else the conceptual and imaginative unity that *Tristram Shandy* possesses: a unity which it would not be inept to describe as poetic.

Characters who exhibit a combination of virtue and impotence can usually be expected to arouse sentimental emotions. Uncle Toby, in the rough outlines of his portrait at least, conforms to this sentimental pattern – so do Le Fever, Maria, the caged star-ling, the old man whose ass has died, and all Sterne's other sentimental figures. But Sterne generally manages to preserve an ironic distance between himself and the figure he is describing, the emotions he is evoking and playing with. He is prepared to enjoy the feelings generated by the contemplation of virtue in distress – or any other pathetic situation – but he is not prepared to suspend his powers of judgment. Sterne's sentimentality is extremely complex.

An excellent illustration of just how complex a thing it is is

[41] For an illuminating discussion of this aspect of Sterne's imagina-tive world see Frank Brady, '*Tristram Shandy*: Sexuality, Morality and Sensibility', *Eighteenth-Century Studies* IV (1970) 41–56.

given by the chapter in which Trim reads the sermon.[42] The text
of the sermon is Hebrews, xiii, 18: 'For we trust we have a good
conscience', and the sermon itself is a well argued and thoroughly
unsentimental attack on the conventionally sentimental motion
that goodness consists solely in following the dictates of the
heart. Sterne begins by stating the normally accepted and comforting view that in the matter of the goodness or otherwise of
our conscience we must surely have certainty, even if we have it
nowhere else;

> In other matters we may be deceived by false appearances . . .
> But here the mind has all the evidence and facts within her-
> self.[43]

As the sermon develops, Sterne goes on to point out that in no
other sphere is it so easy to be deceived: our consciences find it
only too easy to condone in ourselves the commission of those
sins which we find pleasant, and the omission of those acts of
virtue which we find irksome, and to condemn in others the sins
which we have no desire to commit. In words of which Sir
Charles Grandison, that man of principle, would have thoroughly
approved, Sterne states that conscience 'is not to be trusted
alone' – it must be joined to 'another principle'

> if you would form a just judgment of what is of infinite
> importance to you not to be misled in . . . – call in religion
> and morality. – Look, – What is written in the law of God?
> – How readest thou? – Consult calm reason and the un-
> changeable obligations of justice and truth; – what say they?
>   Let CONSCIENCE determine the matter upon these reports;
> – and then if thy heart condemns thee not . . . – the rule will
> be infallible.[44]

[42] Arthur Cash in 'The Sermon in *Tristram Shandy*', ELH, XXXI
(1964) 395–417, gives a full and illuminating account of the religious
and philosophical background to this sermon in particular and
Sterne's ethical thought in general. My reading of 'The Abuses of
Conscience Considered' is generally in agreement with Mr Cash's;
but as will become apparent in my discussion of A *Sentimental
Journey* I have some reservations about his interpretation of Sterne's
comedy.
[43] *Tristram Shandy* 126 (II, xvii).
[44] Ibid. 132–3 (II, xvii).

There is no reason to suppose that Sterne did not hold these views sincerely – justice and truth, together with kindness and tolerance, seem to be the virtues and the qualities which he valued most highly – and the sermon can be read as a theoretical statement of much that is implied rather than openly stated in both *Tristram Shandy* and *A Sentimental Journey*. It puts forward one sort of sentimentalism – the sentimentalism based on a right balance between the head and the heart – in opposition to that doctrine of sentimental morality which maintained that the dictates of pure feeling were the surest guides to virtue. Sterne may have taken the tenderness of his emotions as a sure sign of his possession of a soul – but he realised not only that sympathy was not enough, but also that it could be a fallible guide to conduct. *A Sentimental Journey* can in fact be read as in part an ironical exposition of the tricks our feelings may play on us.

The reading of the sermon is itself a demonstration of the insufficiency of feeling. Dr Slop is moved (not deeply perhaps – but he *is* moved) by the description of the horrors of the Inquisition, but he remains unconvinced: there is not much wrong with his feelings – it is his principles that are at fault: the wretch who perishes in the *auto da fé*, perishes because of a principle: 'this principle, that there can be religion without mercy'[45] – he is killed, in short, because of the intolerance of a system, because he gets under the hooves of a particularly hard-driven hobby-horse. It is significant that when the theoretical point of the sermon is being made (in the paragraph I have quoted above), Dr Slop falls asleep: his heart can be moved, but his reason remains deaf to all attempts to convince it.

The efforts which Sterne makes to engage the feelings of the listeners and the reader – to deliver his 'theologic flap upon the heart'[46] – are worth noticing, for in outline they, too, appear sentimental. The most telling image in the whole sermon is the

[45] Ibid. 139 (II, xvii).
[46] Letter to George Whateley, 25 March 1761. *Letters*, ed. Curtis 134. The context is worth quoting: 'preaching (you must know) is a theologic flap upon the heart, as the dunning for a promise is a political flap upon the memory: – both the one and the other is useless where men have *wit enough* to be honest. This makes for my hypothesis of wit and judgment.'

rhetorical depiction of the wretch condemned by the Inquisition.[47] In itself this is pathetic enough (and it conforms to the sentimental pattern of impotent and distressed virtue: the force of the image comes from the fact that the victim is completely powerless); but its effect is intensified even further by Sterne's decision to endow Trim with a brother Tom who has been a prisoner 'in' the Inquisition for fourteen years. Trim tells the company this before he begins to read – and even sheds a tear or two. The tears are enough to quiet even Dr Slop: 'A dead silence in the room ensued for some minutes. – Certain proof of pity!'[48] (But pity, as we have already seen, is not enough.) A fine dramatic effect is thus achieved when Trim begins to read the description of the helpless victim ('Oh! 'tis my brother, cried poor *Trim* in a most passionate exclamation').[49] The sense of impotence is now redoubled, for Trim, quite unable to help his brother, is forced to listen to the harrowing description of what could well have been his torments. One cannot deny that the feelings of pity, horror and fear are here being deliberately evoked and developed, largely it seems for their own sakes. The scene could very easily degenerate into sentimentalism of the rankest sort. But it does not: it is saved by the presence of Walter Shandy (who exhibits a thorough understanding of everything that is going on); the adamantine determination of Dr Slop to remain unconvinced; the argument of the sermon itself; and the comical distress of Trim. The intellectual argument of the scene indeed seems to work against what might appear at first glance to be its emotional intent. Trim is ostensibly a pathetic figure – his distress after all is real enough, and, as is demonstrated by the excessive tearfulness with which both he and Uncle Toby are presented in some of the versifications and imitations of Sterne which were later produced, it is clear that both of them were regarded by many readers more as pathetic than as comic figures. But although Trim is pathetic he is also ridiculous – just as Partridge is ridiculous when he allows himself to be carried away at the theatre. Trim's distress is thus, like the sermon itself, a demonstration not

[47] By what one can only assume to be an interesting coincidence Adam Smith employs practically the same example in the first chapter of his *Theory of Moral Sentiments*, which was published in the same year.
[48] *Tristram Shandy* 125 (II, xvii).   [49] Ibid. 138 (II, xviii).

only of the power but also of the irrationality of feeling. His tears are a comic revelation of the limitations of innocence and simplicity; and the scene as a whole is a witty and sophisticated commentary on the sentimental notion that the way to virtue lies simply in following the uncorrupted promptings of the heart.

But although Sterne demonstrates continually that he is aware of the fallibility of pure feeling, he also asserts, just as constantly, his faith in it as a source of all that is best in man's relations with his fellow creatures. Trusting to the feelings may lead us into error, but the man who is never prepared to run this risk is a cold inhuman monster. Sterne's distinction as a satirist, and as a creative interpreter of life, lies in his realisation of the positive reality and value of love, tolerance and kindliness. He is aware of the limitations of these things, as he is aware of the limitations of all the endeavours and aspirations of imperfect man; but he never allows his annoyance with cant, humbug and hypocrisy to destroy his own sympathy and affection for other people. The greatness of *Tristram Shandy* as a comic novel rests in this fundamental balance, good sense and lack of rancour. Sterne is in no sense smug or complacent: his view of life is remarkable for its realism and its lack of self-deception. But he acknowledges the existence and the value of sympathy and feeling. He is – in his own, and not the modern sense of the word – a sentimentalist. It is the combination of the satiric wit and the sentimentality – the recognition and evaluation of feeling – that makes *Tristram Shandy* more than just a vast literary joke. Sterne's sentimentality indeed includes his wit: it is a social and a philosophical attitude maintained by a fine balance between reason and emotion, the head and the heart. And *Tristram Shandy*, despite the apparent chaos of its form and the diversity of its discernible motives, is basically a coherent and organically unified expression of Sterne's view of life: like *Clarissa*, *Tristram Shandy* needs to be read not for the story, or, in its case, the learned jokes and the crazy humour of marbled pages and asterisks, but for the sentiment.

3

The Sentimental Comedy:
A Sentimental Journey

I

How sentimental is A *Sentimental Journey*? This is the question which anyone who is at all seriously interested in Sterne's work eventually has to consider. And the attempt to answer the question has called forth some extremely shrewd, lively and subtle criticism. In the twentieth century's reassessment of *Tristram Shandy* most of the critical effort has been directed towards establishing that the novel has an intelligently ordered structure and purpose; in our re-examination of A *Sentimental Journey* attention has been directed almost solely to the problem of determining the nature of the feelings displayed in the book and Sterne's purpose in displaying them. No one today would pose the question as nastily and provocatively as Thackeray did when he asked: 'How much was deliberate calculation and imposture – how much was false sensibility – and how much true feeling? Where did the lie begin, and did he know where? And where did the truth end in the art and scheme of this man of genius, this actor, this quack?'[1] But this, essentially, is the question we are still trying to answer; and the most illuminating of the recent discussions of A *Sentimental Journey* have all been concerned with what might be called the moral status of Yorick's sensibility.

By the time Thackeray came to give his lectures on the English humourists of the eighteenth century there was perhaps some justification for this sort of irritation: A *Sentimental Journey* had been so over-simplified, bowdlerised and sentimentalised by two generations of readers, anthologists and commentators, that it

---

[1] 'Sterne and Goldsmith', Lecture VI in *English Humourists of the Eighteenth Century* (New York, 1853) 240.

must have been difficult to approach it with anything like an open mind. Today we can recognise that, like *Tristram Shandy*, it is an extremely complex work, one which embodies, as Gardner Stout has said, 'a . . . double awareness, combining the subjective experience of "the man of feeling" and the objective vision of the man of infinite jest'.[2] And we read it with the knowledge that when Sterne came to write it he had not ceased to be either a satirist or a priest. There is indeed a deal of 'deliberate calculation' if not 'imposture' in *A Sentimental Journey*, though it is not quite of the sort that Thackeray had in mind. There is also infinitely more 'true feeling' in the book than he would allow.

The 'feeling' in *A Sentimental Journey*, indeed, seems to me its essential and animating principle. I emphasise this, because there is a tendency today among critics to lay a disproportionate stress on Sterne's satiric and homiletic purposes. Arthur C. Cash, for instance, who is in general a most illuminating commentator, wants us to read the *Journey* almost solely as a critical analysis of the way in which we can allow our supposedly generous impulses to act as a mask for fundamentally selfish, particularly sexual, motives. When Yorick feels 'benevolence' for the lady at Calais this benevolence, says Mr Cash, becomes 'part of Yorick's temptation to the sin of carnality . . . its misdirected energy impels [him] in the direction of a sinful act'.[3] This is ingenious but wrong-headed. The real paradox with which Sterne is concerned is not that benevolence leads to carnality but that carnality leads to benevolence. If Yorick had not allowed his heart to fly out before his understanding, if he had not been prepared to acknowledge and to a degree indulge his sexual desire for the lady, he would never have been able to feel benevolence for her. The stoic is the real enemy in *A Sentimental Journey*, not the man who allows himself to feel. Yorick may be ridiculous (often only in a 'worldly' sense) but he is rarely if ever vicious. Certainly he is sometimes weak, vacillating and capricious; certainly he sometimes sentimentally indulges his weakness for tender feelings. But the point still remains that if he had not been willing to be compassionate he could not have been benevolent.

[2] *A Sentimental Journey* Introduction 45–6.
[3] *Sterne's Comedy of Moral Sentiments: the Ethical Dimensions of The Journey,* MHRA monograph, Duquesne Studies Philological Series, 6 (Pittsburgh, 1966) 60.

In Sterne's sermon, 'Philanthropy Recommended', he discusses the Good Samaritan; and as Mr Cash very properly reminds us Sterne emphasises that the Samaritan's impulse of pity was not mechanical or short lived: 'there was a settled principle of humanity and goodness which operated within him, and influenced not only the first impulse of kindness, but the continuation of it throughout the rest of so engaging a behaviour'.[4] 'Sterne's point', comments Mr Cash, 'is just that goodness does *not* depend upon a spontaneous instinctive response or the pleasure it brings.'[5] This is too sweeping altogether: goodness may not depend *entirely* on a spontaneous instinctive response, but without such a response good actions are impossible. The villains in the parable are the Priest and the Levite *who will not allow themselves to feel*: the Priest is 'a sordid wretch, whose strait heart is open to no man's affliction . . .', he '*devoutly* [passes] by on the other side, as if unwilling to trust himself to the impressions of nature, or hazard the inconveniences which pity might lead him into'.[6] The Levite is worse: he looks at the man and then deliberately leaves him: 'It was not a transient oversight, the hasty or ill-advised neglect of an unconsidering humour, with which the best disposed are sometimes overtaken . . . No! – on the contrary, it had all the aggravation of a deliberate act of insensibility proceeding from a hard heart'.[7]

Insensibility and hardness of heart – these are the real evils in Sterne's world, not occasional unchastity or a tendency to let the heart at times govern the head. One of the central arguments of A *Sentimental Journey* is that man must always keep alive in himself the capacity to feel. By doing so he runs the risk both of sentimental over-indulgence and of making a fool of himself – but if he is not prepared to run this risk he will be denying an essential part of his moral nature. 'I pity the man who can travel from *Dan* to *Beersheba*, and cry, 'Tis all barren – and so it is; and so is all the world to him who will not cultivate the fruits it offers. I declare, said I, clapping my hands chearily together, that was I in a desart, I would find out wherewith in it to call forth my affections.'[8] The voice is Yorick's voice but the hands are the

---

[4] *The Sermons of Mr. Yorick* 11th ed. (London, 1773) I 73.
[5] *Sterne's Comedy of Moral Sentiments* 78.
[6] *Sermons* I 67. Italics in the original.
[7] Ibid.　　　　　　　　　　　[8] A *Sentimental Journey* 115.

hands of Laurence Sterne (as is the case, I suspect, more often than not in A Sentimental Journey). Sterne, like Yorick, believed in the primary and vitalising role of feeling – even while recognising that feeling by itself was not enough, and that a willingness to feel could lead to embarrassment and unhappiness.

Although Yorick is a comic and at times a foolish figure, and although Sterne almost certainly realised (indeed probably hoped and intended) that some of his readers would take an unjustifiably solemn and damp-eyed view of his hero,[9] there seems little reason to doubt the genuineness of his – and Yorick's – avowed intentions. Yorick's travels, he tells the Count de B**** as he applies for a passport, are 'a quiet journey of the heart in pursuit of NATURE, and those affections which rise out of her, which make us love each other – and the world, better than we do?'[10] The observation echoes, with an interesting change of emphasis, a remark made by Sterne in a letter to Mrs James: 'I told you my design in it was to teach us to love the world and our fellow creatures better than we do – so it runs most upon those gentler passions and affections, which add so much to it.'[11] In the statement as modified in the Journey particular stress is placed on the naturalness of the affections which make us love each other – and consequently the world. In this context love must be assumed to have the widest of connotations, even though Yorick has just been assuring the Count that he has come to France not to spy out the nakedness of their women but the nakedness of their hearts. Despite his equivocations and his ambiguous concern for his 'virtue' Yorick – and I believe Sterne also – sees agape as inextricably involved with and dependent on eros; and in A Sentimental Journey Sterne gives a comic but sympathetic exposition of the follies and absurdities into which man can be betrayed through the inescapable association of his sexuality and his sensibility.

The answer to the question: 'How sentimental is A Sentimental Journey?' is thus largely to be found, I would suggest, through a consideration of the relationship between the erotic

---

[9] 'My Journey . . . shall make you cry as much as ever it made me laugh – or I'll give up the Business of sentimental writing – & write to the Body'. To 'Hannah', 15 Nov. 1767: Letters, ed. Curtis 401.

[10] A Sentimental Journey 219.

[11] Letters, ed. Curtis 401.

and the moral connotations of 'sentimental'. One of Sterne's purposes in the *Journey* – to my mind it is the dominant one – is to make us acknowledge that our capacity for benevolence, compassion and sympathy – the essential social virtues – is intimately if sometimes ironically related to our capacity for sexual responsiveness. The irony is heightened by the fact that erotic sensitivity can often be associated with sexual innocence and even physical impotence – most notably, of course, in the figure of Uncle Toby. And it is significant that two of the most important – and most ambiguous – incidents in *A Sentimental Journey*, 'The Conquest' and 'The Case of Conscience', focus on just this blend of heightened erotic and moral awareness. *A Sentimental Journey*, as the title suggests, is amongst other things, a book about love.

II

The key to this aspect of the problem of *A Sentimental Journey* is to be found in the enigmatic statement:

> L'amour n'est *rien* sans sentiment.
> Et le sentiment est encore *moins* sans amour.[12]

The sentences occur in the letter from the drummer in his regiment which La Fleur produces for Yorick when he is desperately trying to write a note to the beautiful Mme de L***. The first sentence also appears in a letter written in 1765 when Sterne informs John Wodehouse that he carries on his affairs 'quite in the French way, sentimentally – '*l'amour* (say they) *n'est rien sans sentiment*' – Now notwithstanding they make such a pother about the *word*, they have no precise idea annex'd to it'.[13]

Despite Sterne's disclaimer the French probably had a number of clear ideas attached to the word 'sentiment' in this context; and by the time he came to write *A Sentimental Journey* Sterne obviously had too. As a preacher he knew the value of a good text, and it would not be altogether inappropriate to see the *Journey* as an extended sermon on this verse out of the Epistle from the Drummer Jacques Roque to the Corporal's Wife. At the simplest level we can take 'L'amour n'est *rien* sans sentiment' to mean that love is nothing unless it has a spiritual, moral or

[12] *A Sentimental Journey* 153.   [13] *Letters*, ed. Curtis 256.

intellectual dimension – and all Yorick's flirtations are certainly sentimental in this sense. But if we extend the signification of 'amour' we can take the statement to mean that spontaneous feelings of benevolence, pity or compassion are not worth much unless they are related to some rationally ordered set of moral ideas, unless they are part of some 'settled principle of humanity and goodness'. This is one of the lessons Yorick learns on his *Journey*; and it is when Yorick merely indulges his tender feelings and fails to act in a consistent and principled way that he becomes one of the objects of Sterne's complex and delicate satire.

But the second sentence needs examination also; and – as the italicised '*moins*' suggests – it is perhaps the more important of the two: 'Et le sentiment est encore *moins* sans amour.' At the most obvious erotic level we can take this to mean that spiritual and lofty feelings between a man and a woman are meaningless unless they are grounded in genuine sexual desire – it is the lesson Uncle Toby has to learn when Trim explains to him the true significance of Widow Wadman's 'humanity'. But there is a larger interpretation to be placed upon this text. In the widest sense it means that moral judgments and ideals – (settled principles of *humanity* and goodness) are worthless unless they are motivated by love, by the spontaneous impulses of benevolence which can arise in man only because he is a physical creature (albeit with a soul) with physical – and in particular, sexual – passions and desires. Moral action which comes from the head and not the heart is cold, empty and inhuman; and to assume that sexual feeling does not enter into feelings of benevolence, compassion and pity, especially (but not only) when these are directed towards members of the opposite sex is to indulge in sentimental self-deception.

When Tristram springs out of his chaise to help poor mad Maria, he finds himself sitting between the maiden and her goat. After Maria has looked wistfully and alternately from one to the other, Tristram asks her softly, 'What resemblance do you find?' He goes on: 'I do intreat the candid reader to believe me, that it was from the humblest conviction of what a *Beast* man is, – that I ask'd the question; and that I would not have let fallen an unseasonable pleasantry in the venerable presence of Misery, to be entitled to all the wit that ever Rabelais scatter'd'.

As a result of the encounter he swears to 'set up for Wisdom and utter grave sentences the rest of [his] days – and never – never attempt again to commit mirth with man, woman, or child . . .'[14] In A *Sentimental Journey*, however, Sterne is still committing mirth – if not so obviously – and the point of the comedy is still the ironic relationship between man's moral ideals, his spiritual conception of himself, and his beastliness, his goatish sexuality. And the object of the satire is not Yorick but, as in *Tristram Shandy*, the prurient and puritanical reader.

It is, I think, a gross misreading of A *Sentimental Journey* to take Yorick as on the whole a weak, foolish, gullible and even potentially vicious character. He is certainly fallible, but he is also within recognisable and on the whole acceptable limitations a kind, benevolent, thoughtful and civilised man. To assume that Sterne did not intend him to be admirable as well as charming is unjustified – especially if we are to assume that Sterne wished his own sermons, published as sermons of Mr Yorick, to be taken seriously. But this is not to say that Yorick's charm and virtue are simple: they are, on the contrary, subtle and deceptive. And the point of the deception is to trap the reader into accepting the admirable, charming, sentimental and *Reverend* Mr Yorick as a man with sexual appetites like any other. If the Yorick who tries to free the starling, who pays the *grisset* three Louis d'ors for a pair of ruffles he does not need, who goes in search of Maria, is admirable, it must be accepted that he is the same man who forms an extremely pleasurable connection with the Marquesina di F***, who assists Mme de Rambouliet to pluck her rose, and who catches hold of the end of the *fille de chambre* in the inn on the road to Turin. Indeed Sterne goes further: the real point of A *Sentimental Journey* is to demonstrate that in so far as Yorick is admirable it is *because* he has carnal appetites and is prepared honestly to acknowledge if not always to indulge them. The *Journey* may be a much less bawdy work than *Tristram Shandy*, but it is in some ways much more deliberately and provocatively sexual.

Yorick himself puts the case directly quite early in the book, in the inn at Montreuil, just before he goes out to disburse his eight sous among the sixteen beggars:

[14] *Tristram Shandy* 631 (IX, xxiv).

having been in love with one princess or another almost all my life . . . I hope I shall go on so, till I die, being firmly persuaded, that if ever I do a mean action, it must be in some interval betwixt one passion and another: whilst this inter-regnum lasts, I always perceive my heart locked up – I can scarce find in it, to give Misery a sixpence; and therefore I always get out of it as fast as I can, and the moment I am rekindled, I am all generosity and good will again; and would do any thing in the world either for, or with any one, if they will but satisfy me there is no sin in it.[15]

This is quite straightforward, and there seems no reason why it should not be taken at its face value, especially since it is an echo and expansion of something Sterne had written in one of his own letters. Moreover Sterne himself had good reason to believe in the revitalising power of love. However embarrassingly mawkish the *Journal to Eliza* may be, and however self-deceptively senti-mental the relationship may have been between Sterne and Mrs Draper, it undoubtedly provided him with some of the inspira-tion for *A Sentimental Journey* and with the renewed physical and psychological vigour which he brought to the writing of it. Eliza, in fact, probably helped to keep Sterne alive. And it is possible to read the *Journey* as an extended illustration of the argument. Indeed if we do so certain aspects of the book's struc-ture and tone immediately assume a new significance.

Let us begin by looking at the first set of incidents in the story – Yorick's famous encounter with the Franciscan and the beautiful lady from Brussels. After his first dinner in France, with a bottle of good burgundy under his belt, Yorick feels at peace with the world and with himself and ready to pull out his purse and find an object to share it with. At that instant the Franciscan enters the room to beg something for his convent, and on the whim of the moment Yorick decides to give him nothing – instead he reads him a lecture on true charity. As soon as the monk leaves, however, Yorick feels thoroughly ashamed of himself – 'My heart smote me the moment he shut the door . . . I have behaved very ill; said I within myself; but I have only just set out upon my travels; and shall learn better manners as I get along.'[16] He is presented with an opportunity very soon: as

[15] *A Sentimental Journey* 128–9.   [16] Ibid. 75.

he stands with the beautiful Mme L**** in the street the monk (whom he has seen shortly before in conversation with the lady) comes along. Since he has just been setting himself to consider how he might 'undo the ill impressions which the poor monk's story, in case he had told it her, must have planted in her breast',[17] the meeting is timely; and Yorick effects a graceful exchange of his tortoiseshell snuff box for Father Ambrose's far less valuable one of horn, begging the monk to accept it as 'the peace-offering of a man who once used you unkindly, but not from his heart'.[18] The lady, and the monk, are suitably impressed; and Yorick tells us he still has the horn snuff box: 'I guard this box, as I would the instrumental parts of my religion, to help my mind on to something better: in truth, I seldom go abroad without it; and oft and many a time have I called up by it the courteous spirit of its owner to regulate my own.'[19]

Yorick's motives, of course, are mixed; and it is possible to take the scene simply as a witty and satiric exposure of the way in which a basically selfish action can masquerade as an altruistic one: no matter how sentimental his attitude Yorick's benevolence is essentially self-seeking. But this is a crude and heavy-handed interpretation. Yorick, after all, has already decided to make reparation to the monk (or to the situation) before he meets the lady; and his confession that he had used the old man unkindly *but not from his heart* is, on any reading of the incident, the simple truth. While a certain amount of selfishness enters into the motivation of his action it does express what we can legitimately take to be his true character. When the situation is looked at in this way the presence of the lady and Yorick's willingness to acknowledge her sexual attractiveness can be seen as catalysts rather than causes – they provide the occasion for his elegant and tactful gesture rather than the over-riding reason for it. It is his 'love' for the lady, indeed, which has made it possible for him to make amends for his earlier *gaucherie*, and to learn an effective lesson in true *politesse du coeur*, a lesson moreover with the widest application. Yorick's remark about the instrumental parts of his religion is no doubt an exaggeration, but it would be over-subtle in the extreme to argue that Sterne intended us to take it completely ironically.

Sterne is well aware of all the ambiguities in the situation: he

[17] Ibid. 98.   [18] Ibid. 99.   [19] Ibid. 101.

knows that a middle-aged clergyman flirting with a pretty woman in the street would not normally be taken as an example of virtue. But the reader who assumes that Yorick's carnal desires are his real weaknesses and temptations has fallen into Sterne's comic trap. When Yorick asks himself 'where would be the harm . . . if I was to beg of this distressed lady to accept of half of my chaise?' he tells us that 'Every dirty passion, and bad propensity in my nature, took the alarm.'[20] But there is nothing sexual (as the unsuspecting reader may expect there to be) about these passions and propensities – they are Avarice, Caution, Cowardice, Discretion, Hypocrisy, Meanness and Pride. Those who hate Love, Yorick tells the lady, are the grave, the selfish and the hypocritical – and the hypocritical hate it for religious reasons.[21] Smelfungus and Mundungus also hate, or at least distrust, love. The feelings of Smelfungus are 'miserable', and in Florence he had 'fallen foul' upon the Venus of the Medicis (the goddess of love) 'and used her worse than a common strumpet'.[22] Mundungus 'had travell'd straight on looking neither to his right hand nor his left, lest Love or Pity should seduce him out of his road'.[23] The sentimental traveller, however, yields to the seductions of Love and Pity – indeed actively seeks them – and thus is able to learn better manners as he gets along. These are the 'weaknesses' of his heart; and this is why he writes 'not to apologize for [them] . . . – but to give an account of them'.[24]

In case there should be any doubt as to what Yorick means by love Sterne includes soon after this the 'Fragment', adapted from Burton, in which he tells the story of the reclamation of the town of Abdera from its evil ways by the power of Cupid. The Fragment contains also, it is worth noting, a warning to those who would wish to see Sterne simply as a satirist.

> – The town of Abdera, notwithstanding Democritus lived there trying all the powers of irony and laughter to reclaim it, was the vilest and most profligate town in all Thrace. What for poisons, conspiracies and assassinations – libels, pasquinades and tumults, there was no going there by day – 'twas worse by night.[25]

[20] Ibid. 104.
[21] 'Hypocrites [hate Love]for heaven's [sake].' Ibid. 111.
[22] Ibid. 118.   [23] Ibid. 119.   [24] Ibid. 90.   [25] Ibid. 130.

This depressing situation (for which there is no warrant in Burton – the picture is all Sterne's own) is saved by love and poetry. The townspeople are totally captivated by a speech by Perseus in Euripides' *Andromeda* which begins 'O *Cupid, prince of God and men, etc.*' – 'the whole city, like the heart of one man, open'd itself to Love . . . Friendship and Virtue met together, and kiss'd each other in the street – the golden age return'd, and hung o'er the town of Abdera'.[26]

The placing of the Fragment is clearly significant. It comes between the section in which Yorick announces that in so far as he is a kind and generous man it is because he has been in love with one princess or another almost all his life and the section in which he gives alms to the beggars at Montreuil. This is an important episode – the first 'publick act of . . . charity'[27] performed by the sentimental traveller on his journey. And it is performed after he has been prepared for it both by the lesson in good manners he has been taught by the monk and by the awakening of his benevolent instincts through his gently affectionate and mildly amorous encounter with the beautiful lady from Brussels. Our attention is therefore surely meant to be directed to the question of how well Yorick performs in his role of the man of feeling who is given the chance to exercise his benevolence.

To those who see Yorick primarily as a satiric butt he may not appear to measure up too well – after all there are sixteen beggars, and he prudently doles out only eight sous, plus an undisclosed and much larger sum to the *pauvre honteux* who finally touches his feelings. But we should beware of reading twentieth-century values into an eighteenth-century situation. Yorick does not have much money, therefore he must of necessity place a limit on the amount he gives on each occasion (that he gives at all is important – there are some travellers, as is made clear in the opening paragraph, who solve the problem by saying 'let them go to the devil' and giving out nothing).[28] Moreover it is significant that the beggars amicably recognise the situation Yorick is in, and accommodate themselves gratefully but tactfully both to his generosity and to the bounds he has to set to it. The emphasis for the greater part of the episode indeed is not so much on Yorick and his feelings as on the sophisticated and

[26] Ibid. 131.   [27] Ibid. 132.   [28] Ibid.

civilised manner in which the beggars handle a potentially embarrassing situation. Like Father Ambrose, in fact, they teach Yorick a lesson in *politesse* – 'Just heaven!' he asks, 'for what wise reasons has thou order'd it, that beggary and urbanity, which are at such variance in other countries, should find a way to be at unity in this?'[29] Yorick behaves with prudent benevolence, yielding eventually a little to flattery – and then is moved to make a final absurdly generous gesture by the poor decayed gentleman who is too ashamed to beg –

> Good God! said I – and I have not a single sous left to give him. – But you have a thousand! cried all the powers of nature, stirring within me – so I gave him – no matter what – I am ashamed to say *how much*, now, – and was ashamed to think, how little, then.[30]

The influence of love is not mentioned directly in this episode; but if we set it in its context it is clear that the powers of nature, Yorick's better feelings, can be stirred so easily because he is in love – lightly with the lady from Brussels, and more profoundly as he assures us, rather too self-consciously, with Eliza. ''Twas only in the power', says the Fragment, 'of the God whose empire extendeth from heaven to earth, and even to the depths of the sea, to have done this.'[31]

As Yorick's journey proceeds the references to love and to sexuality and the bodily functions become at one level more direct and forceful and at another more devious and complex. While Sterne wishes to insist that benevolence and the social virtues spring from the same source as sexual passion, at the same time he cannot (and probably did not entirely wish to) present Yorick as a complete sexual libertarian. Despite the open and cheerful reference to his connection with the Italian Marquesina and the occasional invocations of Eliza, Yorick is not and cannot be a completely casual and light-hearted libertine. He is a priest, however insouciantly he may wear the cassock – a priest, moreover, who despite his sprightliness, good humour and sophisticated scepticism is always aware that he is ageing, ill, possibly impotent, and certainly in orthodox Christian eyes a sexual transgressor. It is clear from his sermon on the Levite

[29] Ibid.   [30] Ibid. 134.   [31] Ibid. 131.

and his concubine that Sterne took a fairly optimistic view of
the leniency with which he could expect God to deal with the
carnal weaknesses of an otherwise reasonably virtuous man. But
he is never completely free from sexual guilt. Yorick may
candidly report the account given by the grave and learned
Bevoriskius of the copulative energy of the common sparrow –
but it stains his face with crimson. One may safely assume that
Sterne's face preserved its usual pallor – but the uneasiness,
slight though it may be, is there nonetheless.

It is not surprising then that Yorick's sexuality should begin
to express itself in more complex and less direct ways. The
situations in which he finds himself become more intricately
involved and more ambiguously significant – and to some degree
simply more outrageous; and the language in which they are
presented, while preserving its surface limpidity, takes on new
energy, depth and resonance. Yorick, on his arrival in Paris, for
example, watches the world running at the ring of pleasure –
and the way in which Sterne renders this moment of self-
knowledge combines sexual wit, freshly sensuous observation
and wry, unself-pitying regret in a way that can only be called
poetic:

> I walked gravely up to the window in my dusty black coat,
> and looking through the glass saw all the world in yellow,
> blue, and green, running at the ring of pleasure. – The old
> with broken lances, and in helmets which had lost their
> vizards – the young in armour bright which shone like gold,
> beplumed with each gay feather of the east – all – all tilting
> at it like fascinated knights in tournaments of yore for fame
> and love.[32]

'Alas, poor Yorick!' he says to himself, you will have to solace
your soul 'with some kind *grisset* of a barber's wife'; and
although he throws out the unworthy thought with the resolu-
tion to call on Mme de R**** straight away to present the letter
from his beautiful lady of the remise, Yorick's modest prophecy
proves more or less correct. His role is to watch the world rather
than participate: he feels the pulse of the *grisset*, he slips a
symbolic hand into an equally symbolic glove (the glove does not

[32] Ibid. 155–6.

fit correctly, being too large, – frustration operates even at the fourth remove!), places coins in the beautiful *fille de chambre's* purse – and contents himself with a chaste kiss upon her cheek. The greatest of enjoyments may be 'attended . . . with a sigh . . . and terminated *in a general way*, in little better than a convulsion',[33] but for Yorick, at least in Paris, the convulsion is indefinitely (though not unpleasurably) postponed.

The slightest incidents become rich in implication. When Yorick goes to the theatre, for instance, another priest appears momentarily and on the periphery, as it were, of the main area of our attention:

> It was now my turn to ask the old French officer "What was the matter?" for a cry of "*Haussez les mains, Monsieur l'Abbe,*" re-echoed from a dozen different parts of the parterre, was as unintelligible to me, as my apostrophe to the monk had been to him.[34]

The officer explains that the abbé is the victim of a traditional piece of cruel audience humour: he has been sighted sitting behind a couple of *grissets*, and so the crowd is shouting at him to hold his hands in the air during the performance. Like a guilty *döppelganger* glimpsed on the edge of a dream the poor abbé with his supposedly wandering hands reminds us of his English brother, whose hands, straying over wrists and popping in and out of gloves and purses, have been leading an almost independent sexual life since Yorick met the first of his *dulcineas* at Calais:

> Base passion! said I, turning myself about . . . thy hand is against every man, and every man's hand against thee – heaven forbid! said she, raising her hand up to her forehead, for I had turned full in front upon the lady whom I had seen in conference with the monk . . . Heaven forbid indeed! said I, offering her my own – she had a black pair of silk gloves open only at the thumb and fore-fingers, so accepted it without reserve . . .[35]

But Yorick learns from the incident in the theatre as he learns from every other: the great advantage of travel, the old officer tells him (after explaining why the crowd wants the abbé to hold up his hands) is that 'it taught us mutual toleration; and mutual

[33] Ibid. 228. [34] Ibid. 180. [35] Ibid. 89–90.

toleration . . . taught us mutual love'.[36] 'I blush'd at many a word the first month', confesses Yorick, 'which I found inconsequent and perfectly innocent the second' – [37] and he concludes the chapter and Volume I with his account of Mme de Rambouliet who wanted '*Rien que pisser*': 'I handed Madame de Rambouliet out of her coach; and had I been the priest of the chaste CASTALIA, I could not have served at her fountain with more respectful decorum'.[38] Volume II also concludes with Yorick's hand pointing comically to the naked female flesh:

> So that when I stretch'd out my hand, I caught hold of the Fille de Chambre's
> END OF VOL. II.[39]

Yorick, we can assume, unlike Uncle Toby, knows the right end of a woman from the wrong.

The climax of his Parisian adventures comes in Yorick's encounter with another *fille de chambre*. On a superficial reading it may appear as if his 'conquest' of the young woman is a straight-forwardly sexual one. But although Sterne stretches the double – indeed multiple – meanings of his language as far as possible this seems unlikely, and it would be inconsistent with almost everything else in *Tristram Shandy* and *A Sentimental Journey* if Yorick were to be permitted a simple, satisfactory and uncomplicated consummation. No: Yorick allows himself the maximum amount of physical excitement and psychological titillation and at the crucial moment calls a halt – and does so in such a way as to transform what could have been an embarrassing moment of middle-aged fumbling in a hotel bedroom into an eloquent statement of moral principle.

> Yes – and then – Ye whose clay-cold heads and luke-warm hearts can argue down or mask your passions – tell me, what trespass is it that a man should have them? or how his spirit stands answerable, to the father of spirits, but for his conduct under them?
> If nature has so wove her web of kindness, that some threads of love and desire are entangled with the piece – must the whole web be rent in drawing them out? – Whip me such stoics, great governor of nature! said I to myself – Wherever

[36] Ibid. 181. [37] Ibid. [38] Ibid. 183. [39] Ibid. 291.

thy providence shall place me for the trials of my virtue –
whatever is my danger – whatever is my situation – let me
feel the movements which rise out of it, and which belong to
me as a man – and if I govern them as a good one – I will trust
the issues to thy justice, for thou hast made us – and not we
ourselves.[40]

The passage is remarkable for a number of things. It is, to begin
with, as Stout and Lansing van der Heyden Hammond have
noted, thick with echoes of Sterne's Sermons and the Bible. And
it presents in a vivid, compressed and particularised manner the
argument which Sterne advances at length in his Sermon on the
Levite (who was, like Sterne, a priest) and his concubine – a
couple who form, with the concubine's father, Sterne says, 'A
most sentimental group.'[41] God made us what we are and therefore he must bear some of the responsibility for what we do,
especially in sexual matters where the passions are at once so
strong and potentially so socially valuable. And if we read the
Old Testament with an attentive eye, asks Sterne, what are we
to think?

> O Abraham, thou father of the faithful! if this was wrong,
> – Why didst thou set so ensnaring an example before the eyes
> of thy descendants? and, why did the God of Abraham, the
> God of Isaac and Jacob, bless so often the seed of such inter-
> courses . . . ?

[40] Ibid. 237–8.
[41] *Sermons* III 65. The Sermon on the text Judges xix 1–3, is one
of Sterne's most original compositions. Lansing van der Heyden
Hammond detects only four minor borrowings from one of Hall's
sermons, and he points out that Sterne's treatment of the situation is
completely different from Hall's. See *Laurence Sterne's Sermons of
Mr. Yorick* (New Haven, 1948) 68. There are echoes of this sermon
in two places in *A Sentimental Journey*, one of these being 'The
Conquest'. In view of the importance of this sermon and the attitudes
it embodies and its relationship to *A Sentimental Journey*, I feel it
rather extraordinary that Mr Cash can observe that 'The sexual
passions, which figure so largely in the novels, are not described in
the sermons'. See *Sterne's Comedy of Moral Sentiments* 41 note 6.
Sterne's use of 'sentimental' is interesting. Although the sermon was
possibly written before 1751 it was probably extensively revised
before Sterne published it in 1766. The totally serious way in which
Sterne employs it here almost certainly indicates the connotation the
term carried for him in the mid sixties.

God can dispense with his own laws; and accordingly we find the holiest of the patriarchs . . . accommodating themselves as well as they could to the dispensation.[42]

But Sterne's argument is more than a casuistical appeal to Old Testament examples and God's omnipotence. It is basically a plea to recognise ourselves honestly for what we are – and on the basis of this to act generously and tolerantly towards others, and towards ourselves. And if we should get some enjoyment out of the situation let us again be honest and not shamefaced about it: 'let me feel the movements which rise out of it, and which belong to me as a man' – and leave the rest to God who made us in the first place. And finally let us acknowledge that the threads of love and desire are so inextricably woven into nature's web of kindness that if we rip them out the whole fabric will be torn and destroyed. Man is a sexual and a social being, and these two sides of his nature are necessarily and indissolubly involved with each other. It is not good for man to be alone: God created him as a being who needs and seeks companionship. And if he looks for a companion, part of the motivation will be sexual:

> Let the torpid Monk seek heaven comfortless and alone. – GOD speed him! For my own part, I fear, I should never so find the way: let me be wise and religious – but let me be MAN: wherever thy Providence places me, or whatever be the road I take to get to thee – give me some companion on my journey, be it only to remark to; How our shadows lengthen as the sun goes down; – to whom I may say. How fresh is the face of nature! How sweet the flowers of the field! How delicious are these fruits![43]

'The Levite and his Concubine' is one of the most eloquent and personal of Sterne's sermons; and if we are to assume – as we must – that Sterne means quite unironically what he says here we must also assume that he means us to take at its face value what Yorick says in 'The Conquest', for the message is basically the same.

The full implications of Yorick's encounter with the *fille de*

---

[42] Ibid. III 69.

[43] Ibid. III 73–4. This passage is echoed in 'The Conquest'; see *A Sentimental Journey* 237–8.

chambre, however, become obvious only in the sequel. The master of the hotel lets him know that by entertaining an amateur in his room in the afternoon he has broken the house rules – unless he consents to receive one of the local professionals he will have to seek lodgings elsewhere. Yorick is naturally enough disgusted and annoyed, but he agrees to see the girl with her 'lace and silk stockings and ruffles, *et tout cela*' that evening – although he is determined to take out his annoyance on her and the *maître d'hotel* by buying nothing. 'No man cares to have his virtues the sport of contingencies,' he had observed to himself just before deciding not to give the mendicant Franciscan a single sou – and he obviously has much more justification on this occasion for refusing to act benevolently. But the girl has only been with him for a few moments when he abandons his scheme: he gracefully submits to the ritual of looking at her laces and pays over his money:

> If there is not a fund of honest gullibility in man, so much the worse – my heart relented . . . Why should I chastise one for the trespass of another? if thou art tributary to this tyrant of a host, thought I, looking up in her face, so much harder is thy bread.
> If I had not had more than four *Louis d'ors* in my purse, there was no such thing as rising up and shewing her the door, till I had first laid three of them out in a pair of ruffles.
> – The master of the hotel will share the profit with her – no matter – then I have only paid as many a poor soul has *paid* before me for an act he *could* not do, or think of.[44]

Yorick's action is humane and tactful, and it springs not from the whim of the moment but from that 'settled principle of humanity and goodness' which forms the substantial and enduring part of his moral character. (It is also an example of virtue in distress: in order to act virtuously the man of feeling has to accommodate himself 'weakly' to the demands of worldly convention.) And Yorick is able to act in this way because he is willing to give his sensibility free play, and also because he has learnt the lesson, impressed on him by the old French officer at the theatre, to adapt himself tolerantly to the customs of the country in which he finds himself. There is obviously every

[44] A *Sentimental Journey* 242–3.

justification in comparing Yorick's mode of behaviour here with his treatment of the monk – and the comparison is clearly to his advantage: he has indeed learnt better manners as he has gone along.

There is also a slight but unbroken and highly significant thread linking the two incidents. Yorick is able to make amends to Father Ambrose because he has allowed himself to make love – in the lightest possible manner – to Mme de L****. And it is partly because of his relationship with Mme de L**** that he finds himself able to treat the *grisset* with her laces and ruffles so kindly. The beautiful *fille de chambre*, whom he had been with in the afternoon, coincidentally happens to be employed by the lady in Paris, Mme de R****, to whom Yorick had been given a letter of introduction by Mme de L**** – and when she calls on him in his bedchamber on that 'fine still evening in the latter end of the month of May'[45] she is there on an errand from her mistress. So it could be argued that it is only because of his initial benevolent and amorous response to the lady in Calais that Yorick finds himself alone with this gentle and delightful girl, able both to 'feel the movements which . . . belong to [him] as a man . . . – and govern them as a good one'. And it is certainly because he has been able innocently to enjoy this exercise in sensibility that he is in the basically benevolent frame of mind which permits him to deal so generously with the second girl. Love is demonstrated once more to be the source of virtue.

This, too, is the clear implication of the concluding sections of Volume II. Yorick, worn out by the artificialities of Parisian high society, decides to continue his journey (none of the aristocrats and philosophers he meets is as human a person, it is worth noting, as the humble *fille de chambre* or his valet, La Fleur). Tired of 'the children of Art', he tells us, 'I languish'd for those of Nature: and one night, after the most vile prostitution of myself [the word is aptly chosen] to half a dozen different people, I grew sick – went to bed – order'd La Fleur to get me horses in the morning to set out for Italy'.[46] He travels through 'the Bourbonnois, the sweetest part of France – in the hey-day of the vintage' with his sensibilities fully awakened – 'with my affections flying out, and kindling at every group before me'.[47] But Yorick has no space to tell us about his adventures as he

[45] Ibid. 234.   [46] Ibid. 266.   [47] Ibid. 268.

dances through the vineyards with the sun-burnt daughters and
sons of labour: instead he must give us an account of his visit to
Maria.

If Sterne runs the risk of lapsing into really mawkish sentimentality anywhere in his journey it is here, and it is possible
that he does not altogether avoid it. Maria is the stock sentimental image of distressed virtue: beautiful, destroyed by love
and the world, and now completely impotent and pathetic.
Nothing can be done to help her – neither love nor money can
really assist her. The only tributes she demands are pity and
sympathy. And Yorick, who has deliberately sought her out,
'like the Knight of the Woeful Countenance, in quest of melancholy adventures'[48] liberally offers her both: they sit weeping
together, Yorick wiping alternately her eyes then his, and finally
leaving his tear-damp handkerchief for Maria to dry in her
bosom. The incident teeters on the edge of bathos and absurdity;
and it is only through his superb timing, and the subtlety with
which he hints both at the comic and the erotic possibilities of
the situation, that Sterne succeeds in bringing the scene off. He
does so, I think, and it is his style that enables him to do it. But
the context in which the episode occurs, and its place in the
developing argument of the book are also extremely important.
When these are given their due weight the real function of the
Maria interlude becomes apparent.

Yorick goes in search of Maria because he believes that the
experience of meeting her will reaffirm his awareness of the
existence of his soul. And it has the desired effect: as he wipes
away their tears he is in fact 'turned on' as he had hoped to be:

> I felt such undescribable emotions within me, as I am sure
> could not be accounted for from any combinations of matter
> and motion.
>
> I am positive I have a soul; nor can all the books with which
> the materialists have pester'd the world ever convince me of
> the contrary.[49]

He walks with Maria to Moulines, becoming more and more
conscious all the time of her attractiveness. She may have lost
her wits, but still, he confesses,

[48] Ibid. 270.   [49] Ibid. 271.

She was feminine – and so much was there about her of all that the heart wishes, or the eye looks for in woman, that could the traces be ever worn out of her brain, and those of Eliza's out of mine, she should *not only eat of my bread and drink of my own cup*, but Maria should lay in my bosom, and be unto me as a daughter.[50]

He leaves Maria, and the memory of her sufferings casts a shade across the 'joyous . . . riot of the affections' he had been looking forward to indulging himself in on 'this journey in the vintage, through this part of France'.[51] But it also provides the occasion for his invocation of '– Dear sensibility! source inexhausted of all that's precious in our joys, or costly in our sorrows!'[52] – an invocation that, like the sentimental sketch of Maria, was to be widely anthologised and reprinted.

If this was where A *Sentimental Journey* ended there might be some justification for seeing the whole work as being flawed and, in the pejorative sense, basically sentimental. But there is more to come. This passage is followed by two episodes which quite brilliantly restore the balance, and which allow us (as the Maria passage on its own does not) to give a much more complex, more serious and more positive interpretation of Yorick's fervent praise of sensibility. The first is the supper at the peasant's house and the second is the encounter at the mountain inn between Yorick and the Piedmontese lady and her maid.

The two sections in which the incident at the farmhouse is described are entitled 'The Supper' and 'The Grace', and Parson Yorick sees it and quite deliberately presents it as a sacred occasion: 'a large wheaten loaf was in the middle of the table; and a flaggon of wine at each end of it promised joy thro' the stages of the repast – 'twas a feast of love'.[53] The simple and happy family meal is concluded with a dance in which, says Yorick, 'I fancied I could distinguish an elevation of spirit different from that which is the cause or effect of simple jollity. – In a word, I thought I beheld *Religion* mixing in the dance.'[54] The peasant confirms his intuition:

The old man . . . said, that this was their constant way; and that all his life long he had made it a rule . . . to call out his family to dance and rejoice; believing, he said, that a chearful

[50] Ibid. 275.   [51] Ibid. 277.   [52] Ibid.   [53] Ibid. 281.   [54] Ibid. 284.

and contented mind was the best sort of thanks to heaven
that an illiterate peasant could pay –
– Or a learned prelate either, said I.[55]

The supper and the dance are a simple domestic manifestation
of The Lord's Supper, the central sacrament in the Christian
religion – not so much in its eucharistic sense (although it is
significant that Yorick, the priest, is present) as in its earlier
sense of the feast of love and fellowship. The word used by the
Church Fathers to describe this occasion was *agape* – the 'love
feast': 'a meal (of fellowship to which the poor were invited or
from which charity was dispensed) and a rite (with the use of
bread and wine as an important feature)'.[56] And whether Sterne
was familiar with Hippolytus' *Apostolic Tradition* or not, the
supper and the grace in the Bourbonnois farmhouse are a perfect
example of the traditional love feast – even to the benevolent
dispensation of charity to the wandering traveller.

If *agape* is the informing spirit on this occasion and Yorick
the priest its interpreter, *eros* is the inspirer of the next episode
and Yorick the jester his attendant minister. Obliged to share his
poor room at the inn with a Piedmontese lady 'of about thirty,
with a glow of health in her cheeks' (and an endearing liberality
with her burgundy) and her 'brisk and lively' French maid,
Yorick participates in drawing up a treaty which is supposed to
guarantee the chastity, propriety and comfort of all concerned –
a treaty, says Yorick, 'settled . . . I believe with as much religion
and good faith on both sides, as in any treaty which as yet had
the honour of being handed down to posterity'.[57]

But after they have all retired to bed no one can go to sleep.
Yorick tosses and turns

> till a full hour after midnight; when Nature and patience both
> wearing out – O my God! said I –
> – You have broke the treaty, Monsieur, said the lady, who
> had no more slept than myself. – I begg'd a thousand pardons
> – but insisted that it was no more than an ejaculation.[58]

---

[55] Ibid.
[56] William R. Schoedel, 'Agape' in *Encyclopaedia Britannica* (1971).
He states that 'the classical description of [the "love feast"] is found
in Hippolytus' *Apostolic Tradition*'.
[57] *A Sentimental Journey* 288.   [58] Ibid. 290.

In the heat of the ensuing argument the pins start to fall from the lady's curtain, and the *fille de chambre* comes out of the closet. As the volume – and the book – comes to a close Yorick is left in the darkness with two lively ladies: the Piedmontese by no means giving up her point 'tho' she weakened her barrier by it',[59] and in the narrow passage between their beds the Lyonoise maid who is literally on his hands.

The comedy is complete – and the key word is 'ejaculation'; and since not all ejaculations are pious, the reader is free to interpret it as he pleases. A *Sentimental Journey* ends as *Tristram Shandy* begins with an utterance and by implication at least an action in which the sacred and the secular, spiritual love and carnal, are suddenly and comically but somehow not inappropriately yoked together. 'O my God!' cries Yorick, tossing on his bed at the inn – 'Good G—!' cried my father, making an exclamation, but taking care to moderate his voice at the same time, – *Did ever woman, since the creation of the world, interrupt a man with such a silly question?* Pray, what was your father saying? – Nothing.'[60]

Nothing – and yet everything: in the beginning is the word – and the deed. Mr Shandy, as he begets his son, recalls the creation of the world. Yorick, with his outrageous pun, forces us to acknowledge that the man who is capable of prayer is also capable of sexual desire. The concluding episode in A *Sentimental Journey*, like the book as a whole, emphasises that man is a sexual creature, and that if his capacity to love not only his fellow men and women but also his God is to be properly understood it must be seen in the light of his sexuality. So far as the Christian religion is concerned this is not inappropriate. The gesture of love made by God the Father and Creator in giving his only Son to the world was – indeed by its nature had to be – both a divine and a *sexual* act. In the words of the Nicene Creed (which Sterne would have recited at every Communion service), Christ is 'the only-begotten Son of God, begotten from the Father before all ages . . . begotten not made . . . who . . . was incarnate from the Holy Spirit and the Virgin Mary and became man'. The incarnation is a sacred occurrence, but it is also, and inescapably, a carnal one.

It is the peculiar and characteristic triumph of Sterne in

[59] Ibid. [60] *Tristram Shandy* 3 (I, i).

A *Sentimental Journey* that he is able to make us accept a vision of man which incorporates tenderly, comically and realistically both the carnal and the spiritual aspects of his nature. Yorick the melancholy man of feeling, Yorick the joyful priest and Yorick the ribald lover – these are the three roles in which Sterne presents his hero and *alter ego* in rapid succession in the concluding sections of the *Journey*. If we can accept them all as possible dimensions of his character, and indeed go further and understand that these dimensions are not only possible but necessary, then we can begin to appreciate the real nature of Sterne's sentimentalism. A *Sentimental Journey*, taken as a whole, is in the sense of the word commonly accepted today the least sentimental of books.

And yet, paradoxically, it was from the moment it appeared read almost solely as a sentimental work. Sterne's complex, sceptical and positive vision of man was rapidly softened and sentimentalised by his readers, and imitators, and by the anthologists, into something simple, wistful and pathetic.

In the Preface to his *Journey* Yorick compares himself to the Dutchman 'who first transplanted the grape of Burgundy to the Cape of Good Hope'. The new settler did not know what sort of wine to expect, but he knew it would be 'some sort of vinous liquor' and that it would be alcoholic – and 'he hoped for the best':

> and in these hopes, by an intemperate confidence in the forti-
> tude of his head, and the depth of his discretion, *Mynheer*
> might possibly overset both in his vineyard; and by discovering
> his nakedness, become a laughing-stock to his people.
>
> Even so it fares with the poor Traveller, sailing and posting
> through the politer kingdoms of the globe in pursuit of know-
> ledge and improvements.[61]

And even so it fared with Sterne himself. His readers could not accept his vision of man as being not only tender hearted but also naked, shameless and comic, as being capable of virtue because he was willing to be distressed. The compilers of the extremely popular anthology, *The Beauties of Sterne, including all his Pathetic Tales and Most Distinguished Observations on Life, selected for the Heart of Sensibility*, preferred to forget that

[61] A *Sentimental Journey* 83.

Sterne, Yorick and Tristram were undoubtedly, like Rosinante, masculine animals 'at all points'[62] – however Fate may have dealt with Uncle Toby. Like the sons of Noah they averted their eyes from the old man's embarrassing nakedness,[63] covered him with a blanket, and hoped that he would quietly remain asleep. But Sterne, of course, has obstinately refused to lie down. *Tristram Shandy* and *A Sentimental Journey* remain two of the liveliest, most delightful and most interesting of the works of fiction produced in the eighteenth century. And no matter what the word may mean today the unfailing source of their distinctive life is their sentimentalism. So that if in one sense the *Journey* is the least sentimental of books in another it is one of the most: in its uniquely balanced blend of wit and feeling, scepticism and optimism, it embodies the quintessence of many of the most positive, spontaneous and sophisticated elements in the sentimentalism of the age.

[62] *Tristram Shandy* 35 (I, x). *The Beauties of Sterne*, conveniently equipped with an index, was published in 1782. By 1799 it had gone into thirteen English and four American editions. See *Shandyism and Sentiment, 1760–1800*, by J. T. C. Oates (Cambridge, 1968) 17 and *passim*.

[63] And Noah began to be an husbandman, and he planted a vineyard.

And he drank of the wine and was drunken; and he was uncovered within his tent.

And Ham, the father of Canaan, saw the nakedness of his father, and told his two brethren without.

And Shem and Japheth took a garment, and laid it upon both their shoulders, and went backward, and covered the nakedness of their father; and their faces were backward, and they saw not their father's nakedness.

And Noah awoke from his wine and knew what his younger son had done unto him.

Genesis ix 20–4

4

The Vicar of Wakefield, The Man of Feeling and Werther:

Comic, Pathetic and Tragic Versions of the Distressed and Virtuous Hero

I

When Scythrop, the melancholy hero of Thomas Love Peacock's *Nightmare Abbey* is introduced to the reader he is presented sitting at evening 'on a fallen fragment of mossy stone, with his back resting against [a] ruined wall, – a thick canopy of ivy, with an owl in it, over his head, – and the Sorrows of Werther in his hand'.[1] Later, in one of the climactic incidents in the story, he contemplates following Werther's example and shooting himself because he has been disappointed in love. By the time *Nightmare Abbey* was published (1818) *Werther* was so well known and so popular in England that it could practically be regarded as part of English literature. Moreover it gave the appearance of belonging to a well-established tradition of sentimental fiction: it could be easily grouped together with a number of English novels, including *The Vicar of Wakefield* and *The Man of Feeling*, which had been published round about the same time – between 1766 and 1774.

The Sorrows of Young Werther, The Vicar of Wakefield and *The Man of Feeling* provide an example of what was then regarded as both fashionable and, in a critical sense, respectable. The years between 1766 when *The Vicar of Wakefield* was published, and 1774, when *Werther* appeared, are of particular significance in the history not only of sentimentalism, but also of English fiction. Two other novels of some substance were published within this same period – *A Sentimental Journey* in

---

[1] *The Novels of Thomas Love Peacock*, ed. David Garnett (London, 1948) 362.

1768 and *Humphry Clinker* in 1771. Forty years later, in 1811, Jane Austen's *Sense and Sensibility* was offered to the public; and it would be difficult to counter the claim that within these forty years not one new novel of any major literary importance was produced by a British author. After Smollett the *Cambridge Bibliography of English Literature* includes only two other names in its main list of eighteenth-century novelists – Fanny Burney and William Beckford. Interesting and charming as these two writers may be they are, I think, as inescapably minor as, say, Mrs Radcliffe – and if their names are on the list it is difficult to see why hers is not also.

The works I shall be discussing come then at the end of one stage in the development of the English novel and at the beginning – a delayed beginning it is true – of another. They fall, that is to say, within a period which more than most deserves to be called a period of transition. An investigation of them may, I hope, do something to explain how and why the sentimentalism of fundamentally realistic and tough-minded writers like Richardson and Sterne came to be replaced by the tearful sentimentality of the crowd of now forgotten novelists whose works filled the shelves of the circulating libraries in the last thirty years of the eighteenth century. In the case of *Werther* it may be possible also to suggest, however briefly, some of the ways in which sentimentalism is related to romanticism, and also to other literary developments later in the nineteenth century and in our own day.

The most famous and the most typically representative of all sentimental novels is *A Sentimental Journey*. Both in itself and in its reception by the reading public it offers a paradigm of the whole sentimental movement. Initially extraordinarily popular and, in a catalytic rather than a direct way, influential, *A Sentimental Journey* gradually suffered a decline in reputation. As time went on Sterne began to be cited not as an example of the true voice of feeling but as an example of how the sentimental ideal could be subtly falsified and distorted. Hannah More, for instance, in her poem *Sensibility*, first published in 1782, singled him out as the prime instance of this kind of hypocrisy:

> Oh, bless'd Compassion! Angel Charity!
> More dear one genuine deed perform'd for thee,

Than all the periods Feeling e'er can turn,
Than all thy soothing pages, polish'd STERNE![2]

The man she really admired was Henry Mackenzie, who wrote
The Man of Feeling. Mackenzie's treatment of his hero and
of the theme of virtue in distress is indeed different from Sterne's
handling of Parson Yorick – although not quite in the way
Hannah More suggests. In each of this group of novels sentimentalism in fact assumes a distinct and different form. At the
same time, of course, they share many common characteristics –
and it is to an examination of some of these differences and
similarities that I should now like to turn.

II

The Reverend Dr Primrose, Goldsmith's Vicar of Wakefield, is,
like Parson Adams and Parson Yorick, a Christian hero. He
'unites in himself', says the author in the Advertisement to his
Tale, 'the three greatest characters upon earth; he is a priest, an
husbandman, and the father of a family'.[3] He is moreover the
embodiment of some of the principal sentimental virtues. He is
charitable, humane, optimistic and in general readier to think
well rather than ill of his fellow men. All his family, he tells us,
'had but one character, that of being all equally generous,
credulous, simple, and inoffensive'.[4] Since his moral assessments
of the situations in which he finds himself are spontaneous and
unselfish, he could be described as a man of feeling, but feelings
in his case are always grounded in a coherent set of Christian
principles, and they are always vigorously implemented in positive action. He is a man of sentiment, of sense rather than
sensibility; and his determination to govern his behaviour
according to principle often gets him into comic trouble with
the world. When his son George is about to marry Miss Arabella
Wilmot, Primrose endangers the whole scheme by refusing to
compromise his beliefs on the subject of monogamy which he

[2] *Sacred Dramas . . . to which is added, Sensibility, a Poem* (London,
1782) 285.
[3] *The Vicar of Wakefield: a Tale. Supposed to be written by Himself* (Salisbury, 1766) in *Collected Works*, ed. Arthur Friedman, 5 vols
(Oxford, 1966) I 14.
[4] Ibid. I 21.

discovers to be diametrically opposed to those held by Miss Wilmot's father. Principle again carries the day a short while later when, learning that he has suddenly lost his fortune, Primrose refuses to let the marriage proceed under false pretences.

The purpose of the action in the novel is to display the Vicar of Wakefield in a number of testing situations. 'He is drawn', Goldsmith tells us, 'as ready to teach, and ready to obey, as simple in affluence, and majestic in adversity.'[5] Like Job, he loses his fortune and practically loses his family. At the nadir of his adventures he is presented to us ill, injured, penniless and in prison. His house has been burned down, one of his daughters appears to have been ruined by the local nobleman, Squire Thornhill, and his eldest son George is also in prison, chained and under sentence of death for having sent a challenge to the man who has wronged his sister.

But Primrose never loses his faith nor his moral energy. He preaches to the other prisoners, and once he has got them to listen to him persuades them to spend their time in useful work – i.e. in making small articles which they can sell. 'Thus in less than a fortnight I had formed them into something social and humane, and had . . . brought [them] from their native ferocity into friendship and obedience.'[6] At the same time he consoles his fellow sufferers with the promise that although the rich man may be happy on earth the poor and the wretched who believe in God will be rewarded with an eternity of bliss – a reward which they are much more likely to attain since poverty and imprisonment cut them off from so many dangerous temptations.

But Primrose's virtue is rewarded in a much more immediate and tangible manner. A good fairy arrives in the shape of the cheerful vagabond Mr Burchell, whom Primrose has befriended earlier on in the story. 'Former benevolence [is] now repaid with unexpected interest', as the heading to Chapter XII, Volume II puts it. Mr Burchell turns out to be Sir William Thornhill in disguise, the philanthropic uncle of the wicked young Squire Thornhill. Sir William marries one of Primrose's daughters, he provides a dowry for the other (who turns out to be genuinely married to his nephew), George's fetters are struck off, Primrose's fortunes are restored, and all's well that ends well.

---

[5] Ibid. I 14.   [6] Ibid. I 149.

When Primrose, at the beginning of the novel, sends his son out into the world to seek his fortune he urges him to make the following text his consolation: 'I *have been young, and now am old; yet never saw I the righteous man forsaken, or his seed begging their bread.*'[7] The happy dénouement would seem to be meant to demonstrate the validity of this hopeful statement.

But the whole process of the action of the story has been to negate it. The more virtuously Primrose and his family behave the more cruelly they are made to suffer at the hands of fortune and their fellow men. A synopsis of the plot up to, but not including, the happy reversal with which it is rounded off would make *The Vicar of Wakefield* sound like an episode in Sade's *Justine* – it seems to demonstrate not only that the practices of virtue is not rewarded in this world but also that it is likely to attract the most outrageously bad luck. The burning down of Primrose's house is like the final destruction and violation of Justine by a bolt of lightning – a gratuitous kick in the teeth delivered by the malevolent universe in which we have to live. The structure of *The Vicar of Wakefield*, regarded as a whole, is thus profoundly sentimental, in the modern sense of the term.

Its sentimentality for the most part, however, is not disturbing, and it is interesting to speculate as to why this should be so (the one distasteful element in the fortunate conclusion is the transformation of Squire Thornhill into a suitable husband for Olivia – he is a much nastier character in fact than Richardson's Mr B.). *The Vicar of Wakefield* remains a genuinely charming and delightful book. One of the main reasons for this is that the classically comic plot is so obviously artificial. It has the happy air of a deliberately contrived, almost magical ritual – a charm enacted against wicked men and evil days in which we are cordially invited to take part. Moreover Goldsmith's picture of life in the country is at once realistic and idyllic: the framework may be artificial, but the domestic rural world of the Primroses which it encompasses is rendered with remarkable fidelity, liveliness and good humour. The catastrophes which overtake the family are kept in perspective by the gentle comedy – Primrose slyly tipping the face-wash in the fire, or Mr Burchell, with his

[7] Ibid. I 26 (Psalm xxxvii 25). The text in the Authorised Version is slightly different: 'I have been young and now am old; yet have I not seen the righteous forsaken, nor his seed begging bread.'

chorus of 'Fudge!', undercutting the high-flown sophisticated chatter of the London whores. It is easy to understand how the young Goethe, embarked on his own idyllic holiday with the family at Sesenheim, could feel, as he tells us in *Dichtung und Wahrheit*, that he had walked into the Primrose household itself.[8]

Nonetheless in the final assessment there is something worrying about the novel, a discordant note which all Goldsmith's charm cannot completely disguise. And the source of the discord can be located not so much in the Vicar of Wakefield himself as in his guardian angel, the man who saves him and his family from destruction, Mr Burchell, or Sir William Thornhill in disguise. Sir William Thornhill, as he presents himself through the mask of Burchell to the Primroses, is a melancholy man of feeling. The conversation between him and the Vicar is of unusual interest, and deserves to be quoted at length:

"What!" cried I, "is my young landlord then the nephew of a man whose virtues, generosity, and singularities are so universally known? I have heard Sir William Thornhill represented as one of the most generous, yet whimsical, men in the kingdom; a man of consummate benevolence" – "Something, perhaps, too much so," replied Mr. Burchell, "at least he carried benevolence to an excess when young; for his passions were then strong, and as they were all upon the side of virtue, they led it up to a romantic extreme. . . He loved all mankind; for fortune prevented him from knowing that there were rascals. Physicians tell us of a disorder in which the whole body is so exquisitely sensible, that the slightest touch gives pain: what some have thus suffered in their persons, this gentleman felt in his mind. The slightest distress, whether real or fictitious, touched him to the quick, and his soul laboured under a sickly sensibility of the miseries of others. Thus disposed to relieve, it will be easily conjectured, he found numbers disposed to solicit; his profusions began to impair his fortune, but not his good-nature; that, indeed, was seen to encrease as the other seemed to decay: he grew improvident as

[8] 'The First Visit to Sesenheim', in *Truth and Fantasy from my Life*, ed. J. M. Cohen, trans. Eithne Wilkins and Ernst Kaiser (London, 1949) 124 and *passim*.

he grew poor; and though he talked like a man of sense, his actions were those of a fool.'[9]

In short he began to dissipate his fortune, and also to lose confidence in his ability to assess the characters and motives of his fellow men. In order to repair the damage both to himself and his finances 'he travelled through Europe on foot'. This left him (for some inexplicable reason) 'more affluent than ever'. And now, therefore

> his bounties are more rational and moderate than before; but still he preserves the character of an humourist, and finds most pleasure in eccentric virtues.[10]

Since Sir William Thornhill is so important in the moral scheme of Goldsmith's fable it is interesting to note the terms in which he describes himself. He has a 'sickly sensibility', he has behaved more like a fool than a man of sense, 'he preserves the character of an humourist', i.e. an oddity, and he 'finds most pleasure in eccentric virtues'. 'Eccentric' is perhaps the key word: Thornhill is able to preserve his integrity and also to operate effectively if erratically as a moral agent only by functioning *outside* the society to which he belongs. He does not live on his estates, he moves amongst his tenants in disguise, he is utterly incapable *because of his exquisite sensibility* of playing a normal part in the community. Yet he represents in their most highly developed form the moral ideals of this society from which he is in a sense excluded. Primrose, the 'normal' man, occupies a central place in this same society – husbandman, priest, and father – but it destroys him. Burchell/Thornhill is thus not merely a Haroun-el-Rashid figure, the romantic 'someone in disguise' who turns up in the nick of time to set things right. He is a symbol of alienation, the dispossessed conscience of a sick society. And although like George Primrose (and presumably like Goldsmith in his happier moments) he recalls his travels on the Continent cheerfully enough, his motive for undertaking them was despair. Against the carefree image of the happy wanderer playing his flute to the simple peasants one should set the opening lines of *The Traveller*, which Goldsmith published in 1765 (a year before

[9] *The Vicar of Wakefield* I 29. [10] Ibid. I 30.

the appearance of *The Vicar of Wakefield*) and which bears the
sub-title, *A Prospect of Society*:

> Remote, unfriended, melancholy, slow,
> Or by the lazy Scheld, or wandering Po;
> Or onward, where the rude Carinthian boor
> Against the houseless stranger shuts the door;
> Or where Campania's plain forsaken lies,
> A weary waste expanded to the skies,
> Where'er I roam, whatever realms to see,
> My heart untravell'd fondly turns to thee;
> Still to my brother turns, with ceaseless pain,
> And drags at each remove a lengthening chain.

The implications of *The Vicar of Wakefield*, ostensibly a
sentimental comedy, are thus at bottom as pessimistic and as
elegiac as those of *The Deserted Village* and *The Traveller*. One
feels that for Goldsmith society appears to be so irrational, so
cruel, and so economically inefficient and inequitable, that it is
extremely difficult if not impossible for the ordinary, well-
intentioned, morally responsible man to live the good life. For
Dr Primrose to survive he needs the magical assistance of Sir
William Thornhill. It could be said that Tom Jones similarly
needs the magical assistance of Squire Allworthy – but he does
not need it nearly so desperately. Allworthy in the end merely
represents the good luck which Tom in a sense deserves: it is
easy to believe that he would have had more than a fighting
chance of winning through somehow on his own resources. But
one cannot feel this about the Primrose family. The structure of
The Vicar of Wakfield, and in particular the division of moral
responsibility between the Vicar himself and Sir William Thornhill, reflects a radical disquiet with the nature of man and society,
a disquiet which forces Goldsmith into sentimentality. This disquiet is not apparent in *Tom Jones* nor, for that matter, in
Tristram Shandy or *A Sentimental Journey*. It becomes increasingly apparent, however, in the novels which were produced
between 1770 and the end of the century.

III

Nowhere is the gap between sentimental theory and harsh reality
more glaringly apparent than in *The Man of Feeling* by Henry

Mackenzie and its companion and sequel *The Man of the World*. To the modern reader, and even to some of Mackenzie's contemporaries, they seem far more self-indulgent and superficial than anything Sterne was capable of writing. But he was held by some of his more enthusiastic supporters to be the equal of the English novelist in his power to depict the tender feelings: Sterne and Mackenzie, said Scott, are 'the most celebrated certainly among those [authors] who are termed sentimental'.[11] And there must have been many for whom, as for Hannah More, Henry Mackenzie appeared to be not only the more respectable of the two but also the more sincere. In her poem *Sensibility*, from which I have already quoted, she concludes a scarcely disguised attack on Sterne with a eulogy of his Scottish rival:

> There are, who fill with brilliant plaints the page,
> If a poor linnet meets the gunner's rage . . .
> Who for a wounded animal deplore,
> As if friend, parent, country were no more;
> Who boast quick rapture trembling in their eye,
> If from the spider's snare they save a fly;
> Whose well-sung sorrows every breast inflame,
> And break all hearts but his from whence they came:
> Yet, scorning life's *dull* duties to attend,
> Will persecute a wife, or wrong a friend . . .
> Not so the tender moralist of Tweed;
> His *Man of Feeling*, is a man indeed.[12]

Unfortunately it is just on this score that Harley, the Man of Feeling, is least satisfactory. He is an epicene, impotent, passive, almost completely ineffectual character – a set of tender susceptibilities and conventional moral attitudes rather than a living individual. He accurately reflected the taste of the day, however: the book was popular, and it made Mackenzie's reputation.

The Man of Feeling, as the author himself admitted, is not a conventional novel. It is 'different from most others as containing little plot or incident but merely a sketch of some particulars of the life and sentiments of a man of more than usual sensi-

[11] 'Henry Mackenzie', in *Lives of the Novelists* (1825); see *Sir Walter Scott on Novelists and Fiction*, ed. I Joan Williams (London & New York, 1968) 79.
[12] *Sacred Dramas* 284–5.

bility'.[13] Nonetheless, it had he believed 'something of Nature in it';[14] and it is true that it does possess rather more connection with reality than a great many of the works of fiction that were then being turned out. When Mackenzie wrote the book he was a young Scots gentleman with literary ambitions studying the law in London. His greatest hope was to be a poet; when *The Deserted Village* appeared, for instance, he wrote to Miss Rose, 'How I do envy Dr. Goldsmith's subject . . . I could have made a thousand verses on such a theme.'[15] Like his hero, Harley, he was shy, possibly also a bit gullible, and no doubt lonely and on the defensive as most young Scots in London at that time would have been. *The Man of Feeling*, in so far as it reflects this experience, has a certain liveliness and authenticity. The note of realism is further strengthened by the structure of the book which is in its own way quite sophisticated. The author poses as the editor of a manuscript account of his hero. The manuscript has been given to him by the curate of the parish where Harley had lived and died. He does not know who the author is, and parts only of the original remain, since the curate is in the habit of taking it with him when he goes shooting to tear up and use as wadding.

This serves as a pleasantly amusing and informal introduction to the fragmentary sketches which follow, and through which we are allowed to build up a picture of the Man of Feeling. He is a young country gentleman, without a great deal of money and with no worldly ambitions whatsoever. He is persuaded to go up to London for the purpose of trying to get the crown lease of some land adjacent to his own. He fails in this endeavour, partly through his own innocence and good nature. Whilst in London, however, he meets some interesting characters and has some educative experiences: he visits Bedlam, for example, and is moved to tears by his encounter there with a beautiful young woman driven, like Sterne's Maria, out of her mind through the death of her lover; he is introduced to a misanthropist who tells him that 'man is an animal equally selfish and vain';[16] trusting

[13] *The Anecdotes and Egotisms of Henry Mackenzie*, ed. Harold William Thompson (London, 1927) 186.

[14] To James Elphinston, 23 July 1770. Quoted in *A Scottish Man of Feeling: Some Account of Henry Mackenzie, Esq.*, by Harold William Thompson (London and New York, 1931) 112.

[15] Letter of 2 June 1770. Quoted in *A Scottish Man of Feeling* 87.

[16] *The Man of Feeling* (London, 1771) 80.

like Dr Primrose to his skill in physiognomy, he is fleeced by a
card sharp; and he befriends (and materially assists) a starving
prostitute. On his way back from London he meets an old soldier
whom he also befriends and to whom he eventually gives the
tenancy of a small farm on his estate. He assumes wrongly that
Miss Walton, the woman he loves, is going to marry another,
and so fails to declare his feelings for her until he is on his death-
bed – dying partly from a broken heart, partly from a fever
caught while nursing his soldier tenant, old Edwards, and partly
because he is too good for this wicked world. With tears dropping
from his eyes he assures his friend (the supposed author of the
manuscript) that they will meet again, 'never to be separated',
in a place where his sensibility will be recognised at its true
value:

> There are some feelings which perhaps are too tender to be
> suffered by the world. The world is in general selfish, inter-
> ested, and unthinking, and throws the imputation of romance
> or melancholy on every temper more susceptible than its own.
> I cannot think but in those regions which I contemplate, if
> there is any thing of mortality left about us, that these feelings
> will subsist; – they are called, – perhaps they are – weaknesses
> here: – but there may be some better modifications of them in
> heaven, which may deserve the name of virtues.[17]

At this moment, Miss Walton calls to see him. Knowing that
his situation is now truly hopeless he brings himself to the point
of revealing that he loves her. When she replies that she loves
him too, the news is too much for him altogether:

> "There are, said he, in a very low voice, there are attachments,
> Miss Walton" – His glance met her's – They both betrayed a
> confusion, and were both instantly withdrawn – He paused
> some moments – "I am in such a state as calls for sincerity,
> let that also excuse it – It is perhaps the last time we shall ever
> meet . . . To love Miss Walton could not be a crime; – if to
> declare it is one – the expiation will be made." – Her tears
> were now flowing without control. – "Let me intreat you,
> said she, to have better hopes – Let not life be so indifferent to

[17] Ibid. 260–1.

you; if my wishes can put any value on it. – I will not pretend
to misunderstand you – I know your worth – I have known it
long – I have esteemed it – What would you have me say? –
I have loved it as it deserved." – He seized her hand – a languid
colour reddened his cheek – a smile brightened faintly in his
eye. As he gazed on her, it grew dim, it fixed, it closed – He
sighed, and fell back on his seat. – Miss Walton screamed at
the sight – His aunt and the servants rushed into the room –
They found them lying motionless together. – His physician
happened to call at that instant. Every art was tried to recover
them – With Miss Walton they succeeded – But Harley was
gone forever![18]

One can only agree with the critic in the *Monthly Review*
who, when the book first appeared, observed that 'this performance is written after the manner of Sterne; but it follows at a
prodigious distance the steps of that ingenious and sentimental
writer'. He went on, however, to maintain that *The Man of
Feeling* 'is not . . . totally destitute of merit; the Reader, who
weeps not over some of the scenes it describes, has no sensibility
of mind'.[19] Several of these scenes occur in the story of old
Edwards; and to complete our picture of Mackenzie's sentimentality we should perhaps say something about this, especially
as it was the author's own 'favourite passage',[20] and according
to the gentlemen of the *Critical Review* was 'exquisitely affecting' and 'written in a very masterly manner'.[21]

The impact made by Sterne's Uncle Toby on readers with the
proper 'sensibility of mind' had effectively demonstrated just
how potent a sentimental symbol the figure of the old soldier
could be, and Mackenzie exploited to the full the opportunities
for pathos afforded him by the character and situation of old
Edwards. The scene in which he is first presented to the reader is
a pretty *tableau vivant*, a set-piece of word painting very similar
in style to those in *A Sentimental Journey* (the description of

[18] Ibid. 263–4.
[19] *Monthly Review* XLIV 418 (May 1771).
[20] Letter to Miss Betty Rose of Kilravock, 24 Jan. 1770. He goes on:
'There are some strokes in it which I am prouder of than anything I
ever wrote.' Quoted in *A Scottish Man of Feeling* 110.
[21] *Critical Review* XXXI 483 (June 1771).

Father Lorenzo, for instance, in which Salvator Rosa is also referred to):[22]

> An old man, who from his dress seemed to have been a soldier, lay fast asleep on the ground; a knapsack was rested on a stone at his right hand, while his staff and brass-hilted sword were crossed at his left.

> . . . He was one of those figures which Salvator would have drawn; nor was the surrounding scenery unlike the wilderness of that painter's backgrounds. The banks of each side were covered with fantastic shrub-wood. . . . A rock, with some dangling wild flowers, jutted out above where the soldier lay, on which grew the stump of a large tree, white with age, and a single twisted branch shaded his face as he slept.[23]

The story Edwards has to tell is almost unbearably sad. First, he and his son had been forced by a combination of bad luck and a cruel landlord to leave their farm. Then his son is taken by the pressgang (a scene of high melodrama, this: the young man is seized as he is playing a game of blind man's buff on Christmas Eve). Edwards, however, for the sake of his son's wife and children, goes in his place, and when Harley meets him is returning from service in the East Indies, where he has found the noble and savage natives much more humane than his brutal comrades in arms. The crowning touch is given when he and Harley reach his native village. There they discover that young Edwards and his wife are dead. The children have survived, however, and Harley installs them and their grandfather on a small farm. This act of kindness receives its reward when Harley catches from old Edwards the fever which helps to bring about his own death.

Although there is a certain not unattractive strain of gentle, humorous naturalism in *The Man of Feeling*, it is essentially a mannered, artificial piece of work. And its artificialities, like the pathetic figure of Harley himself, constitute a retreat from reality. They are an admission of despair on the part of the author, a way of escaping from what he clearly felt to be the apparently insoluble moral problems posed by the nature of the society in which he had to live. And it is obvious that both

---

[22] See my article, 'Sterne and Painting', in *Of Books and Humankind*, ed. John Butt (London, 1964) 93–108.
[23] *The Man of Feeling* 172–3.

Mackenzie and his readers found the sort of escape offered by
The Man of Feeling delightful and emotionally gratifying.

By comparison with *A Sentimental Journey* it is genuinely
narcissistic and self-indulgent, and it is much more thoroughly
defeatist and pessimistic than *The Vicar of Wakefield*. Primrose
may be cruelly treated by the world, but he never loses his
resilience, his lively Christian faith or his cheerfulness – if he
goes down he goes down fighting. But Harley gives up practically
without a struggle. Moreover, one is made to feel that society is
actively and malevolently opposed to the virtues he represents –
'There are some feelings which perhaps are too tender *to be suffered* by the world.' The serjeant in charge of the pressgang, for
instance, obviously gets a sadistic pleasure out of seeing the old
man sacrifice himself for his son. When Harley has to leave his
watch as a pledge for the money he has spent on the poor prostitute we are told that he does not notice

> the sneer of the waiter, who, twirling the watch in his hand,
> made him a profound bow at the door, and whispered to a
> girl, who stood in the passage, something, in which the word
> CULLY was honoured with a particular emphasis.[24]

The good man so far as Mackenzie is concerned must inevitably
be a weak man. Simply because he is good he will arouse the
hatred and contempt of the world – he will inevitably be cheated,
he will inevitably be something of a fool or a simpleton.

In so far as a vision of society is made manifest in *The Man of
Feeling* it is of a society which is morally dislocated and disintegrating. This vision emerges even more strongly from *The
Man of the World*, a much more ambitious novel but one which,
even within its own terms, is much less successful. In *The Man
of the World* the sentimental virtues are represented by the
Annesly Family – a country clergyman and his two children, a
boy and a girl. Mackenzie takes considerable care over establishing the characters of the children, and sets out in some detail the
eminently sensible general principles on which their father
attempts to base their moral education. They are not proof, however, against the evil machinations of Sir Thomas Sindall, the
Man of the World. He corrupts and ruins the boy in order to

[24] Ibid. 101–2.

gain power over the girl. Young Annesly commits a stupid robbery and is transported; Sindall abducts and rapes his sister, who dies soon after giving birth to a daughter. Some years later, after a happy and successful life, Sindall is on the point of raping this same daughter just as he had raped the mother, when Annesly returns and kills him (to be fair to the villain, he is not aware until just before he dies that he is the girl's father). This blatantly melodramatic dénouement was too much even for the hardened hacks of the *Monthly Review* who described it as

> such a combination of circumstances as would shock the credulity of a monk. In a lonely hut, on a common, where the villainy of Sir Thomas was to be perpetrated at midnight, the Author brings together the *uncle*, who had been transported to America, the *nurse* who had dropped the girl, and who had been transported too, and *Bolton* the lover. They prevent the mischief; discover all; and turn the heart of Sir Thomas; who, in the stile of the Methodists, is converted, and prays, and goes to heaven.[25]

The one section of the novel which today seems to have any quality is the account given by Annesly of his life amongst the Indians.[26] Like old Edwards in *The Man of Feeling* Annesly leaves the white community and is forced to live with the savages. By stoically enduring torture he wins their admiration and a place in the tribe. Indian society as Mackenzie presents it is hard, cruel and warlike, but by comparison with European civilisation it is honest and honourable. Annesly lives happily amongst them – he is a successful, integral member of his tribe – because he expects them to act as ruthless savages and not as humane, Christian men of feeling. As soon as he returns to his own people, however, he falls into his old mistake of expecting them to live up to their professed good intentions. He is cheated, robbed and almost killed. He survives, a thoroughly disillusioned man, only because of his physical toughness.

The concept of savage nobility is, in its own way, as sentimental as the concept of pure sensibility, and Annesly's story is not altogether free from the artificiality which characterises the

[25] *Monthly Review* XLVIII 268 (April 1773).
[26] See Hoxley Neal Fairchild, *The Noble Savage: a Study in Romantic Naturalism* (New York, 1928) 92 and *passim*.

rest of Mackenzie's work. But Mackenzie's vision of the Indian world is coherent and reasonably well-informed; and his account of Annesly's return to civilisation has a note of harsh bitterness which is reminiscent of Swift and Smollett. Although the tone of this section of the novel is not so tearful and pathetic as the tone of the rest of the book its implications are the same: to be a man of feeling is to invite disaster; and in the sphere of ordinary human activity it is a distinct disadvantage to possess the sentimental virtues. To be virtuous is almost necessarily to be in distress. The only consolation is to know that one is capable of being moved to tears by the pity of it all, for this means that although one may be powerless to alter an evil situation one at least knows that it is evil: one has 'a feeling heart' and 'a mind of sensibility'.

IV

The Man of Feeling and *The Man of the World* are interesting to the modern reader more as examples of what the public taste demanded in the sentimental novel than as works of fiction in their own right. This can hardly be said of *The Sorrows of Werther*. Goethe's novel, despite some obvious defects, is a remarkable artistic and imaginative achievement: its lyrical power, its psychological insight and its dramatic intensity are still unusually impressive. It is also a complex book. At one level it is a tragic love story: Werther, the young romantic, falls in love with the beautiful and admirable Charlotte who unfortunately is already betrothed to the equally admirable Albert. After the marriage Werther still cannot escape from his increasingly obsessive love, and so he breaks out of the eternal triangle by shooting himself. At another level, however, it is a story of self-discovery, self-assertion and deliberate self-destruction: Werther, alienated from society, turns in upon himself in an attempt to create his own world.

He is, however, as much a man of feeling in some ways as he is a pre-Byronic hero in others. And it is the melodramatic and sentimental elements in the story which seem rather embarrassing and ridiculous today – Charlotte's tearful and pious recollections of her dead mother, for instance, at the end of Part I, which Werther finds so profoundly moving. But although

Werther reflects and embodies many of the most fashionable ideas and ideals of the sentimental tradition at the same time it criticises and evaluates them. In this it resembles *A Sentimental Journey*, and Goethe's attitude to Werther is as ambiguous and as puzzling as Sterne's is towards Yorick. The reception which *The Sorrows of Werther* received from the public is also strikingly similar to that accorded Sterne's novel. *Werther* was extraordinarily popular and influential throughout Europe and especially in Germany and England. For the last two and a half decades of the eighteenth century and the early years of the nineteenth there was a Werther cult, almost a Werther madness – 'eine Krankheit, ein Fieber' ('a craze, a fever') as Goethe himself characterised it[27] – which raged throughout Europe amongst the readers of novels and even amongst those who had to have novels read to them. 'Novelists, playwrights, poets, composers, choreographers, and iconographers ranging from reputable painters and illustrators to anonymous waxworkers . . . quickly appropriated its themes to their peculiar talents'.[28] Werther and Charlotte eventually became such well known figures that their names survive, we are told, in German folk-songs. Young men adopted the Werther costume of blue tail-coats and yellow waistcoats, and a few even committed suicide in imitation of their hero.

In this process of popularisation the work which had originally inspired all the fuss tended to be transformed in the general imagination or else lost sight of altogether. The reading public, in taking Werther to their hearts, vulgarised and sentimentalised it, made it over in their own image, just as they transformed and cheapened *A Sentimental Journey*. *Werther* is thus both a key document in the history of sentimentalism and a work of art with its own independent life and integrity. Like *A Sentimental Journey* and the novels of Richardson it needs to be disentangled from the myth it engendered – although the myth itself has its own fascination and importance.

The literary antecedents of *Werther* are equally interesting, for Goethe unhesitatingly located them in English literature. He

[27] *Campagne in Frankreich* 1792. Quoted in *Laurence Sterne and Goethe*, by W. R. R. Pinger (University of California, 1918) 26.
[28] Stuart Pratt Atkins, *The Testament of Werther in Poetry and Drama* (Cambridge, Mass., 1949) 2.

had read Goldsmith and Sterne as a young man – they were indeed amongst his favourite authors and remained so until the end of his life. 'I owe much to the Greeks and the French and I am infinitely ("unendlich") indebted to Shakespeare, Sterne, and Goldsmith,' he told Eckermann in 1828;[29] and his references throughout his life to Sterne are so numerous and so interesting that they constitute in themselves a fruitful area of inquiry.[30] The novels of Richardson, Edward Young's tearful and platitudinous *Night Thoughts*, the poetry of Gray, and the gently romantic pseudo-epic of *Ossian* were all familiar to Goethe and his friends; and no doubt without realising it he probably ensured the book's success by making Werther read *Ossian* to his beloved just before he goes off to commit suicide. The combination of high passion and the most popular and most beautifully melancholy poetry of the day must have been irresistible.

The Sorrows of Werther thus has a special claim to be regarded as a part of English literature.[31] Although it also owes something to Rousseau, it represents the culmination of what was mainly an English sentimental tradition as it was understood by a foreigner; and in writing *Werther* Goethe can be regarded as giving back to the English something which is their own, having refracted it of course through the medium of his own German genius. It is thus not surprising that *Werther* should have become

[29] Quoted by Pinger in *Laurence Sterne and Goethe* 4, 32.
[30] Ibid. 23 note 1.
[31] The History of *Werther* in English is complicated. *Die Leiden des jungen Werthers* was first published in 1774. It was translated into French in 1776 and into English from the French version, under the title *The Sorrows of Werter: a German Story*, in 1779. The first translation into English from the German, with the title, *Werter and Charlotte. A German Story*, appeared in 1786. There were a number of other translations, but it was not until 1854 that an English version appeared in which 'Werther' was spelt correctly with an *h*. In 1782 Goethe began to revise the book extensively. The new version appeared in 1787, and it is the basis for a number of modern translations. But 'the extraordinary thing about [the new version] is that Goethe used as the basis for his revision a pirated and much corrupted edition which had been published in 1779' (*The Sorrows of Young Werther*, newly translated into English by William Rose, London, 1929, xliii). *Werter* as its first English readers knew it is thus different from *Werther* in Mr Rose's translation and different again from *Werther* as it appears in the dual-language translation by Harry Steinhauer, based on the 1787 edition, which I am using.

more popular in England than in any other country outside Germany.

But this is only half the story. W*erther* is not merely the culmination of a sentimental tradition it is also a departure from it, a development of it and in part a rejection of it. In certain respects Werther is a sentimental hero – he is a man of feeling, he is rejected and rendered powerless by the world, he is if not impotent at least sexually defeated, and his ineffectual struggles culminate in his death. The lives of Yorick and Harley fit this pattern perfectly, and there are obvious similarities to the careers and characters of figures in other novels of sentiment – Clarissa and Lovelace, for instance (for although Lovelace is not a man of feeling he *is* a defeated, impotent rebel), Uncle Toby, Tristram and the Vicar of Wakefield. But Werther is more than a man of feeling. Where he differs from all these people – except perhaps, Lovelace – is in his *active* defiance of conventional, established society, in his attempt to assert his individuality, to create his own life for himself rather than merely to defend his right to be himself, and in his decision to commit suicide. Werther, in a supreme gesture of romantic egoism, snatches the fruits of victory from the encroaching world by destroying himself before he can be corrupted, before the forces of convention can render him safe for society. It is perhaps a pathetic rather than a tragic gesture, inspired by bravado rather than courage, slightly ridiculous rather than noble (and it must be remembered that it is due to the mature and balanced manner in which Goethe presents the situation that we are able to assess Werther in this way: it is W*erther* who is pathetic, not W*erther*). But whether his action deserves to be taken at his own valuation or not it *is* an action, and an irrevocable one. This is what distinguishes Werther from the sentimental heroes and heroines who precede him. St Preux and Julie rebel, it is true, but they are eventually smothered into conformism; Clarissa's role is almost purely a defensive one until after the rape; and Yorick (in A *Sentimental Journey*) manages to preserve his integrity by remaining humorously uninvolved, a commentator and an observer rather than a participant.

Werther's suicide, despite its theatricality, is thus an event of some significance. His death moves and distresses the reader, and evokes a genuine sense of loss, of pointless waste. And it does so not merely because Werther has demonstrated in his letters so effectively the sort of person he is – intelligent, receptive, sensitive and to a point creatively rebellious – but also because he has been shown in the process of exploring himself, of attempting to come to terms with himself and if necessary remake himself. 'Ich kehre in mich selbst zurück und finde eine Welt! Wieder mehr in Ahnung und dunkler Begier als in Darstellung und lebendiger Kraft.' – 'I turn back upon myself [or 'in upon myself'] and find a world! But again more in imagination and obscure desire than in actuality and living power.'[32] Edward Young in his *Conjectures on Original Composition* (a work well known at the time among German writers and intellectuals) gives this advice to the man who wants to create original and living works of literature: 'Know thyself! . . . dive deep into thy bosom; learn the depth, extent, bias and full fort of thy mind; contract full intimacy with the stranger within thee; excite and cherish every spark of Intellectual light and heat . . . Let thy Genius rise . . . as the sun from chaos.'[33] Werther at least makes the attempt to do this, and if he fails to release his genius, to make possible the full and fruitful use of his creative powers, we are able to see why. His self-involvement is, in the end, self-defeating because it is based on a false situation which he has himself helped to create: his love for Charlotte has from the beginning been impossible and he should have realised this.[34] But to begin with his retreat into himself has a remarkably energising and stimulating effect. In the opening pages of *Werther* we get the impression of an unfolding imagination, of a mind which is opening wider the doors of its perception and taking into itself, making its own in a creative and enlivening way, the world as it is experiencing it. Werther is deliberately inducing in himself the state which

[32] *The Sufferings of Young Werther/Die Leiden des jungen Werthers* 42–3.

[33] *Conjectures on Original Composition. In a Letter to the Author of Sir Charles Grandison* (London, 1759) 52–3.

[34] Mr John Stowell in a letter to me has commented that '[Werther] would not . . . complain so much about Society, if not so dependent on it – the association of Lotte as much with a possible mother as with a lover is the true cause of . . . his lack of creativity & impotence . . . I think, in fact, that he is massively oedipal'. Goethe's own life and character has been subjected to exhaustive psychoanalytic investigation by K. R. Eissler in *Goethe: a psychoanalytic study* 2 vols (Detroit, 1963).

Keats was later to describe as negative capability – and paradoxically this leads to a heightened, almost ecstatic awareness of
the living world about him. Werther, of course, was not the first
fictional hero to give rapturous expression to his sense of a
mystical communion with nature – St Preux's lyrical evocations
of alpine beauty are amongst the most impressive passages in
La Nouvelle Héloïse. But there is no taint of literary imitation in
Werther's attempts to convey his sense of participation in the
natural world: the note which sounds throughout them is fresh,
original and distinctive:

> A wonderful serenity has taken possession of my whole soul,
> like the sweet spring mornings which I enjoy with all my
> heart. I am alone and am enjoying my life in this region . . .
> When the lovely valley around me is shrouded in mist and
> the high sun rests on the surfaces of the impenetrable darkness
> of my forest, and only single rays steal into the inner sanctu-
> ary; when I lie in the tall grass beside the cascading brook,
> and close to the ground a thousand varieties of tiny grasses
> fill me with wonder; when I feel this teeming little world
> among the stalks closer to my heart – the countless unfathom-
> able forms of tiny worms and gnats – and feel the presence of
> the Almighty, Who created us in His image, the breath of the
> All-loving One who, floating in eternal bliss bears and sustains
> us; my friend! When my eyes then grow misty and the world
> about me and the sky lie wholly within me like the form of a
> beautiful woman – then I often think with yearning: oh, if
> you could express this once more, if you could breathe onto
> the paper what dwells so fully, so warmly within you, so that
> it became the mirror of your soul, as your soul is the mirror of
> infinite God![35]

Unfortunately the full force of this hymn to nature was
rather muffled by the first English translator. Werther's sense of
wonder at the teeming, myriad life in the grass around him is
only barely suggested in the rather lifelessly elegant diction of a

[35] The Sufferings of Young Werther/Die Leiden des jungen
Werthers 35. This seems to me a remarkable foreshadowing of the
passage in Song of Myself (§ 5: 'I believe in you my soul, the other I
am must not abase itself to you . . .') in which Whitman celebrates
his ecstatic sense of mystical communion with God and Nature.

sentence such as this: 'Here, extended on the long grass near the fall of a brook, I admire the infinite variety of plants, and grow familiar with all the little insects that surround me, as they hum among the flowers, or creep in the grass.'[36] Homely touches such as Werther's kissing Charlotte's little brother 'heartily, in spite of his runny nose',[37] or the details of how he cooks his peas as he reads Homer are all smoothed away. There can be no question as to which of the following two passages is the more vivid:

> . . . when I go into the little kitchen and make a soup of them, I figure to myself the illustrious lovers of Penelope killing and dressing their own meat.[38]

> . . . when I then select a pot in the little kitchen, dig out a piece of butter, put the peas on the fire, cover them and sit down nearby to stir them now and then – then I vividly imagine the arrogant suitors of Penelope slaughtering oxen and pigs, cutting them up and roasting them.[39]

No doubt the tamer version seemed more decorus either to the English translator or to the translator of the French version from which he was working.

Despite this coy emasculation of Goethe's prose something of the vitality of the young Werther's personality is still suggested in the versions of the novel which were devoured so eagerly by its first English readers. And it is important that this should have been so, because it is the authority with which Werther's character is established in the opening sections of the book that authenticates the sense of tragedy evoked by his death. When Werther talks to Albert about suicide we feel that he has a right to: if he wants to throw away his life he is at least throwing away something that he has thought about rather more seriously and energetically than most people. When he says that 'man is

[36] *The Sorrows of Werter. A German Story* (London, 1779) I 7.

[37] *The Sufferings of Young Werther/Die Leiden des jungen Werthers* 61. *The Sorrows of Werter* reads: 'I went up to the youngest, who has a most pleasing countenance' (I, 44).

[38] *The Sorrows of Werter* I 70.

[39] *The Sufferings of Young Werther/Die Leiden des jungen Werthers* 77. (The German text of the 1787 edition, of which this is a translation, is in detail slightly different from the text of the first edition but is essentially the same.)

The sentimental vulgarisation of *Werther*: this frontispiece to
The Sorrows of Werter (1801) shows Charlotte weeping at the
tomb of Werther – an incident which does not appear in the
book at all

man and the little bit of intelligence that we may possess is of small account when passion rages and we are driven to the limits of our human condition' (und die Grenzen der Menschheit einen drängen),[40] we feel that Werther at least knows something about the limits of the human condition whilst Albert does not even begin to understand what he is talking about.

Werther, of course, does nothing finally with the genius within himself which he is trying to discover. He becomes another sentimental traveller – 'Ja, wohl bin ich nur ein Wandrer, ein Waller auf der Erde!' (I am indeed but a wanderer, a pilgrim on earth)[41] – and he neurotically commits himself to a situation which in his heart he realises to be hopeless. If this were all that happened, and if Goethe allowed his hero simply to drift into his death, the book would be merely another sentimental novel. But in fact the concluding episodes in Werther's life are rendered with an economy, a dramatic intensity and a degree of psychological realism which unexpectedly lift the work on to another level. Charlotte and Werther are suddenly revealed as characters who have changed and developed in the course of the action and who have arrived at last at some understanding of the sort of people they are, and also of the situation into which they have allowed themselves to drift. The whole affair is brilliantly illuminated when Charlotte says: 'Why me, Werther? Why just me, who belongs to another man? I fear, I fear, it is only the impossibility of possessing me that makes your desire for me so strong' (Ich fürchte, ich fürchte, es ist nur die Unmöglichkeit, mich zu besitzen, die Ihnen diesen Wunsch so reizend macht).[42]

But although Charlotte realises what is happening she is unable to bring herself to prevent the tragedy which she knows is going to take place. It is the way in which Goethe renders her behaviour and her state of mind during this critical period that makes the conclusion so convincing and so genuinely moving. Her feelings are complex: she suddenly becomes aware of what she has been doing to Werther and also of how strong her own attachment to him now is; at the same time she is driven almost unconsciously to acquiesce in his desire and plans for his own

[40] *The Sufferings of Young Werther/Die Leiden des jungen Werthers* 118–19.
[41] Ibid. 170–1.
[42] Ibid. 228–9.

death. The benumbed fascination and perhaps secretly half
delighted horror with which she watches the tragedy develop
are sketched in by Goethe with quick, accurate, highly charged
strokes. The dramatic high point of the action is reached when
Albert receives Werther's request for the loan of his pistols:

> Werther's servant . . . handed the note to Albert, who turned
> calmly to his wife and said: 'Give him the pistols.' – 'I wish
> him a happy journey,' he said to the boy. The words struck
> her like a thunderbolt; she staggered to her feet, not knowing
> what she was doing. She went slowly to the wall, trembling
> she took down the weapons, dusted them off, and hesitated;
> she would have hesitated longer still if Albert had not pressed
> her with a questioning look. She gave the boy the fatal
> weapons without being able to utter a word, and . . . went to
> her room in a state of the most indescribable uncertainty. Her
> heart foretold her every possible terror.[43]

The scene has of course been highly praised many times, especially
(and rightly) for the way in which Goethe has prepared for it
earlier in the book. Even so it is easy to see how close he comes
to the awful chasm of melodrama. The reason for his success in
avoiding it is that the states of mind of all the main characters
now seem to the reader not only understandable but also perfectly justified and inevitable: the stage business of notes and
pistols merely reflects the inner drama in which Charlotte, Albert
and Werther are involved.

One of the things that makes *The Sorrows of Young Werther*
such an interesting book is the way in which it points forward,
hints at what is to come. In these closing scenes there is a clear
foreshadowing of the psychological drama and the psychological
novel of the nineteenth and twentieth centuries. It is not merely
the triangular situation nor the pistol shot with which the action
concludes that makes us think of *Hedda Gabler* or the tortured
domestic dramas of Strindberg. In *Werther* there is the same
revelation of the depths of frustrated and potentially violent
passion which can lie beneath the placid surface of apparently
normal human relationships. And it is not merely because he is
a romantic melancholy hero that Werther seems blood-brother
to Stephen Daedalus, or the solitary adventurers of Conrad, or

[43] Ibid. 263.

Faulkner's impotent and suicidal young Southerners, or indeed any of the crowd of alienated, introspective and often violent outsiders who walk the world of modern fiction reading the book of themselves. It is because the universe presented to us through his eyes is so predominantly, indeed obsessively, his. In *Tristram Shandy* and *A Sentimental Journey* there is a constant and comic interplay between the inner lives of the characters and the outside world. In *The Vicar of Wakefield* there is a similarly ironic relationship between character and situation, although the comedy, as I have suggested, hovers always just this side of tragedy. Some balance, however precarious, is nonetheless maintained. In *The Man of Feeling* and *Werther* the contacts between the character and his world have become so brutal and shattering that this balance is lost – Harley and Werther are forced back within themselves. Unfortunately for Harley and the suffering heroes and heroines of the sentimental novels which quickly followed *The Man of Feeling* there is nothing to fall back upon – they are not characters but a set of shallow, stereotyped attitudes. Werther, however, is a person – a three dimensional, vital individual with depths and mysteries which, like the depths and mysteries we find in the people we know in real life, are capable of surprising, delighting and terrifying us. Stripped of his sentimental and melodramatic trappings he is very much a modern hero. And in the story of his sufferings it is possible to see the modern novel, with its emphasis on the psychological life of the individual rather than on story, emerging from the chrysalis of the novel of sentiment.

5

La Philosophie dans le Boudoir; or,
A Young Lady's Entrance
into the World

'Bring some Madeira.' This cheerful command, with which
Nightmare Abbey is brought to a conclusion,[1] has more to do
with Werther – or Wertherism – than with wine. It indicates
that Scythrop, the melancholy poet and disappointed lover, has
decided not to 'make [his] exit like Werther'[2] with a pint of
port and a pistol, but instead will go on living and console himself with a bottle of Madeira and a boiled fowl. Rather than
allow himself to be defeated by the world Scythrop, even though
he is undoubtedly a man of feeling, makes the best of a bad job
and happily joins forces with it.

Nightmare Abbey was first published in 1818. In the same
year (or possibly in December, 1817) a work with a rather
similar title and in part similar intentions also appeared –
Northanger Abbey, by Jane Austen.[3] Like Peacock, Jane Austen
makes fun of the taste for 'horrid' gothic tales of terror, German
romances and sentimental novels. But she does not extend her
satire, as Peacock does, to the fashion for political enthusiasm
and philanthropic idealism: Scythrop not only sleeps with a copy
of *Horrid Mysteries* under his pillow, but, like the youthful
Shelley (on whom he was modelled) is also 'troubled with the
passion for reforming the world'.[4] There is another difference
between the two works: *Northanger Abbey*, although released in

---

[1] *The Novels of Thomas Love Peacock* 433.
[2] Ibid. 428.
[3] *Northanger Abbey* was announced in the *Morning Chronicle* for
19 and 20 Dec. 1817: see *The Novels of Jane Austen*, ed. R. W.
Chapman, 5 vols (London, 1933) V xiii.
[4] *The Novels of Thomas Love Peacock* 362.

1818, belongs to an earlier period. It had been written in 1797–8, and had remained unpublished for approximately twenty years. We can only speculate as to the reasons for this delay. One of them, however, may have been that the climate for the kind of satire engaged in by Jane Austen in *Northanger Abbey* may have seemed more propitious in 1818 than when the book was written. This may explain why Crosby, the publisher who bought the manuscript in 1803, and who actually advertised the book, decided not to issue it. At all events it is clear that fifteen years later the passion for reforming the world, like many other 'sentimental' notions, had become fair game for the satirist. Peacock's cool, amused scepticism was very much to the taste of an era which had seen the failure, or apparent failure, of the French Revolution and the final defeat of Napoleon; and the horrors of the gothic novel which Jane Austen mocks so effectively must have looked increasingly artificial and unreal in the light of what had happened – and what was supposed to have happened – during the Terror. Even Shelley, contemplating from the maturity of twenty-six the reformist ardour of his adolescence, told Peacock that he was 'delighted with *Nightmare Abbey*' – though he added a characteristic rider: 'I suppose the moral is contained in what Falstaff says – "For God's sake, talk like a man of this world"; and yet, looking deeper into it, is not the misdirected enthusiasm of Scythrop what J.C. calls the "salt of the earth"?'[5]

When Peacock wrote *Nightmare Abbey* it must have seemed fairly obvious that the revolutionary and philanthropic enthusiasms of an earlier period had been misdirected. Indeed post-revolutionary malaise appears to have been a not uncommon intellectual disease. Mr Flosky, for instance, the character in *Nightmare Abbey* based on Coleridge, is presented as a dreamy pessimist whose gloomy ineffectuality stems directly from the collapse of the Revolution:

> He had been in his youth an enthusiast for liberty, and had hailed the dawn of the French Revolution as the promise of a day that was to banish war and slavery, and every form of vice and misery, from the face of the earth. Because all this

[5] Quoted by Garnett in his Introduction to *Nightmare Abbey*, in *The Novels of Thomas Love Peacock* 353.

was not done, he deduced that nothing was done; and from this deduction, according to his system of logic, he drew a conclusion that worse than nothing was done . . .[6]

For anyone concerned with sentimentalism, in all the senses of the term, Mr Flosky's period, the last ten years of the eighteenth century, the decade dominated by the French Revolution, is of particular interest. As I have argued in Part I of this work, the ideology of the Revolution was to a large extent sentimental[7] – and moreover it was recognised to be so both by those who supported it and by those who most deeply opposed it – like the poets of the *Anti-Jacobin*, for instance, who savaged the Goddess of Sensibility.[8] During the revolutionary era sensibility took on the strongest of political connotations; and it did so without losing any of its ambiguities and self-contradictions. The way in which the term was used often combined optimism and pessimism in a peculiarly dynamic fashion, reflecting at once the hope that man, if given the chance to act benevolently, would do so, and the fear that his capacity for rational and humane behaviour was very limited, and that to be endowed with a delicate sensibility was to be cast inevitably in the role of a victim. Mr Flosky's plunge from the peaks of idealistic enthusiasm to the chasm of utter despair is a metaphysical version of a very familiar pattern.

One of the most fascinating aspects of this pattern is the way in which the political connotations now being assumed by 'sensibility' and its associated terms – 'sentiment', 'sympathy', 'feeling', etc. – blended and combined with other connotations which these terms already carried, connotations of weakness, passivity, femininity and impotence. A heightened sensibility could now be taken as an index not only of sexual responsiveness but also of political awareness. Yorick, for instance, on his sentimental journey, demonstrates how his capacity for moral action is directly related both to his erotic sensibility and his sexual impotence: his better feelings are aroused by his allowing himself to become involved in sexual liaisons which he is either unable or unwilling to consummate. Werther exhibits a similar mode of behaviour – but with an added political dimension; amongst other things Werther is a frustrated activist – a man, like

---

[6] Ibid. 360.   [7] See above pp. 56ff.   [8] See above pp. 62–4.

Scythrop, 'troubled with the *passion for reforming the world'*. Jean-Jacques Rousseau, particularly as he presents himself in his *Confessions*, is a similarly complex figure; and it is significant that although the *Confessions* were not published until 1782 (and not in full until 1789) they were written during a key period in the development of sentimentalism, the years from 1761 to 1776. In his autobiography Rousseau puts forward his political and moral idealism as the natural expression of his sensibility – but even while he glories in his possession of a feeling heart he complains that it is the source of all his worldly troubles. His erotic idiosyncracies follow the same pattern: he tells us that he has an almost feverishly acute response to sexual stimulation – or to the prospect of it – but is almost incapable of fully enjoying a woman in any normal way. Born free, he finds complete sexual satisfaction only in his chains.

Rousseau's masochism is clearly a subject to tempt the wildest speculations. Without indulging in anything too extravagant, however, I feel that one is justified in pointing to the closeness with which Rousseau's autobiographical persona in the *Confessions* accords with some of the most pervasive fantasies of the age, in particular with the assumption that a delicate sensibility could be taken as a sign at once of moral superiority or excellence, of a high potentiality for erotic excitability and responsiveness, and of personal weakness and ineffectuality. When such notions are allied to the highest political, ethical and social aspirations it is not surprising that the resulting concept should exercise a powerful fascination nor that, in the wake of the Terror, it should arouse contempt, despair and ridicule.

Simple and sentimentally optimistic notions of human nature had of course been challenged during the eighteenth century long before the Revolution.[9] Sentimentality, both literary and moral, had been laughed at on the stage; and within the novel, as the work of Sterne and Smollett in particular demonstrates, there had long existed a complex relationship between sentimentalism and satire.[10] The dangers both of over-indulging one's own feelings and of placing too great a trust in someone who

[9] See above pp. 65–6.
[10] Ronald Paulson's *Satire and the Novel in Eighteenth-Century England* (New Haven & London, 1967) is particularly illuminating on this matter.

appears, deceptively, to be endowed with a genuine sensibility, became a favourite theme. A great many novelists would have been happy to claim, as Mrs Jane West does in her dedication to *A Gossip's Story*, that their aims were 'to illustrate the Advantages of CONSISTENCY, FORTITUDE, and the DOMESTICK VIRTUES; and to expose to ridicule CAPRICE [and] AFFECTED SENSIBILITY'.[11]

Caprice and affected sensibility are also among the objects of Peacock's satire. Indeed, by the time he came to write his comic novels, the first of which appeared in 1815, there was already in existence a sizeable body of anti-sentimental fiction, although for a variety of reasons much of it was unpublished.

Towards the end of the eighteenth century – ironically enough during the period of warmest revolutionary enthusiasm – the clichés of the novel of sensibility and its cousin-german the gothic novel had begun to be burlesqued, inverted and parodied within underground variants of the novel form itself – in some cases by people who were themselves producing or who went on to produce the very material they were satirising. Matthew Gregory Lewis, for instance, author of the most notorious of all gothic novels, *The Monk*, which appeared in 1796, wrote when he was sixteen a brief and unfinished skit called *The Effusions of Sensibility*. Courtney Melmoth, a most prolific sentimentalist, and William Beckford, author of *Vathek*, both wrote parodies of the genre. And Jane Austen began her career as a writer with a series of little burlesque novels which she produced in her early teens for the private amusement of her family. The most substantial of these, *Love and Friendship*, written when she was about fourteen, is a surprisingly accomplished work, and despite its brevity the best and most thoroughgoing of all the burlesques of sentimental fiction.

One of the most interesting things about these parodies is the spontaneity with which they appeared. Young 'Monk' Lewis and the younger and even more precocious Jane Austen were not following any set satiric tradition when they produced their skits – they were merely amusing themselves by playing with the worn-out formulae of popular fiction. Nor did they write for publication: Lewis's piece was not printed until 1839, some time

[11] *A Gossip's Story, and a Legendary Tale* (London, 1796) I Dedication.

after his death,[12] *Love and Friendship* with the rest of Jane Austen's juvenilia remained in manuscript until this century, and even *Northanger Abbey* which, although it contains elements of parody, is a novel in its own right, did not appear during the author's lifetime. As I have already mentioned, the book, which had been written in 1797-8, was not published until 1817, the year in which Jane Austen died. It is, if nothing else, an interesting coincidence that almost simultaneously and quite independently these two young writers should have decided to send up the novel of sensibility. The coincidence becomes even more interesting if we take into account another and in many ways very different work which was published at the same time – *Justine, ou les Malheurs de la Vertu*, the first edition of the Marquis de Sade's first novel. The manuscript of *Love and Friendship* is dated June 13, 1790; *The Effusions of Sensibility* was written in 1791; and it was in this year that *Justine* first appeared, although the first draft of the book had been completed in 1787. *Justine*, of course, is more than a mere skit; but like all of Sade's fiction it can be regarded as at once an extension and development of the novel of sensibility and the gothic novel and a parody of these forms – a parody the purpose of which is to invert and attack the values which they embody and express. The same can to some extent be said of Jane Austen's novels, especially the early ones, *Northanger Abbey* and *Sense and Sensibility*, which are most closely related to the parodies she wrote as a girl.

The ways in which Sade, both as a writer and as a human being, differs from Jane Austen are so glaringly obvious that it may seem rather embarrassingly pointless to look for any similarities at all. Nonetheless some points of resemblance do exist, and they are, I believe, of some interest and significance. To discover one of the simplest one needs look no further than the opening pages of *Justine*, Sade's first novel, and the corresponding section of *Sense and Sensibility*, which Jane Austen commenced in 1797, and which, when it appeared in 1811, became the first of her novels to be published.

[12] *The Life and Correspondence of M. G. Lewis,* [by Mrs Margaret Baron-Wilson] (London, 1839) II 241-70. For an excellent account of this and other parodies of the novel of sensibility see *The Novel in Motley: a History of the burlesque Novel in English,* by Archibald Bolling Shepperson (Cambridge, Mass., 1936).

Each novel has for its central characters two sisters (there is also a third in *Sense and Sensibility*, but she is not very important), and the situations in which they are revealed to us at the beginning of their stories are basically the same. Justine and her sister Juliette, at the tender ages of twelve and fifteen, are suddenly bereft of their parents and their fortune: their father dies a bankrupt, his wife soon follows him to the grave, and after 'two distant and heartless relatives [have] deliberated what should be done with the young orphans'[13] they are given a small legacy and thrust out into the world to fend for themselves. Jane Austen's two sisters, Elinor and Marianne Dashwood, are not in such desperate straits as Juliette and Justine, but like them they have lost their father, they have been deprived of the money they could reasonably have expected to inherit, and they are treated with high-minded selfishness by their brother and his wife.

The parallels do not end here. Each author makes a point of contrasting the characters of his heroines in rather similar terms. Elinor Dashwood, Jane Austen tells us, 'possessed . . . strength of understanding, and coolness of judgment . . . her disposition was affectionate, and her feelings were strong; but she knew how to govern them'.[14] Her young sister, Marianne, however, was 'sensible and clever; but eager in everything . . . she was generous, amiable, interesting: she was everything but prudent . . . Elinor saw, with concern, the excess of her sister's sensibility'.[15]

No one could say that Juliett's 'disposition was affectionate', but in her own utterly libertine way she certainly exhibits 'strength of understanding and coolness of judgment' – she has, Sade tells us, 'a philosophic acuity far beyond her years'.[16] Justine's resemblance to Marianne is much more direct: 'Full of tenderness, endowed with a surprising sensibility . . . she was ruled by an ingenuousness, a candor, that were to cause her to tumble into not a few pitfalls.'[17] Like Elinor, though for somewhat different reasons, Juliette also 'saw with concern, the excess

---

[13] *Justine, or Good Conduct Well Chastised*, in *The Marquis de Sade: the complete Justine, Philosophy in the Bedroom and other Writings*, comp. and trans. by Richard Seaver & Austyn Wainhouse (New York, 1966) 459 [hereafter, *The complete Justine*].
[14] *Sense and Sensibility* (London, 1811) I 10.
[15] Ibid. 11.   [16] *The complete Justine* 460.   [17] Ibid. 459.

of her sister's sensibility'. 'She rebuked her for her sensitiveness (*elle lui reprocha sa sensibilité*); she told her . . . that in this world one must not be afflicted save by what affects one personally; that . . . true wisdom consists infinitely more in doubling the sum of one's pleasures than in increasing the sum of one's pains; that, in a word, there was nothing one ought not do in order to deaden in oneself that perfidious sensibility from which none but others profit while to us it brings naught but troubles.'[18]

Elinor's 'sense', though very different from the amoral or anti-moral 'reason' represented by Juliette, is not altogether unrelated to it; and if we allow for the obvious dissimilarities there still remains a real parallelism between the situations in *Justine* and in *Sense and Sensibility*: both Sade and Jane Austen are concerned (though for somewhat different ends) with exposing the weakness of sensibility, and the folly and danger of trusting completely to it. There is nothing very original in their attempting to do this: in the novels written in the last thirty years of the century the heroine who has to learn how to keep her sensibility under prudent control and how to distinguish between true and false sensibility becomes something of a stock figure. It is during this period, some time in the eighties, that '*sensiblerie*', the French word for affected, hypocritical sensibility – '*sensibilité feinte et stérile*' is a definition given in a work published in 1799[19] – appeared in the language. Even the device of two sisters with contrasting characters, one of whom is distinguished by her sensibility, appears to have been to some extent conventional. A novel called *The Twin Sister; or the Effects of Education* was published in 1788; *Melissa and Marcia, or the Sisters*, appeared in the same year; and Jane West's *A Gossip's Story*, which is also concerned with two sisters, and which has been called 'an embryo *Sense and Sensibility*',[20] was published in 1796. Even more profoundly conventional – so well-established indeed as to warrant

[18] Ibid. 460.
[19] Mercier, *Le Nouveau Paris* (1799) II lxx. Quoted in *Dictionnaire alphabétique et analogique de la langue Française*, par Paul Robert (Paris, 1966). Mercier places the appearance of the word in the eighties, when 'quelque temps avant la Révolution, les gens de bon ton avaient adopté une certain philosophie *sentimentale* qui était l'art de se dispenser d'être vertueux'.
[20] J. M. S. Tompkins, *The Popular Novel in England, 1770–1800* (London, 1932) 99.

our calling it a 'fantasy' – is the dichotomy reflected in Jane Austen's title: the conflict between sensibility and sense, heart and head, the passions and reason, men of feeling and men of the world, innocence and experience, nature and art, is one of the most pervasive and persistent of all themes in the literature and thought of the eighteenth century.[21]

The situation in which Sade and Jane Austen initially involve their heroines is also conventional: the situation in which a young innocent heroine is suddenly thrown on her own resources 'at this period crucial to [her] virtue', as Sade puts it.[22] It is a situation, of course, which has fascinated man's imagination ever since he has had the leisure and opportunity to think about young and innocent heroines. But in the eighteenth century it assumed a special significance; and it did so partly because the status of woman was undergoing a revolutionary change – it is in the eighteenth century, significantly, that women's liberation as well as the liberation of slaves may be said to begin – and partly because of the particular complex of values which were attached, as I have suggested, to the concept of sensibility. There were no doubt other reasons as well – among them the special relation, both as writers and readers, in which women stood to the novel – but those I have mentioned are the most obviously important. But for whatever reason, the entrance of a young lady into the world – which is the sub-title to Fanny Burney's *Evelina* as well as to this chapter – became an established and enduring theme in eighteenth-century fiction, and one which was to exercise the imagination of the novelist until at least the beginning of this century. We see the final and fullest development and exploration of the theme probably in some of the novels of Henry James – *Portrait of a Lady* and *The Wings of the Dove* particularly.

It was, of course, a social ritual of considerable importance. When a young lady made her debut – either through presentation at court or through her first formal appearance at a country

[21] This is reflected in titles such as *Sense and Sensibility*; *The Man of Feeling* and *The Man of the World*, by Henry Mackenzie; *Songs of Innocence and of Experience, showing the Two Contrary States of the Human Soul*, by William Blake; *Man as he is* and *Hermsprong, or Man as he in Not*, by Robert Bage; and *Nature and Art*, by Mrs Elizabeth Inchbald.

[22] *The complete Justine* 459.

ball or a ladies' tea party – it indicated that she was on the marriage market. It also indicated that she was fair game for every scoundrel who might wish to seduce her before she was safely wedded. It is an old story – but in the eighteenth century this familiar *rite de passage* assumed an unusually wide significance. A stock description of a stock situation may suggest just how great this significance was. It comes from the first chapter of *The Monk*. When *The Monk* appeared in 1796 it seemed remarkably novel and daring, but what is really striking about the book is the way in which it brings together into one work so many long established fictive patterns and devices. Nothing could be more conventional than the warning Lorenzo, a young gallant, issues to one of the heroines, Antonia, who has just felt an equally conventional and sentimental thrill of sympathy for Ambrosio, the monk. 'Surely', she cries, 'the warmth of sympathy cannot have deceived me?' Indeed it has, for Ambrosio eventually rapes and murders her. She would have done well to heed Lorenzo's warning:

> You are young, and just entering into life . . . your heart, new to the world, and full of warmth and sensibility, receives its first impressions with eagerness. Artless yourself, you suspect not others of deceit; and viewing the world through the medium of your own truth and innocence, you fancy all who surround you deserve your confidence and esteem. What pity, that these gay visions must soon be dissipated! What pity, that you must soon discover the baseness of mankind . . .[23]

The universal significance with which the situation is invested is perhaps the most notable feature of this statement. Lorenzo is not merely warning her – as so many girls in so many songs and stories have been and still are warned – that in affairs of the heart men are deceivers ever. What he is saying is that once Antonia enters the world or life – the terminology could not be more sweeping – she will not only lose her innocence but also

[23] *The Monk* (London, 1796) I 28–9. *The Effusions of Sensibility*, Lewis's juvenile parody, is also concerned with the theme of a young lady's entrance into the world. Honoria, the heroine, leaves the country and goes to London. At her first ball she too '[discovers] the baseness of mankind': tripped by a jealous rival she falls and sprains her great toe.

because she is innocent she 'must soon discover the baseness of mankind', – the baseness, that is, of humanity as a whole. In making her entrance into the world this young lady – like a great many of the young ladies in eighteenth-century fiction – will symbolically represent not merely sexual innocence or the supposedly mystical power of virginity but something more. Pamela and Clarissa, the archetypal heroines from whom Antonia is descended, are not just young women attempting to defend their honour in difficult situations – they are representatives of a whole constellation of social and moral values which include but transcend the merely sexual. The debates between Clarissa and Lovelace, like the debates and lectures which precede and follow practically every rape and orgy in Sade's fiction, are debates about fundamental moral and metaphysical issues. The status of individual human beings – are they free, are they fallen, are they innately good or innately evil, have they inalienable rights? – the question of whether there is or is not a God – these questions are discussed at the theoretical level by lovers, or by rapists and victim, and the conclusions they reach are often given a practical demonstration through the way in which the sexual relations between these people are brought to a conclusion. Ambrosio, the monk of Lewis's novel, is deliberately presented as a Faust figure – but he is not tempted by the chance of exercising absolute power, as Faustus is, he is tempted by love and by the desire to lead a life of sexual freedom and fulfilment. Since this too is what most of the other characters in the novel want, Ambrosio is also something of a revolutionary and Promethean hero: his destruction placates the terrible authoritarianism of the Church which has been presented as the most repressive instrument of organised society. And his temptations, and the theological and philosophical analyses to which he subjects them, take place, not surprisingly, for the most part in the bedchamber, although for Ambrosio and his unfortunate mistresses the bedchamber tends more often than not to be cold, damp, stony, and occupied by corpses and the things that feed upon them.

One could say that the association of philosophical speculation and debate with sexual activity goes back to the Garden of Eden; or, if one wishes to be classical rather than Christian, to Plato's *Symposium*. But *La Philosophie dans le Boudoir*, the title chosen by Sade for one of his briefer and perhaps for this reason more effective pieces, assumes a special significance in the seventeenth and eighteenth centuries. To be libertine meant practically from the beginning to be both sexually a free liver and philosophically a free thinker;[24] and the salon was both symbolically and often actually the antechamber to the boudoir. It is no accident that Diderot should have located his thoroughly philosophical exploration of the concept of *sensibilité* in d'Alembert's bedchamber, – even though, ironically enough, it was probably no boudoir in the erotic sense. Practically all Sade's philosophising takes place in the boudoir, or at least amid scenes of sexual intercourse, and while this association of activities reflects Sade's own obsessive preoccupation with sex it also represents – like so many other things in Sade's work – the logical culmination of much that is implicit in the philosophy and the fiction of the preceding century. *'Il y a un peu de testicule au fond de nos sentiments les plus sublimes et de notre tendresse la plus epurée'*,[25] Diderot once remarked. It was Sade's purpose, pursued with manic energy, to demonstrate that this, though true, was only half the truth. In Sade's view, the sentimental image of man denied not only the sexual elements in his nature, but also his inherent violence, aggressiveness, selfishness and cruelty. Long before the Terror Sade was suggesting that the sentimental ideals by which the Revolution was inspired were based on a grossly inadequate account of human nature; and the force of his criticism was not lessened by the deficiencies and distortions in his own view of man.

The point of the satire in Jane Austen's *Love and Friendship* can be seen, in this context, to be remarkably sadistic; and the

[24] The original meaning of 'libertine', which goes back to Roman times, is simply 'a freedman; one manumitted from slavery' (OED). But in the sixteenth century 'libertin' (French) and 'libertine' were applied to religious freethinkers – 'The name given to certain antinomian sects of the early sixteenth century, which arose in France and elsewhere on the Continent' (OED). By the 1590s the word could mean 'a man who is not restrained by moral law, esp. in his relations with the female sex' (OED); and in the seventeenth century the word both in French and English became firmly identified with philosophical scepticism and sexual freedom. It is at this time that pornographic prose fiction first appears in Europe – see David Foxon's *Libertine Literature in England, 1660–1745* (London, 1964).

[25] In a letter to Falconet, July 1767. Quoted by Charly Guyot, in *Diderot par lui-même* (Paris, 1953) 37.

work even has a connection – unhappy and fortuitous – with
the Revolution. Jane Austen dedicated the little novel to 'Madame
la Comtesse de Feuillide'. The countess was her cousin Eliza,
and Eliza's husband, Jean Capotte, Comte de Feuillide, was to be
guillotined four years later during the Terror. This unfortunate
occurrence is not out of keeping with the argument of *Love and
Friendship* which is, basically, that sensibility as such has nothing necessarily to do with moral worth, and that human beings
are fundamentally selfish – or, rather, that to believe that men
in general are basically *unselfish* is to be dangerously deluded.
The heroes and heroines in *Love and Friendship* are all creatures
of the most exquisite sensibility and the most ruthless and unscrupulous selfishness. 'A sensibility too tremblingly alive to
every affliction of my Freinds, my Acquaintances and particularly
to every affliction of my own', confesses Laura, the main
character, 'was my only fault.'[26] Her husband Edward and her
friends Augustus and Sophia are 'Exalted Creatures [who]
scorned to reflect a moment on their pecuniary Distresses &
would have blushed at the idea of paying their Debts.'[27] They
do not blush to rob their parents and relatives, however, and
purely out of principle they marry in defiance of their parents'
wishes. Having 'constantly refused to submit themselves to such
despotic Power', they disentangle themselves 'from the Shackles
of Parental Authority' and then contrive to live with the help
of 'a considerable sum of Money which Augustus had gracefully
purloined from his Unworthy father's Escritoire'.[28] Sophia, of
course, like Laura is 'all Sensibility and Feeling'[29] – so much so
that when Augustus is finally removed to Newgate she cannot
bear to visit him: 'my feelings are sufficiently shocked by the
recital of his Distress, but to behold it will over-power my
Sensibility'.[30] Deserting their husbands Laura and Sophia flee to
Scotland where they are given shelter by Sophia's 'relation'
MacDonald. In return for his hospitality they rob him and
corrupt his daughter. She had been happily going to marry a
young man of whom he approved, but, says Laura, '[Janetta's]
errors in the Affair had only arisen . . . from a want of proper
confidence in her own opinion, & a suitable contempt of her
father's. We . . . had no difficulty to convince her that it was

[26] *Volume the Second*, ed. B. C. Southam (Oxford, 1963) 5–6.
[27] Ibid. 24.   [28] Ibid. 23–4.   [29] Ibid. 20.   [30] Ibid. 27.

impossible she could love Graham, or that it was her duty to disobey her Father . . .'[31] They soon pack her off to Gretna Green with a lover who is suitably sentimental – that is, a man who is in her father's opinion, which is doubtless justified, 'an unprincipled Fortune-hunter'.

The four main characters in this story all marry in defiance of the wishes of at least some of their parents; they behave in thoroughly anarchic and self-centred ways; and, with one exception, they come to a variety of sticky ends (Laura survives with a reasonably handsome annuity). They do enjoy a period of complete happiness, however, and this is when they are able to live together as a group quite cut off from the world of normal social responsibilities. 'In the Society of my Edward & this Amiable Pair', writes Laura, 'I passed the happiest moments of my Life: Our time was most delightfully spent, in mutual Protestations of Friendship, and in vows of unalterable Love, in which we were secure from being interrupted, by intruding & disagreeable Visitors . . .'[32] It would be too much to describe this as a commune of sexually liberated swingers, but it does bear some interesting resemblances to the isolated groups of criminals and libertines which are a dominant feature of Sade's fantasies.

The same pattern appears in the reunion of Laura with her cousins Philander and Augustus towards the end of the story. Although they have robbed and deserted her, she finds her unscrupulous cousins much more congenial than her other companions: 'whilst the rest of the party were devouring Green tea & buttered toast, we feasted ourselves in a more refined & Sentimental Manner by a confidential Conversation'.[33] In the course of the conversation she learns that this small *Societé des Amis du Crime* has had a typically Sadean inception: the commission of a criminal act which leads to the death of their parents. Their mothers, they tell Laura, were sisters and always lived together.

They were neither of them very rich; their united fortunes had originally amounted to nine thousand Pounds, but as they had always lived upon the principal of it, when we were fifteen it was diminished to nine Hundred. This nine Hundred, they always kept in a Drawer . . . for the Convenience of having it always at Hand. Whether it was from this circum-

[31] Ibid. 35.   [32] Ibid. 22.   [33] Ibid. 60.

stance, of its being easily taken, or from a wish of being inde-
pendant, or from an excess of Sensibility (for which we were
always remarkable) I cannot now determine, but certain it is
that when we had reached our 15th year, we took the Nine
Hundred Pounds & ran away . . . to London & had the good
luck to spend it in 7 weeks & a Day . . . [We then] began to
think of returning to our Mothers, but accidentally hearing
that they were both starved to death, we gave over the design
& determined to engage ourselves to some strolling company
of Players, as we had always a turn for the stage.[34]

The most obviously sadistic passage in Jane Austen's work
does not, however, occur in *Love and Friendship*, although it is
included in the collection of juvenilia, *Volume the Second*, in
which *Love and Friendship* appears. It is a short piece which
bears the title, 'A Letter from a Young Lady, whose feelings
being too strong for her Judgement led her into the commission
of Errors which her Heart disapproved.' It begins as follows:

Many have been the cares & vicissitudes of my past life, my
beloved Ellinor, & the only consolation I feel for their bitterness is that on a close examination of my conduct, I am convinced that I have strictly deserved them. I murdered my
father at a very early period of my Life, I have since murdered
my Mother, and I am now going to murder my Sister. I have
changed my religion so often that at present I have not an idea
of any left. I have been a perjured witness in every public
tryal for these past twelve Years; and I have forged my own
will. In short there is scarcely a crime that I have not committed. – But I am now going to reform.

She is going to reform because she has just helped Colonel Martin
of the Horse Guards defraud his brother of eight million pounds.
'The Colonel in gratitude waited on me the next day with an
offer of his hand –. I am now going to murder my Sister. /Yours
Ever. /Anna Parker.'[35] With its family murders, irreligion, and

[34] Ibid. 61–2.
[35] Ibid. 202–4. *Volume the Second* also contains a brief piece,
'Letter the first From A Mother to her friend' (153–7), which gives
an account of the 'first entrée into life' of two sisters – they go to
drink tea with a neighbour and her daughter, but not before receiving the conventional warning: 'You are this Evening to enter a

a crime involving an enormous sum of money this reads like a synopsis of one of the episodes in *La Nouvelle Justine*.

From the novels Jane Austen went on to write it is abundantly clear that she did not believe that everyone was like Anna Parker, or even that everyone was so thoroughly selfish as the characters are in *Love and Friendship*. But she knew that all of us, even the most amiable, have a streak of Miss Parker in our make-up and that to pretend otherwise is a sentimental delusion. One of the few really chilling moments in her fiction comes in *Northanger Abbey* when we are made simultaneously to realise both that General Tilney is not a murderer out of a gothic novel and that he is a ruthless, self-centred man who, given the right provocation and the right circumstances, could possibly be tempted to kill someone. It is her ability to include the potential cruelty and nastiness of ordinary people together with their more admirable and pleasant qualities in one balanced image of humanity that in part makes Jane Austen a great novelist.

The Marquis de Sade, although he is a literary figure of major importance, is not a great novelist, and the image of humanity presented in his writings can hardly be called balanced. As a philosopher he is both highly intelligent and, I think, fundamentally confused, although the confusion is a fruitful one so far as his imaginative work is concerned. His novels, which are all in a sense one novel, are the result of a continuous and unrelenting attempt to resolve the radical inconsistencies in his position, inconsistencies which stem directly from his sexual peculiarities. Simone de Beauvoir has observed very perceptively that 'it is neither as author nor as sexual pervert that Sade compels our attention; it is by virtue of the relationship which he created between these two aspects of himself. Sade's aberrations begin to acquire value when, instead of enduring them as his fixed nature, he elaborates an immense system in order to justify them.'[36] And because of the particular character of his

---

World in which you will meet with many wonderful Things: Yet let me warn you against suffering yourselves to be meanly swayed by the Follies and Vices of others . . .'

[36] 'Must we burn Sade?', in *The 120 Days of Sodom and other Writings, by the Marquis de Sade*, comp. and trans. Austyn Wainhouse and Richard Seaver (New York, 1967) 6 [originally published as 'Faut-il brûler Sade?', *Les Temps Modernes* Dec. 1951–Jan. 1952].

aberrations Sade's attempt to justify them led him into direct conflict with that complex of ideals, fantasies and theories about the
nature of man and society which can be called sentimental.
Against the image of man as a social, sympathetic, generous,
benevolent and good-natured being Sade sets his diametrically
opposed image of man as an isolated, anarchic, selfish, cruel,
violent and aggressive being. Yet he shared with sentimentalism
the belief that all knowledge and all systems of value stem
basically from the individual experience; and that the ideal
society is one in which individual men and women can determine
as freely as possible their own destinies.

It is not surprising then that Sade should have been preoccupied with the theme of a young lady's entrance into the
world – just as so many 'sentimental' novelists were, particularly Richardson, for whom, like Jane Austen, Sade had an un-
qualified admiration. The entrance of a young lady into the
world is an occasion on which the individual comes directly into
conflict with society, and on the outcome of this conflict depends
the degree of independence and freedom with which the mature
individual, the adult woman and the values she represents, can
lead her life. In its basic form it is an act of sexual initiation; and
when the conflict between the desire for freedom and the pressure
to conform is violent, as it is in *Clarissa*, the act of initiation can
itself be violent and painful. The rape of Clarissa by Lovelace is
one of the most significant actions in the whole of eighteenth-
century fiction. The threat and possibility of rape lurk in the
background of most sentimental novels; and Sade, of course, was
obsessed with the subject. Justine, the heroine of his first novel,
is raped continuously. Every sexual act to which she submits is a
violation – she remains, metaphorically at least, a perpetual
virgin who is forced again and again to enter the world, a
symbol, like Clarissa, of the impossibility of ever completely
reconciling the values of the world with the sentimental and
Christian ideal of virtue. For Juliette, her sister, however, the act
of sexual initiation is liberating: she becomes free, powerful and
criminal – instead of being crushed by the world she dominates
it.

The most successful of Sade's works of fiction is *La Philosophie
dans le Boudoir*, and since its subject is the sexual initiation of a
young woman this is understandable. Also it is relatively short,

it has a single coherent dramatic action – it is presented as a dramatic scenario rather than a novel – and it is much more tightly controlled than any of Sade's other explicitly sexual pieces. The philosophical debates are brief, lucid and pointed, no one is actually killed, and that feature of his perversity which, as Gilbert Lely observes, 'belongs . . . to the sphere of real lunacy',[37] his coprolagnia, is for the most part kept out of sight. It is even at times, in Sade's own black way, grotesquely funny; and one has the reassuring feeling that Sade on this occasion was sufficiently distanced from his subject to be aware of the fact. At the height of one of his incredibly complicated group acts of coition, when everyone is uttering the usual Sadean screams of joy, pain, ecstasy and execration, he remarks with unusual tact that 'the fear of appearing monotonous prevents us from record- ing expressions which, upon such occasions, are all very apt to resemble one another'.[38]

La Philosophie dans le Boudoir is powerful and disturbing, and despite the simplicity of its structure, unusually complex. It is also in some ways, like The Monk, remarkably conventional; and it is to these conventional aspects of the work that I should like briefly to draw attention. The central character is a young girl, fifteen years old, of great sensibility, Eugénie de Mistival, and in the course of the action she is introduced by a group of libertines to practically every form of sexual activity. She is an apt and eager pupil, and her sexual education is accompanied by a series of philosophical discussions in which the generally accepted notions of religion and morality are systematically destroyed. The situation in which, as Barry Ivker observes, 'the heroine's philosophic inquiries . . . parallel her discoveries in the sexual sphere',[39] had already become well established as a

---

[37] The Marquis de Sade: A Biography, trans. Alec Brown (London, 1961) 304. Originally published in Paris in 1952, Lely's biography gives a sympathetic account of Sade. Lely notes that while more than half the six hundred sexual incidents related by the female story tellers in Les 120 Journées de Sodome involve the eating of excrement, Krafft-Ebing lists only one example of coprophagy in his nine hundred case-histories.

[38] Philosophy in the Bedroom, in The complete Justine 272.

[39] 'Towards a definition of libertinism in 18th century French fiction', Studies on Voltaire and the eighteenth century LXXXIII (1970) 231. Mr Ivker's extremely informative article and David

convention in libertine fiction; and Sade himself, in a footnote to
the third version of *Justine*, draws attention to some earlier
examples of the genre: Argens's *Thérèse philosophe*, Chorier's
L'Académie des dames, Latouche's *Le Portier des Chartreux* and
Mirabeau's *L'Education de Laure*. But Sade goes much further
than his predecessors in his emphasis on the natural savagery,
selfishness and cruelty of human beings. And in *La Philosophie
dans le Boudoir* he takes particular pains to demolish the notion
that sensibility, especially in women, can be taken as evidence
of a generous, benevolent, kind, humane disposition. On the
contrary, argues Dolmancé, one of the most eloquent of Sade's
libertine philosophers, it is a sign of a capacity for exercising the
most exquisite cruelty.

> [This] species of cruelty, fruit of extreme organic sensibility,
> is known only to them who are extremely delicate in their
> person, and the extremes to which it drives them are those
> determined by intelligence and niceness of feeling; this
> delicacy, so finely wrought, so sensitive to impressions, re-
> sponds above all, best, and immediately to cruelty; it awakens
> in cruelty; cruelty liberates it.[40]

This is too much for Eugénie, who is driven into a frenzy of
sexual excitement by Dolmancé's remarks. Taking her in her
arms, Mme de Saint-Ange, her female instructress, cries out:
'Adorable creature, never have I beheld a sensibility like yours,

---

Foxon's *Libertine Literature in England, 1660–1745* (New Hyde Park,
N.Y., 1965) provide an excellent account of libertine fiction (before
Sade) in the seventeenth and eighteenth centuries. Donald Thomas's
Introduction to *The School of Venus* (New York, 1971) is also very
helpful. The main works in the libertine tradition appear to be Pietro
Aretino's *Sonnetti Lussuriosi* (1527) and *Ragionamenti* (1534–6);
La Rhetorica della Puttana (1612); *La Puttana Errante* (c. 1650),
probably by Niccolò Franco; *L'Escole des Filles* (1655) by Michel
Millot and Jean L'Ange (translated as *The School of Venus* some
time before 1688); *Le Meursius Français ou L'Académie des dames*
(1680; Latin version, *Satyra satodica*, 1660) by Chorier; *Venus dans
le cloitre* (1633), by Jean Barrin; *Le Portier des Chartreux* (1743), by
Latouche; and *Thérèse Philosophe* (1748), by the Marquis d'Argens.
Many of these works and even exact bibliographical details concerning them are hard to come by, and I have not yet been able to read all
of them.
40 *Philosophy in the Bedroom*, in *The complete Justine* 255.

never so delightful a mind!'[41] And indeed it is in the mind, in her imagination, that Eugénie experiences her greatest ecstasy. Inflamed once more by Dolmancé's calm dismissal of 'the useless virtues of generosity, humanity, charity, all those enumerated in the absurd codes of a few idiotic religious doctrines' and his argument that the individual has the right to assert himself against society by criminal acts, Eugénie exclaims, 'wild-eyed', 'I want a victim.'[42] The victim she wants is her mother, and the mere thought of what she may now be at liberty to do to her is enough to bring this delicate creature with her exquisite sensibility to a sexual climax. Later the mother appears, and in the concluding scene she is raped, beaten, infected with venereal disease and kicked out of the door.

Remarkably unpleasant and grotesquely fantastic as all this may be it has an inner psychological and dramatic coherence and an intellectually ordered development which make it in its own terms convincing – and for that reason rather more disturbing than the gory extravaganzas which crowd the interminable pages of Sade's longer works. It is, of course, quite patently Oedipal or Electral in its structure; and it is in this pattern (of which the education of the heroine in philosophical libertinism may be seen as a variant) that what I have called its conventionality may be seen basically to lie. But what is involved is more than the simple destruction of a parent – it is the implications with which this act is charged that are really troubling. The point is that Eugénie is already free when she tortures and humiliates her mother – but in order to validate and authenticate her liberty she needs this ritual confirmation of the fact, just as Dolmancé, like Sade's other atheist libertines, feels the need to blaspheme at the moment of sexual triumph, even though he is convinced that God is a 'disgusting fiction'.[43]

Precisely the same pattern may be seen to operate throughout *Love and Friendship*. Jane Austen's loving couples are absurd

---

[41] Ibid. 257.   [42] Ibid. 287–8.

[43] Ibid. 241–2. ('Be not astonished at my language: one of my largest pleasures is to swear in God's name when I'm stiff. It seems then that my spirit ... abhors, scorns this disgusting fiction; I would like to discover some better way to revile it ... and when my accursed musings lead me to the conviction of the nullity of this repulsive object ... I would instantly like to be able to re-edify the phantom, so that my rage might at least fall upon some target.')

because they defy and disobey their parents *when there is no
need to.* 'My Father . . . insisted on my giving my hand to Lady
Dorothea,' says Edward. 'No never exclaimed I. Lady Dorothea is
lovely and Engaging; I prefer no woman to her; but know Sir,
that I scorn to marry her in compliance with your wishes. No!
Never shall it be said that I obliged my Father.'[44] The deaths of
the mothers of Philander and Augustus and the way in which
their unscrupulous sons accidentally learn of the fact and light-
heartedly dismiss it has a similar tone. 'The DISTRESSES that
may attend the Misconduct Both of PARENTS and CHILDREN, In
Relation to MARRIAGE', as Richardson describes it on the title
page of *Clarissa*, was of course a theme of enduring interest to
novelists and their readers in the eighteenth century. There are
some fairly obvious reasons why this should have been so,
especially in view of the fact that the majority of novel readers
were women. But the determination of the proper relationship
between child and parent had a significance that extended beyond the question of whether a daughter or a son had the right
to choose her or his own marriage partner. It comprehended – to
quote again from the title page of *Clarissa* – 'the most important
Concerns of Private LIFE', it comprehended, as Sade felt his work
comprehended, the whole issue of the liberty and the rights of
the individual.

And it is in *Clarissa* that we find the closest parallel to the
situation in *La Philosophie dans le Boudoir*. Clarissa is initiated
into the world by Lovelace when he rapes her. The rape, like the
sexual initiation of Eugénie, is carried out before a group –
Lovelace is assisted by Mrs Sinclair, the keeper of a high-class
brothel, and her girls. Clarissa, of course, cannot accommodate
herself to Lovelace's world – she preserves her freedom, and dies
– going, as she says to Lovelace ambiguously, to wait for him at
her father's house. But her freedom, like the liberation of Eugénie,
is also accompanied by the ritual destruction of figures of
parental authority. Her own parents survive – Richardson con-
triving as always to have his cake and eat it – but their surro-
gates, Mrs Sinclair the bawd and Captain Tomlinson Lovelace's
assistant, both die. Clarissa's experience in the brothel can be
read very convincingly as a nightmare analogue of her experience
at Harlowe Place – Mrs Sinclair and her helpers force, cajole and

---

[44] *Volume the Second* 11.

trick her into submitting to Lovelace just as her own mercenary and selfish parents had tried to force, cajole and trick her into marrying the repulsive Mr Solmes. The agonising and physically horrible death of Mrs Sinclair cannot be exactly equated with the destruction of Mme de Mistival, but it certainly performs an analogous function in the symbolic structure of the story.

The implications of *Clarissa*, like the implications of everything Sade wrote, are saddening and disturbing – and when they are set in this context so too are the implications of Jane Austen's otherwise delightful burlesque. An excessive indulgence in sensibility or a blind faith in man's capacity to follow the dictates of his heart, to act in accordance with his better feelings, is foolish and deserves to be ridiculed. But to cast doubt on – or to attempt to destroy entirely, as Sade does – the ideals embodied in the concept of sensibility is to attack something which must be regarded as fundamental to any view of man that is at all rational or hopeful. 'It suffices that man is what he is', wrote d'Holbach, 'or that he is a sensible being [i.e. a being endowed with sensibility] in order to distinguish what gives him pleasure or displeasure. It suffices that one man knows that another man is a sensible being like himself, to perceive what is useful or hurtful to him . . . Thus the feeling and thinking being has only to feel and think, in order to discover what he must do for himself and others. I feel, and another feels like me; this is the foundation of all morals . . .'[45] This is stating in its most optimistic form the enlightened, the *sentimental* assumption; and if this is not in some sense true, no matter how limited that sense may be, then there is not much hope for mankind. Sade, with his eerily prophetic visions of genocide and universal annihilation, obviously wants us to believe that there is not; and if we were to read *Love and Friendship* as tragedy rather than comedy we could perhaps come to a similarly bleak conclusion. Seen in a balanced rather than an unduly pessimistic light, and read in the context of the revolution, these works do of course suggest that the sentimental ideal, though a noble and indeed an essential one, is frail and delicate; and that for man to realise it, to achieve his

---

[45] From *Good Sense* (1772), an abridged version of *Le Système de la Nature* (1770), trans. J. P. Mendum, included in *The Enlightenment: The Proper Study of Mankind*, ed. Nicholas Capaldi (New York, 1967) 51.

potentially humane destiny, he needs to be protected from the more ferocious and self-centred elements in his humanity.

These parodies of sentimentalism go further than this, however, in their implication that there is a connection between the experience of and the desire for freedom and the urge to cruelty and destruction. This makes them particularly disturbing to people who read them, as we do today, in an atmosphere thick with the rhetoric of dissent and revolution and charged with the threat of violence. The simple explanation of and excuse for the bloodshed which can accompany social revolution is that it is a political or military necessity: people have to be killed so that objectives felt by the revolutionaries to be legitimate may be achieved, objectives which have been rendered otherwise completely unattainable by repressive and inflexible authority. Revolutionary violence can thus be seen both as an expression of frustration and disillusionment, and as something which is intended to serve a functional purpose. Sadean cruelty can partly be explained in this way: his great criminals like Juliette and St Fond commit atrocities in order to gain power and wealth. But these 'necessary' acts of cruelty are far less important in Sade's world than the murders, tortures, blasphemies and desecrations which accompany the sexual activities of people who are already in a state of complete liberty, who no longer need to attain freedom.

Ritual cruelty and violence are of course essential elements in the fantasy life of psychopathological sadists. They can also be essential elements in the fantasy life – and the real life – of societies. The Terror, like many political purges, was in part symbolic: as Hazlitt very beautifully observes in his *Life of Napoleon Buonaparte*, 'it was the phantom of kingly power that was struck at, that tottered and fell headless with Louis XVI'[46]

[46] *The Life of Napoleon Buonaparte* (London, 1830) I 269. H. M. Stephens in his *History of the French Revolution*, records that during the Terror 'little guillotines were worn as brooches, as earrings, as clasps, and the women of the time simply followed the fashion without realizing what it meant. Indeed, the worship of the guillotine was one of the most curious features of the epoch. Children had toy guillotines given them; models were made to cut off imitation heads, when wine or sweet syrup flowed in place of blood; and hymns were written to La Sainte Guillotine, and jokes made upon it as "the national razor".' *A History of the French Revolution* (New York, 1902) II 359–60.

(and decapitation itself is, quite fortuitously, a highly symbolic mode of execution). Sade reminds us continually of the social and political significance of anarchy, violence and cruelty; and this reminder is all the more ominous when we bear in mind that he had established his intellectual position and written much of his work during the period of greatest revolutionary hope and enthusiasm, the period which culminates in the Declaration of the Rights of Man. Sade was himself, in his own way, a political revolutionary, and in La Philosophie dans le Boudoir he includes a substantial political manifesto, 'Yet another Effort, Frenchmen, if you would become Republicans.' It has been suggested that this destroys the unity of the work,[47] and it certainly has a distinct identity since it was apparently extracted and distributed widely as a pamphlet during the revolution of 1848. But Sade, who was highly conscious of the relationship between sexual and political activity, clearly intended I think to place it where he did; and the reading aloud of the document by Dolmancé forms an ironically fitting climax to the philosophising which has gone on in Mme de Saint-Ange's boudoir.

The causes of and motivations for social and political violence are extraordinarily complex; but Sade suggests more vividly than most writers one of the areas in which an explanation of these things can be sought. Moreover the line of approach which Sade opens up has a quite special relevance to what is happening today. I am touching here, of course, on the fringes of an enormously complex subject; but it is worth observing that the new radicalism, not only in the United States but possibly in all urban, highly industrialised societies, is openly and at times aggressively sexual, extremely sentimental – both in the good sense, in its commitment to humane values, and in the bad sense, in its self-pity and self-deception – and increasingly violent. A thoroughly anarchic and libertine document like Jerry Rubin's Do it!, for instance, which is sub-titled Scenarios of the Revolution and which chronicles the transformation of the relatively sentimental Berkeley hippy into the activist Chicago yippy, presents a very familiar pattern to anyone who has read Sade. (In other ways – in its good humour, in the use of the physical appearance of the book to reflect its apparent anarchy and

[47] Introduction to Philosophy in the Bedroom, in The complete Justine 180.

incoherence, and in its zany charm, *Do it!* is also very reminiscent of *Tristram Shandy*).[48] Let me cite one more example: *Defiance*, the first issue of 'A Radical Review', published in October 1970. It is interesting, in the context of this present discussion, for a number of things. First, it is concerned to a surprising degree with what, in eighteenth-century terminology, would have been called the difference between true and false sensibility. Richard Poirier, for instance, in an extremely thoughtful essay – which contrives, nonetheless, to give somehow the impression that the eighteenth century never occurred – begins by asserting that 'the future induces even more sentimentality than does the past', and arrives at the conclusion that while 'there has probably never been a time before . . . when there were such irresistible demands on feeling . . . what is probably being discovered are the possible restrictions of human compassion, sympathy and feeling'.[49] Second, it is remarkable in how many of the semi-documentary reports from the revolutionary front contained in *Defiance*, political conversion or illumination is presented as being associated with an act of sexual initiation. And today, as Dotson Rader, the editor, suggests in his sombre article 'On Revolutionary Violence', the world is once more proving too much for the young lady: 'Violence on the left . . . [arises out of] sexual disorder compounded by a sentimentalist, neo-Romantic sensibility available in the literature of revolt'.[50] The idealistic enthusiasm of the civil rights struggle of the fifties has soured. Now, says Rader, the 'English majors handling dynamite . . . are beyond despair, and death has claimed their vision. For they have understood that to destroy all limits is, in a perverse sense, to be truly free. To destroy is to *feel* free.'[51]

Sade himself could have written that final sentence. 'Il faut toujours en revenir à de Sade, c'est-à-dire à *l'homme naturel*, pour expliquer le mal',[52] Baudelaire confided to the pages of his journal. Sade may not explain evil, but he certainly shocks us into a fresh awareness of its existence. Natural man undoubtedly has

[48] *Do it! Scenarios of the Revolution* by Jerry Rubin, Introduction by Eldridge Cleaver (New York, 1970).

[49] 'Escape to the Future'. *Defiance: A Radical Review* no. 1 (New York, 1970) 163, 178–9.

[50] *Defiance* 202–3.   [51] *Ibid.* 201.

[52] *Romans et Nouvelles*, in *Oeuvres Complètes* (Paris, 1952) XIII 12.

elements of sadism in him – so does civilised man – and to return to Sade is to be made painfully conscious of our potentiality for cruelty, ferocity and selfishness. If the heavenly city of the philosophers is one possible and imaginable condition of man's existence, the hellish dungeons beneath the snow-bound castle of the Duc de Blangis, running with blood and excrement, provide us with another: and any balanced view of mankind must somehow take them both into account. The Marquis de Sade, limited and horribly distorted though his own image of man may be, forces us as few other writers do to acknowledge this. But if we must return to Sade we should also return to Jane Austen, for even in the slightest and most inconsequential of her works she offers us, as does Peacock, the reassurance that with wit, intelligence and a sense of humour it is possible – at least for most of the time – to contemplate and even bear the condition of being human.

6

Epilogue: Decline and Fall –
a Note on Courtney Melmoth,
Professional Sentimentalist

Sade, Jane Austen and Peacock are all anti-sentimentalists; and the response which each of them makes to sentimentalism is, in the first instance at least, satirical – although with all of them, even Peacock, the satirical exposure of sentimental and romantic absurdities soon develops into a more complex, more extensive and more widely-based rendering of life. That these three very different writers, together with a number of lesser ones, should have reacted in this way to sentimentalism is highly significant. It suggests to begin with that this complex of ideas and ideals, or at least some of the ways it was by now manifesting itself in literature and in social and political action and ideology, invited and to a degree deserved satirical attack and exposure.

Nothing indicates more convincingly just how thoroughly the attack was merited than the life and writings of Samuel Jackson Pratt. Yet at the same time nothing demonstrates more clearly the validity and necessity of many of the basic sentimental assumptions about man and society and the complexity and underlying vitality of the whole sentimental movement. Pratt was a second-rate hack who made his living by exploiting the growing concern with philanthropy. From the number of editions which some of his works went through – the poetical essays *Sympathy* (1781), *Humanity* (1788) and *Cottage-Pictures; or The Poor* (1801), for instance – he also seems to have been fairly widely read and respected. That a writer so bad could have been so successful indicates very compellingly the strength of the attitudes and feelings to which he was appealing.

Pratt, who wrote mainly under the name of Courtney Melmoth, lived from 1749 to 1814. He produced poems, novels, plays, essays and journalistic pieces, and edited anthologies and selections of his own and other people's work. His writings are indeed, as the rather acerbic article on him in the *DNB* says, 'voluminous'. They are also topical, unoriginal and almost indescribably mediocre. The first of his works listed in the *DNB* gives a good indication of the line his career was to follow: '"The Tears of Genius, on the Death of Dr. Goldsmith. By Courtney Melmoth", 1774; written a few hours after Goldsmith's death, and containing imitations of him and other popular authors.' The appeal to tears, the exploitation of an obviously pathetic situation, the imitation of other writers – the patently second-hand and manufactured quality of the whole thing – are all typical. Pratt went on to write a number of plays (most of which failed) and several sentimental novels, including the obligatory imitation of Sterne – *Travels for the Heart*, supposedly written in France (1777). His poems seem to have been popular, as were his rambling descriptive essays of life and society in various parts of England which he published under the title *Gleanings*. By 1805 he was clearly not only popular but at least in a social if not a literary sense respected and respectable. In that year he made a 'positively last appearance' in a sumptuously produced three-volume production entitled *Harvest-Home: consisting of Supplementary Gleanings, Original Dramas and Poems, Contributions of literary Friends, and select Republications, including Sympathy, a Poem.* The work is dedicated to the Prince of Wales, and the subscription list of approximately two hundred and fifty people is headed by Their Royal Highnesses the Duke of York, the Duchess of York and the Duke of Kent. What these distinguished subscribers got for their money was a collection of unsuccessful plays, indifferent verse, and pious, benevolent, platitudinous, sentimental journalism.

But there are some solid grains among the chaff: the third volume concludes with a survey of that 'which of all others', Pratt announces, 'is the most prominent and beautiful feature in the magnificent portrait of Great Britain. – Is it necessary again to say I mean its Charities . . . the numberless palaces which my country has raised to the unfortunate; and to whom Pity's angel, bearing the commission of God himself, administers . . .'[1] What follows is a factual guide to the charitable institutions of London – the Foundling Hospital, the Asylum for the Reception of Friendless and Distressed Orphan Girls (founded by Sir John Fielding), the Royal Cumberland Free-Mason School, the

[1] Op. cit. III 530–1.

Magdalen Hospital for the reclamation of prostitutes (with the founding of which Samuel Richardson had been associated), and several other asylums, infirmaries, hospitals and benevolent organisations. The list is brought to a resounding if ungrammatical conclusion with Pratt's account of

> [that] sublime institution 'the centre of philanthropy, whose rays, with genial energy, are directed to a boundless circumference', and whose object in the language of some great and benevolent characters, who continue to reanimate 'the rigid limb, the clay-cold skin, the silent pulse, the breathless lip, the livid cheek, the fallen jaw, the fixed staring eye;' 'to rouse the lethargy of opium;' to restore the wretched victims of intoxication; to restore 'life to the infant that had lost it at its birth;' to rekindle it in those who had suffered by lightning, by apoplexies, by damps, by excessive cold, suffocation, poison; to prevent, what is of more consequence than all, 'the being confined to a coffin, or committed to a grave', ere the vital spirit had departed.[2]

– in other words, the Humane Society.

Pratt's prose may leave something to be desired, but there is nothing wrong with the causes he champions. His poetry is even less distinguished than his prose – but again the ideas and ideals he expresses are admirable. In *Sympathy; or a Sketch of the Social Passion*, he attempts to demonstrate that all living things are by nature sociable, and that the bond which unites them all is Universal Sympathy, a quality which manifests itself most clearly in men. Unfortunately man is capable of denying his own nature, of acting in an unsociable, unsympathetic manner; and in *Humanity, or the Rights of Nature* Pratt goes on to consider the inhuman ways in which men can treat each other – especially through the practice of slavery:

> HUMANITY requires that the RIGHTS OF NATURE should be enjoyed by every *Human Being*. It is therefore against the shocking barbarity, the unquestionable cruelty, and the too well-attested horror, growing out of [the slave trade], that I contend. – An abolition of *these enormities* is absolutely

[2] Ibid. 551–2.

necessary. For the rest, whether the commerce flourishes or falls, is a matter of no moment to the Philanthropist . . . it is sufficient to Him that the happiness of the *species* in *general,* is made independent of the tyranny of *particular indivi- duals . . .*[3]

Humanity, to be fair, does have some liveliness and energy: Pratt is always happier in writing about 'the *species* in *general*' than '*particular individuals*' – the further away the object of his pity the more clearly he seems to see it. He writes better in *Humanity* about the Indian tricked into slavery than he does in *Cottage- Pictures;* or *The Poor,* about the dispossessed slaves of the new industrial system and the outmoded rural social structures in his own country. Pratt believed in 'the laws of subordination',[4] and while he was happy to assert that

> *The rights of man by nature still are due,*
> *To men of ev'ry clime and every hue;*[5]

neither he nor his aristocratic patrons would have wished to see the lower orders in Great Britain lay claim to these natural rights in too insubordinate or revolutionary a manner. Nonetheless in *The Poor,* as in *Humanity,* he is concerned with a real social evil; and if the ways of dealing with it which he proposes are palliative rather than remedial they are in their intentions genuinely compassionate. As one reviewer commented, 'the author of this Poem has felt for the miseries of the Poor, and expressed good feelings on an important topic . . . his advice is always humane and generally judicious'.[6]

It was regarded as 'judicious', of course, because it nowhere suggested that it was the system which was at fault: Pratt could safely 'recommend much practical improvement in the comforts of cottagers'[7] without ever implying that some basic restructur- ing of the social order might be necessary if the evils of poverty were ever to be eliminated. Indeed it is clear that he believed no

---

[3] *Humanity, or the Rights of Nature, a Poem* (London, 1788) iii (Preface).   [4] *Ibid.*   [5] *Ibid.* 29.

[6] *Critical Review* Jan. 1802 (cited by Pratt in a selection of 'Critiques on the Poem').

[7] *Supplement to the Gentleman's Magazine* Dec. 1801 (also cited by Pratt).

such radical solution to the problem was possible: thus the strongest feeling in all his work is *generalised* pity and philanthropy. Universal compassion is a fairly safe attitude to adopt – and it is this basic complacency that makes him a sentimentalist in the pejorative sense – this and the impression he cannot help conveying that he is *using* for his own purposes both the situations about which he is writing and the feelings of his readers. There is about Samuel Jackson Pratt more than a touch of the Reverend Mr Stiggins in *Pickwick Papers*, with his scheme 'for providing the infant Negroes in the West Indies with flannel waistcoats and moral pocket-handkerchiefs'. The patronage of the aristocracy and the public acknowledgment of his own benevolence and good heartedness were, one feels, as important to Pratt as Mrs Weller's hot rum and pineapple were to Mr Stiggins.

Samuel Jackson Pratt, alias Courtney Melmoth, was a sanctimonious fraud – albeit an intelligent one. He knew how to appeal to the 'better feelings' of his readers without forcing them into any embarrassing confrontation with the harsh facts of social injustice: one could read Pratt and enjoy the luxury of armchair philanthropy and theoretical benevolence without ever actually having to do anything about the state of the world – which was, in any case, irremediably sad for the unfortunate. The assumption that the poor will always be with us can be as comforting and reassuring as it is distressing. This aspect of Pratt's sentimentality appears in its purest form in two small volumes of selections from his own writings: *Pity's Gift: a Collection of Interesting Tales, to excite the Compassion of Youth for the Animal Creation* and its sequel, *The Paternal Present*, which were published respectively in 1801 and 1802, and which subsequently went through several editions. The selections, according to the title-pages, are made by a Lady (although the *DNB* suggests that Pratt made them himself); and the books are tastefully printed, and charmingly decorated with woodcuts by Bewick. Of the two, *The Paternal Present*, which is not concerned solely with kindness to dumb animals, is the more interesting: it is a small anthology of sentimental literature. It contains poems with titles like *Compassion, Hospitality, Sensibility, Tenderness*, and *Friendship*, a note on *The People of Colour*, and a number of sentimental sketches and fables. Two of these are of particular

significance because of the example they afford of how sentimental themes which in Richardson and Sterne had formed the
basis of a realistically tragic or comic exploration of life, have
degenerate into nothing more than clichés, cheap formulae for
producing moral platitudes and exacting easy tears. *The Earthquake or, Virtue not exempt from sublunary Ills*, for instance,
may be regarded as an essay on that theme which Richardson
stated *Clarissa* was meant to illustrate: the theme of virtue distressed on earth but rewarded in heaven. The heroine, Signorina
Ramoni, marries secretly a poor student. By accident her father
discovers at the same instant that his daughter is married and
that she is about to become a mother. The shock is too much,
and he dies of an apoplexy. A few days later the Signora learns
that her husband has died of the plague in Rome. Their child is
born, but fate strikes again, and he is killed when the house
collapses during an earthquake. This last stroke is more than the
poor woman can bear: 'without a groan, her spirit winged its
way to that heaven, where virtue will find its ultimate and
eternal reward'.[8] But there is nothing remarkable about the
heroine's virtue – it has withstood no trials, and has not been
called forth in any way by the vicissitudes she has endured.
Moreover her sufferings are almost all completely accidental –
they do not result in any direct way from her character or from
the situations in which she places herself. These things do not,
however, deter the author from breaking with all apparent conviction into the usual sentimental apostrophe:

Ye who have felt the ardour of genuine regard, the exalted
glow of genuine affection; – ye who have tasted the luxury of
love repaid ... To you I need not attempt to describe what the
sterility of language denies; and to such as derive their happiness from insensibility, I disdain to address myself. This frame,
which is feelingly alive to every distress; this heart, which
vibrates to every impulse of pity – wretched as it is from
the keen reflection of losses not to be recovered, and the
prospect of ills that still menace a fall – shall never pay
homage to unamiable indifference, or seek for shelter in sullen
apathy![9]

[8] *The Paternal Present* 96.
[9] Ibid. 83–4.

The sentimental theme of the impotence of virtue receives an even more melodramatic vulgarisation in *The Beggar and the Angel, an Oriental Story.* The story begins with the wonderfully optimistic sentence: "'And vindicate the ways of God to man.' Nothing so easy –.'[10] The vindication consists in the story of a beggar outside the gates of Baghdad who has suffered practically every conceivable ill – the loss of wife, children, fortune, a leg, an arm and an eye. Not unnaturally he sometimes rails against fate. One day an angel (in disguise) proves to him that he is much happier than he thinks he is: his disabilities have prevented him from committing all sorts of sins which, had he been as other men, he would have certainly committed: his eyes are opened and he beholds the universe 'as one prodigious theatre, filled with criminals, assassins and unfortunates'.

> 'Suffer patiently,' said the Angel. 'After death, thou shalt commence a new career, where every happiness shall be complete and uninterrupted . . . thou shalt have an immortal character, and everlasting felicity.' Nahamir . . . thanked heaven, with all his heart, that he was *old, deformed, blind, crippled, and limping; without fortune, without a wife, and without children.*[11]

Nahamir is not presented as a particularly likeable character, and he is obviously not expected to evoke the same sort of affectionate emotions as Uncle Toby does; but like Toby he is a symbol of the ineffectiveness of virtue. He stands at the end of the century, an ugly litle image of utter disillusionment.

And yet – and yet: cheap huckster and self-pitying defeatist though he may have been, Pratt was concerned with social and moral issues of the utmost importance. In the end, perhaps, his work should be judged less by the silliness and bathos of his sentimental stories than by the good sense of his sentiments. For instance, his note on *The People of Colour or the Blacks* (portion of which I have already quoted), is intended 'to excite and expand the *principle* of *sympathy* and the *practice* of benevolence beyond our own country',[12] by the enunciation of the following 'grand truths':

[10] Ibid. 97.   [11] Ibid. 120–1.
[12] Ibid. 24.

1st. That the happiness of the species in *general* should be made independent of the tyranny of *particular individuals*. 2dly. That the laws of *subordination* in the different classes of SOCIETY should not violate the laws of humanity. – 3dly. That so much of liberty should be allowed to every man, as that he should feel a consciousness of his being a link in the great chain of the community; – and, 4thly, That till by some act of his own . . . it shall become necessary that the individual should be considered as an outcast of that community, he is by the rights of nature, of reason, and of God, entitled to protection from insult, oppression, and death.[18]

This is to be sure a safely conservative interpretation of *Liberté, Egalité, Fraternité* – but it is, nonetheless, a precise enunciation of certain principles and ideals to which lip service at least is now paid throughout the world. It was in the eighteenth century that these principles received their first clear formulation; and it is in the great sentimental novels of the period that the implications for individual people of these general notions of human rights were explored and illuminated. Sentimentalism degenerated into sentimentality, it is true – and the reasons for this decline are extremely complex. But it was a temporary aberration of taste, and one that could not destroy the positive values of the sentimental ideal.

If the sentimental writers of the eighteenth century erred in their estimation of man they erred (to use one of their own words) generously. It *is* better to be a man of feeling than a man of the world; better to pay some tribute, however small, to the rights of other people than to disregard them with complete cynicism; better to sympathise with another than to repress feelings which are, as the sentimentalist insists, natural; it is better, in short, to be not only human but humane. This is the lesson of the eighteenth century; and unless we learn it soon not only shall we lose our chance of becoming fully human but humanity itself may cease to exist. 'To assail the sun, snatch it out of the universe, make a general darkness, or use that star to burn the world! Oh that would be a crime!'[14] cries one of Sade's

[18] Ibid. 25–6.
[14] Quoted by Simone de Beauvoir in 'Must we burn Sade?', in *The 120 Days of Sodom and other Writings, by the Marquis de Sade* 32.

anti-sentimental heroes. Man, with his capacity for global annihilation, now has it in his power to realise an essential part of the Sadean nightmare – just as he also has the power to bring about the sentimental dream of a truly humane society. As never before he has the opportunity to realise to the full either the most selfish or the most altruistic aspects of his own nature. In the novels of the eighteenth century this dual and ambiguous potentiality of the human personality is presented and explored with unprecedented and prophetic clarity. It is this above all, perhaps, which makes them significant and valuable.

Index